GARDEN WIZARDRY

Richard C. Davids

GARDEN WIZARDRY

CROWN PUBLISHERS, INC., NEW YORK

To Bob and Lorry,
whose questions during their first glorious year
of gardening led to this book

Published in the United States of America

Published simultaneously in Canada by General Publishing Company Limited

Designed by Manuela Paul

Library of Congress Cataloging in Publication Data

Davids, Richard C
    Garden wizardry: short cuts, tricks, and
gleanings from a lifetime of growing all kinds of
vegetables and flowers.

    1. Gardening. 2. Vegetable gardening.
3. Flower gardening. I. Title.
SB453.D35   1976   635   75-45129
ISBN 0-517-52519-4

preface:
a word
from
the wizard

A package of seed to me is like the smell of a cork to an alcoholic. I can't help myself.

The day a seed catalog comes, I am numb to the world over new cosmos, more buttery beans, cucumbers that outperform all others. I am powerless to resist. I must have them all, especially the new and untried.

I garden not for food or flowers or exercise or anything but the fun and excitement of it. Much as I like growing prize carrots or perfect cucumbers, I would rather try the untried plant, one from some distant, mysterious land. This book is partly a record of my experimental gardening.

It is also a practical book to help you cut food bills, plan a kitchen garden, store vegetables all winter, make sauerkraut, keep down weeds, get by with less watering, find garden space you never knew you had.

It aims to reintroduce gardening to America as the way of life it was from the day our earliest Americans tended their fields of corn, sharing generously with alien immigrants at Jamestown, Plymouth, and Wilmington, and thereby rescuing them from starvation. It aims to re-create the pleasures that made gardening the overwhelming passion of Washington and Jefferson and many another Founding Father.

It aims to shore up the courage of the timid male who fears that gardening and flower-growing may be something not quite manly—a worry that doesn't bother me, since as one reviewer of a previous book said, "Davids looks big enough and mean enough to play left tackle for the Minnesota Vikings."

For you who like to experiment, I hope this book may suggest new gardening pleasures. Grafting is something I'd like you to try. Convert your old-fashioned lilacs into sumptuous French types in a single year. And for very little money, have a pool with cascading water and a fountain that will make you feel like Louis XIV in your own Versailles.

It's about time I finished writing this book. It began so long ago I can barely remember. I had been taught to read and write by five big brothers and a sister, and during the lonely hours when they were at school, I started recording in a diary all the flowers I would grow when summer came, from hollyhocks and abutilon at the back, descending in careful steps to alyssum in front. My finances didn't stand up to my plans, nor did the weather, but that hasn't stopped my gardening. I've been at it ever since. This book is a chronicle of my gardening, including my failures.

And believe me, I have failures. In fact, here are some plants I just can't seem to grow. Others grow too well and are simply weeds. Still others aren't worth the space. It seemed time for a candid book to expose these black sheep of the botanical world, some of which have been blatantly overpromoted.

Many garden books make me feel like a yokel. I don't have a gardener, or even a greenhouse, pergola, or gazebo (whatever that is). Too many garden books are bloodless, lifeless, funless, and this is tragic because gardening is not a chore but a way of living, of creating beauty, of achieving peace.

I hope this book may spread the joy of gardening to every American, introduce him to a pastime that awaits just outside the door, that greets him at the end of every long commuter ride.

To a gardener, every morning is a red-letter morning, every spring and summer day a holiday. A walk around the perennial border before breakfast is a festival.

If the reader finds a single dull, opaque, or unbiased line in the entire book, ship it back to the publisher for a cheerful refund.

Here then is the Davids School of Practical (and Impractical) Gardening that puts fun into the fundamentals.

Contents

1
the
healing
hoe

The day I plant my garden I feel like a cosmic force of nature—as much a part of it all as the spring winds blowing past my face, as the wet earth into which I sink step by step, or as the soft sun that warms my bald head. I let the peas drop evenly into the waiting soil. I am a necessary part of the whole mysterious process. If I had worries when I began, they are forgotten now. There is healing in planting and tending a garden. Excitement, too.

I think I know the excitement my prehistoric ancestors felt when they watched the first blades of corn pushing up from the seeds they planted outside their caves. I think their eyes must have shone as they watched the little plants reach up and grow thick and tall, the sun glinting from their leaves. And when the young ears began pushing out of the stalk, their excitement was something beyond the promise of food: a glimpse into the essence of creation, magic beyond all comprehending. And what made it all the more awesome was that they had had a part in it.

Perhaps at other times in their lives, our ancestors felt the power of a divinity, but probably never stronger than at spring planting when they put in the earth a part of their treasured supply of corn or wheat, trusting the whims of whatever corn-god or earth-god was on hand to increase it. Burying food to make more food must certainly have been one of mankind's earliest gambles.

Planting a garden is an act of faith, and I doubt there is a gardener who hasn't felt it. A radish seed is lost in the soil even before I cover it, and when I look at the row I have just covered and tramped on, I wonder if anything can possibly come of it. The seeds are so small. The weather is so cold. There might be no rain. There might be frost. Most of all, will that awesome power once again awaken the seeds and start them pushing up? Maybe the seed is old or overheated.

And yet, amazingly enough, it does sprout and grow and flower and fruit, to the pleasure of everyone.

Gardening is a way of playing second fiddle in the magnificent orchestra of nature, of adding one small sound to the symphony of existence. You'll have to excuse me if gardening stirs me to poetry.

In one seed catalog there is an amusing photograph of a Tennessee gardener who has grown the most bizarre gourds on a trellis above his head. Each gourd is like a bamboo pole six or seven feet long, but with a jug-shaped bottom. Obviously he has grown them just for fun, but he feels impelled to say, "You can make a good many useful and ornamental things from them." He doesn't say exactly what useful and ornamental things, and I'd be hard pressed to help him, unless he has an open well and needs a six-foot dipper for it.

No need to apologize for growing gourds, any more than for spending an afternoon on the golf course or taking a Sunday drive or a tramp in the woods. Unfortunately, our Puritan ethic dictates that gardens produce food, and most people haven't revised that dictum. I haven't yet grown bamboo-pole gourds, but I aim to. Someday, too, I will grow yard-long beans and spaghetti squash, without apology.

To the beginning gardener: I hope that this book will take you by the hand through that first wonderful year of growing things, steering you away from temperamental plants toward faithful performers.

I hope that it may help both novice and old-timer to become expert—whether at marigolds, potatoes, or eschscholtzia—by asking them to experiment, observe, and try to distinguish folklore from fact.

Gardening, unfortunately, has fallen prey in the last few years to a motley crew of scientific charlatans, merchandising sharks, and oddballs who would have you pray over plants and talk to them. Surprisingly, some people take them seriously. Yet gardeners and gardening will survive all this. Because gardening is more than hobby or pastime or sport. It is an inborn urge, fundamental, essential.

There is considerable honest misinformation about gardening, too. For instance, some garden books maintain that clematis vines need a handful of lime around them every now and then all summer. Mine seldom got that treatment, only because I wasn't around to get it done. Yet they grew beautifully. The reason for such success through neglect is that America got its clematis from England, where soils are often intensely acid and require lime, and garden authorities simply repeated the mistake, generation after generation. This book tries to correct another error by not promoting plants that are usually failures: ranunculus, anemones, gloriosa lilies, to name a few.

So many garden books are without opinion that it's time for one that exposes some of the truth of the botanical world: some plants are just not worth planting. This volume guarantees to name names and be biased throughout. Other garden books with snob appeal presuppose a paid gardener or, at least, a greenhouse, pergola, and gazebo. This one has dirt under its nails (mellow loam, I am happy to say).

Let's face it. I'm hooked on gardening. Maybe you are, too. If so, we're in the best of company. A word about that now.

Washington, Jefferson, and Me

Could you guess who penned these words: "I am particular always in my seeds, because nothing is more to be regretted . . . than to sow seed that does not come up. . . ."

That statement is from a letter dated December 8, 1799, at Mount Vernon, and went to Colonel Clement Biddle, Philadelphia business agent for the Father of our Country. It was the sixth to the last letter he ever wrote, and it belongs to my esteemed friend, Wheeler McMillen, expert on the life and times of Washington.

Basically, Washington was a farmer who, pressed into military life, excelled in that realm, too. He loved his farm, and he loved to walk or ride through his fields and woods. But probably the most absorbing of his interests, Wheeler says, were plants and trees themselves. He grafted English mulberries onto wild ones, new improved cherries onto old ones, and he imported Siberian wheat. He wanted for Mount Vernon every kind of native tree or shrub noted for its form, leaf, or flower.

He wrote his agent: "I shall begrudge no reasonable expense that will contribute to the improvement and neatness of my farms, for nothing pleases me better than to see them in good order, and everything trim, handsome and thriving about them; nor nothing hurts me more than to find them otherwise."

Suddenly, I understand that man! I used to think of him as a crotchety old man, unwilling to smile because his wooden teeth rubbed the gums raw, a slave owner and someone insensitive to his soldiers' suffering at Valley Forge. I know now that I wronged him.

In his travels as a young man Washington rubbed shoulders with the cultured of America and Europe, and he learned landscaping. While riding around his farm, he laid down plans for a serpentine road flanked with contrasting shade trees. With each ride through his woods and pastures he would note in his diary some new tree or shrub that pleased him. On a day in April he wrote: "The flower of the Sassafras was fully out and looked well—an intermixture of this and Redbud I conceive would look very pretty—"

As he rose to prominence in the Colonies, his friends sent him plants. From his friend Governor Clinton of New York came linden trees; from "Light-Horse Harry" Lee, twelve horse chestnuts and twelve cuttings of tree boxwood (perhaps the same that now delight visitors to Mount Vernon). That same spring, George planted aspens, black gums, catalpas, crabapples, filberts from his sister Betty Lewis, hemlocks, holly, locusts and honey locusts, seeds of the Kentucky coffee tree, magnolias, a live oak, papaws, sassafras, serviceberries, a row of shellbark hickories, hawthorns, and yews.

How he must have waited for them to come. The spring was a dry scorcher that year, and business kept him absent for several days. What he records on his return is a majestic dirge:

> Most of my transplanted trees have a sickly look.—The small Pines in the Wilderness are entirely dead.—The larger ones in the Walks, for the most part appear to be alive (as yet)—almost the whole of the Holly are dead—many of the Ivy, wch. before looked healthy & well seem to be declining—few of the Crab trees had put forth leaves; not a single Ash tree has unfolded its buds; whether owing to the trees declining or any other cause, I know not. . . . The lime trees, which had some appearance of Budding when I went away, are now withering—and the Horse chestnut & Tree box from Colo. [sic] Harry Lee's discover little signs of shooting.—the Hemlock is almost entirely dead, & bereft of their

leaves;—as are the live Oak.—In short half the Trees in the Shrubberies
& many in the walk are dead & declining.

How could a man like that be anything but sensitive and kind! I really mean
that. I would like to have known that man!

Seeds in those days came largely from England and Holland, and George was
forever entreating his British suppliers to get the captain "to keep the seeds in the
cabin, or out of the ship's hold, at any rate, as they never fail to heat and spoil
when put there." But the results were almost always the same. "The seeds arrived," he wrote, "but some of them were injured (as will always be the case) by
being put into the hold of the vessel."

Benjamin Franklin was another who was interested in plants. That old ap-
ple-a-day man promoted American apples in England and helped start an export
business. He is said to have first brought rhubarb to the Colonies. John Quincy
Adams was still another. He ordered his consuls to send home any promising
plants, and he tended his own garden at Quincy carefully. At the old Adams's
house there still blooms—or did when I was last there—a rose that his mother
brought from England in 1788 or 1789.

Thomas Jefferson was as hooked on plants as Washington. His sixty-year
diary of gardening, published by the American Philosophical Society in 1953, is a
marvel of minute observation as well as precise, vivid writing. Reading it, along
with some of his letters, you must conclude that it is no accident that the
Declaration of Independence is a masterpiece of the English language. Jefferson
seriously proposed that gardening be considered not a skill or a trade, but a fine
art, along with painting, sculpture, and music.

Come join the club. Gardening is for the great, the illustrious, the energetic,
the creative. I don't promise that it will make you that way, but it can't hurt.

A Word from Today's Experts

Although man has been gardening for at least a few thousand years, it's
surprising how little even acknowledged experts really know about it. I shall never
forget my shock at seeing one of the nation's garden authorities consult a seed
catalog to familiarize himself with a plant I had known intimately since childhood. After many years of buying garden articles for national magazines, I came
reluctantly to the conclusion that nobody—not even the garden greats—can be
expert on all phases of gardening.

The first time I met Alfred C. Hottes, author and editor of books on gardening,
it was something like an audience with the Pope. Since childhood, I had pored
over his articles and books, honoring his every commandment. Later, working
down the hall from him, I was dumbfounded to find that he didn't know the
answer to every garden problem. Nor did he make any pretence of knowing.

"Leave it to the experts," he would say.

Louise Bush-Brown, another renowned author of books on gardening, has
much the same to say. The more you experiment, the more you realize how vast
are the gaps in our knowledge of how to make things grow. This is part of the
excitement of gardening.

Fred Rockwell, nationally known gardener and author and his wife, Esther Grayson, also widely known, say that at most you can speak with authority on only a handful of plants, and then only for your own soil, rainfall, weather, and latitude. Most experts therefore confine themselves to a single study, such as day lilies. There is so much to learn, even in a practical way—about culture and breeding, let alone the chemistry, morphology, genetics, and other scientific disciplines—that few people can master more than one or two plant families.

So don't expect an expert on glads to tell you how to cover roses for the winter. He won't know. Nor will anybody, for that matter, because there is no good way. Professionals in rose culture will tell you how they care for their roses, with reasonably good success, for most winters. But now and then all techniques fail. Even experts admit that in their own specialties there are large unknowns.

The result is both exasperation and challenge. Perhaps you will be the person in horticultural history who can dream up the right way to winterize a rose. A plastic spray? A new kind of insulation? A different way of planting? The answer, when it comes, won't confer a fortune on the originator, and that's probably one reason why more research hasn't been directed at the question.

How do you stop an epidemic of aster yellows? How do you grow rutabagas without worms? There are empty niches in the gardener's Hall of Fame waiting for the nonprofessional with enough skill and patience—and luck—to solve these riddles.

In all honesty, though, I must admit that my interest in gardening is less scientific than exploratory. Much as I like growing a prize carrot or a perfect cucumber, I would rather try the untried plant, one from some distant, mysterious land.

The Adventure of Gardening

I am too fat to climb Everest, too timid to raft the Pacific, too old for space travel, and I have no quarrel with lions or tigers or wild buffalo. But I explore and adventure just the same, without the exertion, the heat of the tropics, or the travails that beset the traveler's digestive tract.

The charm of travel to me is largely in the exotic plants I find—and many of them I can grow in my own garden. The edelweiss looks just as it did on the Jungfrau in Switzerland. The calla lilies are exactly like those I saw being carried in great armloads by Quechua Indian women along the streets of Quito.

The Peruvian daffodil (also called spider lily, *Ismene calathina*) isn't exactly showy, but it takes me back to a pleasant week of beachcombing in the Bahamas, where it grows wild in dense clumps just behind the sandy beach. It takes me even further away, to the island of Bali around the world from me, to a land where men are unashamed of decking themselves with flowers, and often sport a spider lily bloom above one ear. Every morning that I rose to watch the sun come up over the Indian Ocean, a bouquet of these flowers would be waiting in a pewter vase on the porch railing of my seaside cottage, along with a pot of freshly steeped tea.

Other plants take me to places I have never seen. *Tigridia*, or Mexican shellflower, grows wild in Mexico, where its starchy tubers are a favorite of certain Indian tribes. I can see it blazing in the Mexican sun, along with the beautiful

Mexican sunflower, or tithonia, which grows head-high and blooms on the fiercest days of summer.

I like the voodoo lily, or snake palm *(Hydrosme rivieri)*. Where it comes from I don't know, but it must be some evil, dangerous, distant part of the universe. Its foul-smelling blossom is something I have only read about. Mine have never bloomed. But their snakelike stalks are otherworldly, despite the handsome swirl of the leaf atop each one. I can see it growing in some moist jungle. Try a bulb this spring and see. My plants grow only knee-high, but in good soil with lots of water, they're supposed to be four and five feet tall.

Devil's-claw (also called unicorn or proboscis plant) is another that suggests life on another planet, although I understand it grows wild in southeastern United States. Its leaves are big, lusty, and squashlike, the flowers are funnel-shaped, lavender, and rather pretty. The whole plant is soft, almost sticky, and queasy to touch. The fruit pods have curving, beak-shaped hooks. It's not the kind of plant you continue to grow, but for one summer anyhow, it's an interesting garden adventure.

Another is datura, the big improved version of the jimsonweed, which makes a giant plant hung with lilylike trumpets; it transports me to the great West of frontier days. A flat of cactus grown from seed, too, is a pleasant adventure into the Old West.

Sometimes my sense of geography gets a sharp jolt. In formal gardens in Cairo I saw flowers I knew didn't belong anywhere but at Rockefeller Center in New York City. I wondered why Egypt—poor as she is—could afford such obviously expensive plants. Each flower was a cluster of blue on a tall lilylike stalk, and the leaves were long and lilylike, too. I cudgeled my brain for the name of it, and slowly it came to me: agapanthus, or blue lily-of-the-Nile. Even then, for a time I didn't associate the name with my location. I was on the bank of the Nile! When the plant blooms in my garden, though, it takes me to Manhattan, where I first saw it growing.

Years later, on a trip by foot and jeep in headhunter country in the Andes, on a small tributary of the Amazon, I saw a dazzling lily growing along the path —exactly like those I saw at Rockefeller Plaza surrounded by splashing fountains. How could it ever have come here, to the edge of a forest in one of the remotest spots in the world? It was knee-high, and each stem had a cluster of white narcissuslike blossoms. It seemed woefully out of place here among the Auca Indians, who not long before had killed five missionaries. Who could have planted it here? Once again I searched the musty mental closets into which I toss such dubious knowledge as the scientific names of plants. Like a distant echo came the sound: eucharis, or Amazon lily. The thinking part of my brain was not as responsive. It was half an hour later before I realized that the flower belonged here and not at Rockefeller Center. I was indeed in its home in the headwaters that fed the Amazon.

2
how to
hurry up
spring

Even though it's still winter, you're on fire to get started. By all means, do start. Buy petunia seeds, the best you can find, some potting soil, and a tray.

Spring starts the moment you pour that soil into a container, tamp it firm, and water it, thereby releasing that glorious smell of moist earth.

Off to a Quick Start

Depending on where you live, February or March isn't too early for petunias and perhaps snapdragons. Six to eight weeks before it's time to plant outside is about right for those slow growers. For fast growers like zinnias and marigolds, start them no earlier than six weeks before they go outdoors.

I like shallow plastic trays as containers for seedlings, big cake-sized ones that give you enough area so seeds don't need to be crowded. As for planting materials, I have tried vermiculite, peat moss, and sphagnum, but my favorite is the rotted wood that I scoop out of the center of an old hardwood stump. It holds moisture like a sponge, is light and well drained, has enough food in it to support plants, and seems not to have the usual soil-borne diseases. If I don't have any tree stump handy, I buy potting soil that has been heated to kill off plant disease spores. Then I see that the soil is moist.

I plant seeds directly on the surface, cover the top of the tray with plastic, and store it in a warm place. (That's generally under a bed beside a hot-air duct.) Bigger seeds I cover slightly by crumbling soil between my palms and letting the fine particles sift over them. Then I cover with plastic. There is no need to water again.

The day the seeds sprout, it's important to remove the plastic and get seedlings into the strongest possible light. The next few days are as crucial as the first days for an incubator baby.

The Secret of Keeping Plants Growing

Fluorescent lights are the answer. They make garden experts out of amateurs. A single forty-inch fixture with two bulbs will start all the petunias you'll ever need, and do it better than your gardening Grandma ever dreamed of doing on her kitchen windowsill. I must have made gifts of fluorescent lights to a dozen people, especially to the shut-in and the elderly.

Fluorescent bulbs give light with little heat, so you can lower the bulbs to within an inch or so of the emerging seedlings, flooding them with the energy they need to push up ahead of the damping-off organisms that topple seedlings just after they emerge. If you drape a sheet of plastic over the fixture and down over the sides, you'll hardly need to water. Leave a few cracks in the plastic tent to allow fresh air inside. I haven't found that too important, though, perhaps because someone is always lifting the plastic to look in. The important thing is to keep the lights within an inch or two of the tops of the plants.

Since the strongest illumination is toward the middle of the bulbs, that's where you'll want your emerging plants. As soon as the seedlings get their first true leaves, they're fairly safe from damping-off and you can move them toward the ends. Some people keep their lights on night and day, to speed growth. Mine are set to go on at seven A.M. and snap off at midnight, for no other reason than that those hours coincide with my day.

With all those hours of light, petunias stay squat and deep green, the way I have never been able to grow them on a windowsill. Instead of sending up a main stalk, many of them begin to stool—that is, send out side shoots. Before long, with this system, you'll need to transplant them so they don't crowd one another. And soon you'll meet another problem—no more room under the lights. This is the time when you'll need another fixture. And since then you'll have room to spare, you plant another tray or two of seeds, and before long you'll need another fixture.

With lights, the fun never ends.

Books have been written to capitalize on the interest in gardening under lights. Buy one if you like. But they won't tell you much more than what I'm setting down here.

The ordinary white fluorescent bulb works as well as the kind specifically designed for plants. Perhaps in the total absence of any daylight—as in a windowless basement—the tubes would need added red light. It's easier without the red lights, though. The trouble with incandescent bulbs is that they burn a plant if placed very close. This was the trouble my sister-in-law had with her handsome commercial console model equipped with incandescent red bulbs. She no longer uses the red bulbs because they burned the leaves.

How Do You Set Up Indoor Lights?

Setting up for fluorescent gardening is hardly more trouble than plugging in the fixture. Deciding where it should go may take more time. The best place is some unused room that you can keep on the cool side, and where a bit of mess won't show, and where you have some outdoor light. Basements are all right, but they tend to be a bit airless and often a trifle too cool. The living room isn't so good either, since some bulbs, no matter what you do with them, produce a constant humming. On top of that, gardens under lights aren't attractive enough to warrant the living room, since plants are so close under the lights that you can't see them very well.

Perhaps in the future we'll have fluorescent bulbs of higher intensity that will allow you to keep the fixture a foot or so above the foliage. General Electric has been working with such a high-intensity bulb, but to date it is expensive and comes without any mounting.

A single forty-inch fixture, on the other hand, is easy to install. I suspend mine from ceiling, wall, or other support, using brass chains so I can raise and lower the fixture. In my previous home, a Philadelphia apartment, I used steel shelving, supporting a light below each of three shelves. In that contraption I grew cinerarias and gloxinias, and I started petunias, coleus, marigolds, lilies, plumepoppies, bletilla orchid, butterfly weed, chives, thyme, and many others. With three lights I could arrange plants of the same height under one light.

Don't expect to grow certain tall plants effectively under lights. Tomatoes, for instance, will start with ease and grow fast, but they need more light than the fluorescent bulbs can furnish. For starting plants, though, a fluorescent garden is nearly perfect. You can control the humidity, drainage, and sunlight as you never can do outdoors.

Midwinter Gardening

Maybe you don't mind having mediocre plants on the windowsill all winter. I do. I get tired of nursemaiding a few geraniums that tease with a furtive flower or two. I like healthy plants or none at all. That's where my lights come into play again.

How much better to keep houseplants out of sight in a spare room under lights, where you can care for them quickly, where they will prosper in a cool, moist environment with ample light. As each plant comes into bloom, you can take it to your living room when it's at its height. With a fixture or two, you can have flowers in bloom for your table all during those cheerless dark days. I recommend no other practice quite as urgently as midwinter gardening under lights.

If you know of a shut-in or semi-invalid who likes to grow things, by all means install a light for such a person at once. You could do him no greater kindness.

How to Jar Some Seeds into Sprouting

Some seeds need to go through a winter before they sprout. Many of the lilies are like that. A spell of cold seems to improve germination in many different plants and is mandatory for others.

These seeds need chilling in order to sprout properly: lupines, snapdragons, phlox, pinks and carnations, sweet alyssum, sweet peas, clarkia, candytuft, and stocks. Give them a stay in a jar in the refrigerator in a mixture of moist sand at a temperature in the 40s for a month if you can. Or else plant them in the fall or very early spring. Larkspurs and delphiniums start best in cold soil, but more important, the seed should have been kept cool before you bought it. Delph seeds lose their strength fast in ordinary storage, but will last for months when kept cold and dry.

It's possible that some seeds don't need chilling as much as they do careful storage at 45 to 50 degrees.

Perhaps cold induces a chemical change in the seed coat that makes it permeable to moisture. Or it might be that cold works a change within the embryo itself. In the buds of apple trees, for instance, a hormonelike substance, which researchers call dormin, or abscisic acid, dissipates little by little during the winter until it has all but disappeared by spring, permitting new growth to begin, which is probably why you can't force branches of flowering shrubs and trees until late winter or early spring. The same kind of reaction may occur with seeds.

One of my gardening friends puts seeds that are usually slow in germinating—like larkspur—in the ice cube tray of the refrigerator for a month or so, then plants the ice cubes in the garden, with good results. More cowardly, I keep my cold-loving seeds in their unopened packages in the freezing compartment for a couple of weeks, then in the crisper until ready for planting. In most gardening matters, however, I am not generally that cautious.

Sweet peas need a cold treatment to germinate properly. I put mine on moist sand in a glass jar in the refrigerator, but I won't boast about my results. They germinate better when I pop them into the ground in late fall.

Pansy seed is something different. It won't germinate until it has undergone wide fluctuations in temperature. The bigger the fluctuations the better. This is the reason that pansy seeds germinate best in autumn, when nights are cool following hot days.

Again, some seeds will germinate well for a few months after they are gathered, then go completely dormant for a few months, then germinate well. This is the case with primrose seed.

(These flowers like warm soil: zinnias, marigolds, morning glories, nicotiana, salvia, ageratum, balsam, cleome, dahlias, columbine. Either wait until the weather gets warm to seed them, or start them indoors where the seed flat will stay above 68 degrees.)

How to Keep Seeds Another Year

Seal any leftover seed in its own package and store in a closed coffee tin in a basement that's cool, to slow down their metabolism. Most seeds that are kept in a cool, dry place will germinate well a second and a third year. Germination of carrots and parsnips—always a little uncertain—is often improved after a year of storage.

How Do You Plan a Garden?

I'm glad you raised that question . . . because my answer is: Don't bother to plan. Those elaborate blueprints you see in some garden books make me smile. They're the work of an amateur or, at least, a dreamer. The perfect gardens are always on paper: hollyhocks at the rear, then steeplechase larkspur somewhat lower, and on down like a grandstand of spectators all the way to alyssum in front. When I was six, that was how my garden would look. We had just moved to the farm, and I had all the space I wanted. What a challenge to my creative juices! Let my five brothers grow the vegetables. I would have 15 rows of flowers in my garden. At 5¢ per pkg. my order was 75¢, with another 15¢ for postage. The only trouble was that my seeds didn't come up—not my row of rhododendrons, nor my petunias, nor my larkspur. And though the hollyhocks came, they didn't bloom. A few stocks finally sprouted, but they sat all summer like gray-green ghosts. All I can remember of that first garden was a profusion of brachycome or swan river daisy, hardly eight inches tall, a few plants of calliopsis and California poppies and a row of the most magnificent purple pansies I had ever seen. Pacing across my vacant rows gave me the feeling of walking in a cemetery.

Go ahead and plan your garden on paper, whether it be a border of perennials or a formal bed, but don't be surprised if it isn't what you expected. It never is. Sometimes it's much better. The summer may be so kind to petunias that they overwhelm the place. Other years the four-o'clocks decide to become trees. Some years drying winds or flooding or cutworms kill off young seedlings and you have bald spots here and there. That's when you have room for a few flats of annuals from your nursery or the supermarket.

The only planning I do is to see that annuals get full sun. This means that lusty growers like tithonia, the Mexican sunflower, should be planted to the north of lower growers. So too should sweet corn. Rather than regiment flowers by height—as the cavalry officers lined us up at Fort Riley—I suggest you vary the heights as well as textures and colors of plants. Landscape architects say that the best planned gardens don't show all at a glance, but tease the imagination. There are corners to travel around before you see more.

The average gardener will probably insist on some concessions to color—a hang-up that I, being color-blind, fortunately don't have. I would rather put contrasting shapes side by side—tall foxgloves beside bushy daisies—and contrasting leaf colors and textures side by side.

I am afraid that my planning is based mostly on what plants or shrubs or trees I want to try out. After I cut the twine on my nursery stock or open the package of seeds, I start then to decide where things will go, and my decision hinges primarily on where things will thrive best and only secondarily on whether or not something will cut off the view or enhance it. My last consideration is how troublesome it will be to mow around. My own practice, though, is something I would denounce in others.

What I am saying about garden plans is that they are fine on paper and sort of fun, but don't be too embarrassed if—in midsummer—you chance to run across the sheet of paper that set down your springtime plans. I am convinced that the old landscape architect with his exquisite plans for pergolas and balance is a trifle pathetic, probably because the garden tools he knows best are compass, square, and drafting board—not the hoe.

3
the magic story of seeds

A seed package is like the jacket on a book of fiction, suggesting what's inside and what's in store for you. But from there on, the analogy falls apart. When you open a novel to read, you're a passive spectator. In gardening, you're part of the scenario.

Dust with a Destiny

Seeds are amazing, even awesome. Consider that inside each seed is life suspended in a sleep that might last as long as ten years, a hundred years, or even a thousand in the case of the lotus. Each is a spark of life, with precise instructions to produce not just a petunia, but the exact variety described in the catalog, a foot high, with ruffled edges in exact colors. All this comes in a particle much smaller than a mote of dust—in the case of begonias for instance, where a million seeds weigh one ounce. Besides that, each seed carries along its own packsack of food, carefully formulated to supply the embryo with its precise needs until the baby plant begins feeding itself through its roots.

Seeds are a unique way for plants to survive deadly cold and searing heat, months or even years of drought. Seeds are a way for plants, anchored to the same square foot of soil, to spread around the globe. Seeds of the dipper gourd, for instance, survive in salt water for a year—long enough for the gourds to drift across an ocean.

If seeds germinated at once when exposed to moisture and warmth, plants would have succumbed long ago to frost and drought. Many seeds therefore have delay mechanisms. Only prolonged cold weather will ready some of them for germination when warm weather comes. (Such seeds can be tricked into growth by an ersatz winter of a few weeks in the refrigerator just above freezing.) A waxy coat on morning glory seeds keeps them from soaking up moisture quickly and germinating before winter. Some weed seeds won't germinate without light, lying dormant for years until you and your tilling machine bring them topside.

Our pioneer grandfathers laboriously herded the cattle and hogs and sheep that were seed stock to the flocks that sprang up along the way west. Inside the covered wagon in bags was corn, oats, wheat, and barley enough to feed the family and its livestock, and to plant crops for the coming year. How much more convenient and manageable were the seeds of plants than the starting flock of animals. Tied up in bits of cloth and handkerchiefs were the pole beans and carrots and pumpkins and marigolds and mignonette and hollyhocks that would feed the westward travelers, body and soul, and help ease the loneliness of a new life far from home.

Even as they traveled west with their treasured seeds, a new kind of business was evolving in the East, one designed to make our pioneers less happy about their favorite varieties of food crops and fruit trees and flowers.

Our Earliest Seedsmen

Perhaps America would have discovered the American way without its seedsmen—but certainly not as soon.

Just as Cornwallis was calling it quits at Yorktown, a young Englishman named David Landreth left for the New World, arriving in Quebec (too cold for him there), passing through New York (a "mere hamlet"), finally arriving in the glamorous capital of Philadelphia, where he set up a seed store in 1784. Up till then, nearly all seeds came from Holland and England, and as one customer, George Washington, would have told you, you just couldn't depend on foreign seeds.

Almost at once, Landreth began growing his own, began advertising, and began casting discreet aspersions on his competitors—all part of the growing American way. His ad in an early newspaper ran:

> Just imported in the ship Fame, from London, and for sale by David and Cuthbert Landreth, at their seed shop in Market near Twelfth Street, being the next house to the French minister's, and at their stall . . . a general collection of kitchen garden and flower seeds. They have likewise a considerable quantity of their own saving, which are very good. They have tried the imported seeds, and will sell none but such as are found to grow.

Something new Landreth had for his buyers in 1790—a freestone peach, as well as strawberries in two colors, both red and yellow. His Virginia Green Grass soon became the talk of all visitors to the capital. Not long after, he unveiled a new flower, the zinnia, found growing wild in Mexico. No wonder the Landreth store was popular with Washington, John Quincy Adams, and Jefferson, who undoubtedly made gardening a highly social avocation. Gentlemen gathered at Landreth's to discuss their favorite vegetables. Except for sweet corn, our Founding Fathers had them all, plus a few others: corn salad, a green; orach, used somewhat like spinach; rocambole, a garliclike plant; skirret, a root used like salsify; plus several dozen herbs.

Now this much is conjecture on the part of a few historians, but it seems possible that it was in Landreth's seed house that Jefferson, with his fascination for new plants, planned a trip of exploration over the vast land known as Louisiana, which he had just bought from the French, and that one of the explorers he sent—Meriwether Lewis—was a trained botanist. Seed of the Osage orange that he found along the Osage River was sent to Landreth's for propagation, and was touted as a hedge plant in the catalog they later produced. In the best American tradition, business cooperated with government. And so through five generations of Landreths, the American way continued to take shape.

Down the competition: "Cheap seed is always nasty seed," said Landreth's. "Don't be shanghaied into buying seed because it is cheap." Their seed cost five cents a package, but included postage. A field of beets pictured in their catalog bore the caption: THREE HUNDRED SAMPLES FROM ALL OUR COMPETITORS. MANY HORRIBLY BAD."

One by one, other seed and nursery firms started up: Dreers' in 1838; Vaughan's in 1877; and Star Roses' in 1897. But it was not until Luther Burbank that seedsmen achieved the ultimate in American hyperbole. Burbank himself wrote in his catalog:

> World travelers find my seed under cultivation by the temples of Hindustan, near the pyramids of Egypt, the Botanical gardens of Java, Western China and on Pacific Islands. Burbank fruits and flowers are household words everywhere. My 65,000 customers live in Iceland, Brazil, and Australia, Patagonia, Alaska, China, Tasmania and far-off Cathay. Is it necessary to say more?

Not really. But he did.

"I have tested the best grains from all over the world, and mine yield nearly double." Without a blush, he offered Burbank flax, Burbank peppers, and the earliest tomato in the world—naturally enough, the Burbank. "Luther Burbank," we read in his own catalog, "is unquestionably the greatest student of life and living things in America if not the world."

It was inevitable that Burbank share his wisdom in a book, *The Training of the Human Plan,* and in so doing, he formulated a new kind of language—a language for American political lightweights. He wrote:

> By placing ourselves in harmony and cooperation with the main high potential lines of human progress and welfare we receive the benefit of strong magnetic induction currents. We are now standing upon the threshold of new methods and new discoveries which shall give us imperial dominion.

And yet, thank God for seed catalogs! Without them, we'd probably be planting the same seeds as the Colonists did. And we'd be depending on friends and neighbors for our new ones—worst fate of all!

Before you delve into the pages of a seed catalog, a few footnotes to the literature of that limpid language.

How to Read a Seed Catalog

I've never met a seed catalog writer, and I'm not sure I'd like to. Just as I feel uneasy around poets, I suspect I'd be uncomfortable around them, too. Like poets, they aim at mood, not fact. Here, one sings of the dark red trillium, biggest of all trilliums, and in the very next paragraph calls the showy white trillium the largest. Did the same man (or high school senior) describe them both? Or did two inspired poets cross pens? Ah, bless their pow-rous prose!

Let's turn the page to petunias. In this catalog, each is the proudest creation, the most vivid, the surest to dazzle, the most floriferous. So what do you do? Just enjoy the wonder of each description, then shut your eyes and poke a pencil somewhere. A word of help, though. The F_1's—from hand-pollinated matings of inbred parents—will give you the biggest blooms, perhaps. F_2's are seeds from the love match of F_1's, unassisted by man. They'll vary more in color, but may have more blooms. (More of this later.) It doesn't really matter which you order. You'll probably buy plants at the supermarket when they come in.

It is among the glowing pages of Burpee marigolds where you feel the need of a Seeing Eye dog. Here are dwarf giants and giant dwarfs, each more stupendous than the next. Some are pale gold, some lemon, some orange. There are Burpee's best, Burpee's finest, Burpee's latest. The only kind I've never tried are those that no longer smell the way a marigold ought to. Why not order a Mammoth Super-Duper Glorious mixture of them all? Next year you might decide which you like best. I never do. Because the following year, the descriptions, the pictures, the names are richer than ever.

Just as Shakespeare needs footnotes, so do these other literary works. Here are a few tips that may help you comprehend them better:

"A gem for the rockery." This is a way of saying that if you want to enjoy the flower you must get down on all fours and confront it—bifocals to sepals. Otherwise you may never notice it. The only place for such gems is a niche in a rock wall, at eye level. There, indeed, some of these "gems" are exquisite.

"Once established." What this means is that this plant may take years before you even notice it. Climbing hydrangea is a plant like that. You plant it for your grandchildren's sake. The only climbing hydrangea I've seen in bloom is at Hyde Park; it was probably planted by FDR's ancestors the moment they arrived from Holland.

"Wilt-resistant asters." My asters have never been bothered with wilt. It's aster yellows that kills them off, year after year.

"Likes full sun." Don't put this one anywhere else!

"Likes shade." This means a spot dappled with a few shadows now and then, not the full-time shade of a house. There are few plants that can take full shade with little or no sunlight.

"Good for naturalizing." Sound the alarm! This one needs the same care you'd give a lion on your place. Or measles. Give it a chance and it will take over your garden. The trouble is that many of these *are* beautiful and are worth planting.

Fifteen years ago—it seems much longer—I ordered all five colors of tradescantia (otherwise known as spiderwort) from Wayside Gardens, an excellent nursery house, which described the plant as "good for naturalizing." Too late would I learn what that phrase meant.

Each tradescantia was beautiful and swiftly became a clump, and then started clumping all over the place, sneaking into the heart of a cluster of prize lilies, its leaves almost indistinguishable from them. For fifteen years now I have been uprooting every tradescantia I can find, and still they keep coming. Someday they may invade the basement and creep up into the living room.

Beware of these others, all "fine for naturalizing": physostegia, certain campanulas (the kind you get as gifts), and most but not all violets. If you must try these plants, put them in quarantine in a remote part of the garden. Perhaps in your climate and soil, they may behave. But then again, it may be too late. You may have unloosed a plague.

"Prefers a moist soil." Japanese iris are among these. I have seen them the size of dinner plates (as the catalog says), but only under the care of full-time gardeners, who apparently soak them every day. Mine grow all right, and I like their cattail foliage, but their blossoms, if any, are more the size of saucers. I thought one spring I'd plant them in the marsh beside my spring. There they would have the moist soil they prefer. But they didn't. I think what they really prefer is a full-time paid gardener, and I don't quite qualify.

"May be left undisturbed for years." Change that word "may" to "must" and the description is more accurate. In fact, unless you leave them undisturbed for years, you won't notice them. In this category: ranunculus and fritillaria (crown imperial). I must have disturbed both of them somewhere along the line. Neither one has ever appeared.

"Best grown in clumps of three or more." A single plant is as inconspicuous as a sparrow in a hen house. That wild flower of the West, the camas, is one like that. One alone looks weedy. A dozen in a tight clump are pleasant.

"Hardy as an oak." Pen in hand, I am poised above the seed catalog about to order a new flower—when I read a final assurance: "hardy as an oak." I quickly cool. What that phrase means is that most such plants generally succumb to cold, or, at least, have earned that reputation, and that this strain is somewhat hardier.

"May be divided." If you *don't* divide them up, they'll quickly choke themselves to death.

If my cautions sound harsh, I am sorry. Sometimes we criticize most what we love most, and seed catalogs are among my favorite things. Do enjoy them. Remember, even Shakespeare enjoined us occasionally "to gild the lily, to throw a perfume on the violet."

All-American Winners

Here's one notation in a seed catalog that means something. To qualify for this label, a new variety must be tested at thirty sites across the country, each representing different climates and soils. Only those that flourish and are a distinct improvement over the nearest existing variety can win the citation. In the average year, only a handful of winners are picked.

F_1 Hybrids, F_2—What's It All About?

Mules are F_1 hybrids. If mules could reproduce, their offspring would be F_2 hybrids. That's what those terms mean. The *F* stands for filial or offspring, the digit for the generation. Just as mules have greater vigor than either parent, so have hybrid plants. In general, they grow faster, bigger, and more uniform, and they bear more flowers and fruit. That's especially true of the F_1 generation. Offspring of those F_1 plants—the F_2 generation—often have more vigor and uniformity than regular plants, but less than the F_1.

The trouble with F_1 hybrids is that the seed is expensive. It's bound to be because, in most cases, seedsmen can't let bees do the pollinating, but must brush the proper pollen on by hand. F_2 seed doesn't require hand pollination, so is less costly.

Breeding the right parents of hybrids is what takes the time and talent and perseverance. A seedsman wants an all-season pansy, for instance, one that doesn't give up in hot weather. He already has one that holds up in the heat, but its flowers are nondescript. His hybridizers set to work on that one, fertilizing each blossom with its own pollen, then enclosing each one in a paper sack to keep out pollen from other plants. All offspring that don't stand up to hot weather are rogued out, and the best survivors mated to themselves, generation after generation, until hybridizers achieve what they call a pure line in which one plant doesn't vary a scintilla from the next. But generations of these incestuous matings have done frightful things to the plant. It is scraggly and weak. About its only virtue is that it blossoms all season. In another plot is a pure strain with big flowers.

Now then comes the magic. Cross the two pure strains and you may get plants with supernatural vigor, that defy both heat and cold, blooming during winter as well as summer. The flowers are giants—far bigger than the large-flowered parent.

The reason for such vitality is a puzzle. Early pioneers remarked about the strength and endurance of "half-breeds," and anthropologists today wonder whether the increase in size of successive generations of Americans isn't partly owing to the effects of hybridization between recent newcomers to our melting pot, as well as improved nutrition.

Henry A. Wallace, our former vice-president and a man who figured largely in the development of hybrid corn, confessed to being as mystified as any about the miraculous boost that results from crossing two inbred parents. His analogy of hybrid vigor, though, is as good as any. He sees it as a power within every cell of a plant or animal, a kind of spark that leaps from pole to pole. The bigger the difference between the poles, the bigger the spark. You see that vital power in a certain few men and women, he says, whose every cell is bursting with energy and drive. They can no more help being active than can another man with a weak spark help being lethargic.

Vigorous hybrid plants sometimes pass on part of their vitality to the next F_2 generation. More often, though, seed kept from hybrids is disappointing. That vital charge is lost. It is hard for many people to understand this. Agronomists in

Africa and South America and Asia, for instance, are less interested in hybrid seed than in nonhybrids, or so-called open-pollinated, strains because they know that farmers will save seed from the phenomenal hybrid plants regardless of how often they are enjoined not to. Sometimes F_1 hybrids don't succeed in a climate different from the one in which they were developed. For that reason, agronomists are working with corn-hybridizing almost everywhere in the world, developing types best suited to their locations. I have met with corn hybridizers in Egypt, Jordan, India, Pakistan, and Ecuador, all striving for better hybrids, as well as ways of producing the seed in quantity to bring the costs down and to make their nations independent of imported hybrid seed. The hybrid you buy, however, has generally been field-tested widely to insure results in most climates in the United States.

Sometimes the term *hybrid* is used in a less specific sense to mean any cross of different strains, either natural or man-made. Thus, rutabagas are thought to be a natural cross, or hybrid, between turnips and some other member of the cabbage-kale family. People who hybridize lilies or day lilies or irises are crossing one variety or subspecies with another and saving the best offspring.

Like the mule, some hybrids are sterile. One example is a hybrid marigold, which, because it doesn't set seed, blooms without faltering until frost. Other hybrids, like the new cucumbers, are as diligent in their duties as rabbits, and set fruit within an inch or two of the place where they emerged from the soil.

And How About Tetraploids?

Scientists have other ways of changing plants. Seeds or plants exposed to atomic radiation are often grossly changed. A drug, colchicine, extracted from the fall-blooming crocus can profoundly change plants too, sometimes doubling the number of chromosomes in every cell, so that a normal diploid becomes a tetraploid. Such plants may have enormous vigor, bigger blossoms, and bigger fruit. The brown-eyed Susan of the meadows was treated with colchicine to become the vigorous and beautiful Gloriosa daisy, a tetraploid. Other tetraploid flowers are Blue Mink ageratum, Glamour phlox, and tetraploid snapdragons and zinnias.

The small French marigold has double the chromosomes of the big American type. Crossing the two results in an intermediate triploid kind that is sterile and, failing to produce seed, continues blooming with great vigor all season.

Are Pelleted Seeds Better?

For a little extra you can buy petunia seed in pellets the size of fine shot, which are easy to sow in flats and which often germinate and grow much better than usual. Pellets contain a little plant food as well as seed disinfectant, which should help keep the seedlings from damping-off. More important than that, though, is the fact that you can space the seeds, so you are spared the disagreeable job of thinning—and for the average person that's a big help. A main reason for failure of flat-grown plants is that they smother one another.

My experience with pelleted seeds has all been good, and I would recommend you use them.

Should You Gather and Save Your Own Seeds?

Those cucumbers that started bearing an inch from their roots and never stopped are probably hybrids, or you might say freaks. Tremendous as they are, their offspring won't be worth growing. This isn't some cheap merchandising trick of seed companies to sell fresh seed every year, but the price of hybrid progress. Seeds from hybrids generally produce poor plants (as we mentioned earlier).

Home-saved seeds more often than not will disappoint you, even though the plants are normal nonhybrids. Plants have the same excuse for getting into trouble as mothers a generation ago used to explain their unmarried daughters' pregnancies: They sat in a cold draft. Well, plants are always standing in a draft that may sweep the neighboring male's pollen past them, or it may be carried in by bees or whatever. It's as hard to keep a plant pure as it is to keep your cat a virgin.

And, generally, the prowling pollen is of the alley-cat variety. Last spring I made gifts to our entire local garden club of hollyhock plants grown from the finest double hollyhocks I had seen. This summer they bloomed. Not one was double. Younger plants that I had grown from seed direct from George W. Park Seed Company (Greenwood, South Carolina) bloomed in my own garden as spectacularly as ever. I don't blame my friends if they feel I gave them castoffs.

Geneticists say that highly improved varieties—doubles, exotic colors, and the like—are generally less able to reproduce themselves and are often less vigorous than the traditional varieties. So the amateur who saves his own seed, gradually, and sometimes swiftly, finds himself back to the unimproved.

There's good reason why seeds are grown in irrigated valleys in California and comparable places. Each new strain is in strict isolation, encircled by miles of blazing desert too hot and dry for wandering bees or pollen to survive.

Old-time gardeners who keep seed of their own squash—and swear by it—do so partly out of loyalty and pride, but more likely because they haven't tried the newer varieties that keep popping out of hybridizers' silk hats.

One reason I don't save seed is that by the time the seed is ripe, the flowers or vegetables look so ratty that I've forgotten how good they were. Finally, there's a practical reason why I don't keep my own seed. I simply can't figure out where or in what container I should keep them. All year I save aspirin bottles and the glass tubes that toothbrushes come in, and an assortment of bottles and packages, which I stumble across when I'm looking for something else. When I need them, they're not to be found. I come inside with my fists full of grape hyacinth seed. Where are my bottles? All I can find for my seeds is a business envelope. I have stored seeds in everything from an old sock to a strongbox. Ten years later, when I discover them, the seeds are still there, but the time is midwinter or midsummer.

Each time I vow I'll have just one place to store seeds, but somehow I can't live up to my promise. I vow too that I'll label them more carefully, but I can't seem to do that either.

Right now I have in an empty coffee can an envelope of "ex tung 1968." Was I gathering tung seed? Was I even in the South in 1968? Another envelope is marked "bilf" and in clear writing an added note, "excellent." So that if I ever choose to grow excellent bilfs or bilves, I know exactly where I can get the seed.

In spring when the ground is mellow and ready, like King Midas counting his gold, I take out my golden packets of Park's originals and my Burpee packets resplendent with color. Every package calls out, "Plant me!" What chance does my "bilf," though excellent, stand against such competition?

4

the facts
of life
for gardeners

Unless you were blessed with a gifted gardener as a progenitor, you probably learned the facts of gardening life the hard way, by trial and error. You thought your peas were blighting—when the trouble was aphids. You thought that kids were breaking off your tomatoes—when it was cutworms. Your garden just didn't grow—all it needed was water. Some people garden for years without learning about the basic needs of plants. They ascribe their success or failure to luck. It was either a good or a bad year.

Let's run through a few of the fundamentals.

A Bill of Rights for Plants

Most plants are busting to grow and flower and fruit, and all they need is an understanding gardener to help them along. You probably know their needs in general, but do you know them all? Better check yourself with these ten commandments for plants.

1. *Treat seeds like eggs.* Don't let them get too warm, and especially don't let them get wet. Moisture and warmth are their clues to start growing. So store seeds before planting in a tight coffee can in a dry, cool place. If you're in doubt about how early to plant, hold off. In cold soil, many seeds rot. For most flowers and many vegetables, it's better to plant too late than too early. Look at directions on the package. If the instructions say to wait until the ground is warm, do just that. When seedlings break through the soil, treat them like the babies they are. Water gently and often until their roots strike down deep.

2. *Give plants sun.* Don't expect them to do much unless they have full or nearly full sun. That means practically constant sunlight. Houseplants will tell you when they're short of light; they creep along the window ledge looking for it. Outdoor plants grow spindly and lean toward the sun. Their flowers or fruits are inferior. If you're short of sun, chop down the old lilac hedge or else prune it back, cut down the old maple. Or else try growing plants that can stand some shade.

3. *Keep plants weeded.* Weeds do more than steal food and water. They cut down on sunlight, the energy that keeps plants growing. They cut down on the supply of air. Grass is a weed that chokes other plants. So too are trees, whose roots may be wolfing all the food and water for as far out from the trunk as the trees are tall. Some weeds even poison certain neighboring plants.

4. *Don't crowd your plants.* The surest mark of the beginner is a garden that hasn't been thinned. To a marigold, other marigolds are weeds when they crowd too close. You simply can't grow decent plants if you don't thin according to the instructions on the seed package. Wait until the cutworms have done their thinning; then you thin, and thin mercilessly.

5. *Give them water, lots of it.* The best favor you can do them is to soak them weekly with water. In hot weather when plants are growing fast, a garden needs prodigious amounts, especially on sandy soils. Conversely, the best favor you can do your houseplants indoors is to be stingy with water. In small containers, roots quickly get waterlogged and short of air.

6. *Don't let them suffocate.* Clay soil is so dense that it can't breathe, and roots tend to suffocate. It quickly gets too much water, and plants grow spindly and yellow. Give clay soil all the peat moss and compost you can muster. More about this later.

7. *Keep them fed.* If your neighbor grows bigger and better flowers and vegetables, he's either watering more or feeding better, whether with liquid fertilizer like fish emulsion, compost or chemicals. You can grow a garden without feeding, but a better one with feeding.

8. *Don't trim off leaves.* Leaves are the food factories. The more leaves a plant has, the more food it can produce. Cut off stems or leaves and you slow down the assembly line. It's as simple as that. Yet people wonder why their crocuses in the lawn don't bloom when they mow off the leaves. Or why lilies don't bloom the year after they picked off the whole stalk for an arrangement. Plants that throw up new stems after you pick them—like asparagus, rhubarb, spinach, and most annual flowers—can recover and do, but even these need a rest. When you pick flowers from your perennial border, see that you leave plenty of leaves for feeding the roots for next year's blooms.

9. *Don't let them go to seed.* Seed production exhausts a plant. A plant packs its all into seeds. Every one is an embryo, plus a concentrated supply of food to get it started. Seed production costs the plant a lot of strength. This is the reason most flowers stop blooming unless you pick off seedpods. This is the reason you nip off tulips as soon as the petals fall, shear off lilac heads, keep old bean pods removed.

10. *Don't condemn them for failing.* Don't always blame the plant if it dies out over winter, or if it barely grows, or if it doesn't ripen before frost. Not all plants prosper in your climate. Our cultivated plants come from all over the globe: from mountainsides and valleys, the far north and the tropics, from rain forests and deserts. It's not strange if they don't flourish everywhere. This is especially true of trees and shrubs that can't sleep under the snow of winter.

Enough of preliminaries. Let's roll up our sleeves and start to work. The time is ready for getting out in the dirt.

How to Set Out Your Young Plants

You've bought a flat or two of petunias, a flat of tomatoes or peppers. There are a few tricks in giving them the right start in the world.

Keep in mind that leaving a greenhouse and being planted outdoors is a shock to a plant almost equal to germination and birth itself. Think of transplants as patients that need to go into intensive care. You can get them ready for the shock by watering them well, but transplanting is still a major operation. Regardless of how carefully you break apart a flat of soil and plants, many roots are broken off. More important, the young plant comes from the moist air of a greenhouse into the hot drying wind outside, which sucks moisture out of leaves and buffets them as well.

The prudent and methodical gardener (not me) will harden off plants before setting them out. That means placing the flat in a half-shaded spot protected from the wind for increasing periods of time until the plants are ready for the rigors of the outdoors. This might require as long as two weeks of minute attention to watering; it also means moving the flats in and out of the sun. Not many people I know are that painstaking. I know I'm not, nor am I around every day to nursemaid them.

My favorite aids in protecting transplants are pieces of shingle, two to a plant, stuck in the ground to the south and west of each plant to cut off nearly all wind and block out most of the sun. Each time I water, I tilt the shingles back to give a little more light and air, but I leave them in place for perhaps two weeks or more, because our winds are dry and searing.

Even with such treatment, transplants often dry and burn and appear to collapse, but they revive every night as the sun moderates.

To insure that my young plants are well fed, I use a tablespoon or so of a fritted fertilizer, mixed into the soil at the bottom of the planting hole. This granular kind of plant food is constructed to release nutrients so slowly that there is practically no danger of burning. Generally I water my transplants with what some gardeners call a starter solution—a mild solution of fertilizer—that probably speeds up recovery and the formation of new root hairs.

Hotkaps are good in transplanting, too, especially when you want to have early tomatoes, peppers, or watermelons. It's surprising how the little caps retain the ground's heat, even when nights go considerably below freezing.

Now for what could be the most important of all considerations in transplanting: watering.

How Do You Water?

Here you have as many experts as you have men with hoses and favorite spray heads.

Ideally, water should flow along the surface and soak in, but since my soil erodes too fast for that, I use overhead sprays. I have a real assortment of sprayers, but the one I generally use is a kind that alternates back and forth. To water the border beside the house I dig in my spading fork and hang the spray head from it so that the water goes horizontally left and right along the house.

Soil-soaking perforated hoses (or canvas) sometimes work all right, but I find it a little troublesome to keep moving the hose. I have toyed with installing shallow pipe in an automatic sprinkling system, but so far I haven't decided if I want to be tied down to such an inflexible system.

The handiest garden gadget I own is a coupling with a cutoff valve between two lengths of hose or at the end of the hose, which allows me to turn off the water at the hose end without going all the way back to the hydrant. You can buy such a valve at any hardware or nursery store for fifty cents or so.

I like to water in the morning so that I don't lose too much by evaporation, but if plants are wilting badly I water any time of the day. Evening watering sometimes encourages mildew, especially in humid climates.

How to Save on Watering and Weeding

The answer is to mulch, which means to blanket the ground with something. What that something ought to be I wish I could tell you. There is no best mulch. All I can do is tell you some mulches that have worked fairly well for me.

A three-inch layer of leaf mold or compost is great. It's fluffy enough to insulate the soil, keep it both cool and moist. The trouble is that it's hard to get, it breaks down in a year or so, and it does let weeds through. In fact, weeds glory in it.

Peat moss stops evaporation and keeps down weeds, for the most part, and it doesn't break down. So what's wrong with it? It sheds water or soaks it up so completely that, after a sizable downpour, the ground below it is bone-dry. The best place for peat moss, therefore, is mixed in the soil around the plant roots.

I thought for a while that black plastic was the answer to a gardener's prayer. Weeds under it die out for lack of light, it's cheap, and it keeps evaporation to zero. Small holes that I poked through it here and there let the rain seep through. But black plastic is an eyesore, the like of which you can't appreciate until you have watched it flap forever in the breeze, glinting black and shiny by turn until it drives you mad. You throw soil on it and it still glints, until in desperation you cover the whole surface—enough so that weeds begin to grow on top of it. How do you get rid of it? Plowing and cultivating won't do. It's there forever, or so it seems. Plastic I put down a dozen years ago still keeps tangling my cultivator. I have a roll I'll sell real cheap.

Speaking of eyesores reminds me of another kind of mulch—newspaper. A single Sunday edition of *The New York Times* was enough to coat a big part of my perennial border about six-ply. It looked terrible, so I watered it down to its essential pulp. It looked exactly like newspapers watered to a pulp. Looks aside, it worked fine all summer until in a fury of cleaning up the garden I pulled up the giant spitballs and burned them. Cardboard boxes don't look as bad, and they do the job equally well. It could be that I'll try them again someday.

Straw works, too, but it must be all of a foot deep to keep out weeds, and sometimes the straw brings in some of nature's most heroic weeds—thistles and quack grass. It has the virtue of improving the soil texture when you plow it down.

Hay, especially marsh hay that is free of upland weeds, is effective, but slow to rot, and it must be removed when you want to plow or cultivate.

The sophisticated mulches—buckwheat hulls and tanbark—may have fewer faults. I wouldn't know. I've never been able to find them. I have tried wood shavings and sawdust, which are effective, but they must always be used with extra nitrogen or the plants they surround will turn yellow and die off. Years ago my brothers and I mulched half an acre of raspberries with sawdust and killed them off.

So what am I going to use next year? I have been watching some leaf mold piled up by a bulldozer that widened a road through a woods. If no one else beats me, that will be my mulch for the year. If I can't get that, I'll use straw.

Staking Plants

Don't toss away the lilac stems you thin from an old clump full of suckers. They're ideal for propping up a variety of weak-kneed plants. Poke a stem deep alongside each giant marigold you set out, and let the plant grow up through the stiff arms atop the lilac stub. In short order you won't see the lilac, and if you've poked the stem down six inches or so, you'll have the marigold supported better than you've ever seen it done. Lilac trimmings work fine with other sprawlers, like some of the campanulas, snapdragons, and carnations. They're the best kind of support for low climbers like sweet peas, cardinal climber, and canarybird vine.

Other trimmings I have found useful: plum, which is stiff and strong and lasts the season well, and hazel brush. There are probably many others.

5
weed and bug clinic

If I can't teach you to admire weeds, maybe I can suggest you understand them. Or cook and eat them. Whether or not weeds bother you is a matter of attitude—physical and mental.

The Trouble with Adam's Garden

Adam had a garden, too, but I can't believe he enjoyed it the way most gardeners do. You've got to invest a little sweat and planning. As I understand it, Adam had only to walk around and gather his food (with certain restrictions) and enjoy the beauty of the flowers the way we do when we stroll through a public park. That's pleasant enough, but the real fun is growing your own, midwifing each plant into the world and nursing it to a healthy maturity.

We might long for an Eden without weeds or aphids or blight or dogs, but I suspect that if plants grew that easily, part of the attraction would be gone. Every garden needs a little adversity. That proclamation sounds all right in midwinter; I'm not sure I'd admit authoring it during an onslaught of chickweed.

Anyhow, I offer you here these practical helps for your dark hours of gardening.

Meet the Enemy

Every story must have its villains, every sport its obstacles, and in gardening the enemy is weeds—a whole Mafia of them that steal light, moisture, air, and soil nutrients.

For the most part, all you need do about weeds is extract them like an ailing tooth—and then keep on extracting and extracting as others spring up to replace them.

I can't help but admire the way weeds get along on their own without benefit of planting, cultivating, spraying, and fertilizing, without greenhouses or hybridizing. You've got to admire any street urchin like that. I'll even have to admit that my archenemy—quack grass—quickly greens over the bare spots in my spring lawn. I guess weeds have immigrant vigor. Much as I cuss them, I can't help but give them grudging respect.

Some beginning gardeners chop a hole in sod and plant seeds, expecting them to thrive. The sad truth is that it won't work. Only weeds will prosper among weeds. Plants reach out and draw food and moisture from a long way around them. If your garden is near an elm or tulip poplar or other fast-growing tree, you'll soon understand that. Such a tree that crowds your soil with rootlets is therefore a worse weed by far than anything else in the garden.

Some weeds do more than starve plants for food, water, and carbon dioxide. Have you ever noticed a clump of the woolly wild everlasting? Nothing else grows among them, even when they are no more than an inch high. The roots secrete a toxin that poisons other plants. Walnut roots poison certain plants, too. And my nemesis—quack grass—even poisons the soil so that plants are weak and yellow for a couple of years after I've pulled out the last root.

Ugly Foreigners

At the risk of giving aid and comfort to xenophobes, let me offer a gardening footnote.

Almost all America's worst weeds came from abroad. Some, like lamb's-quarters and burdock and chickweed and Frenchweed, probably came as stowaways in grain cargoes. But just as many probably came with our immigrant forefathers, the seed knotted in handkerchiefs to help bring something familiar to the new shores. Butter-and-eggs—a pleasant little yellow snapdragon—came that way. So too did that survivor of abandoned old gardens, bouncing Bet, that looks like a white sweet William. Wormwood-scented yarrow with its flat white blooms and fernlike foliage is another. Oxeye daisy, Queen Anne's lace (or wild carrot), creeping Jennie, camomile, cockle and knapweed are others that must have brought cheer to our homesick great-grandmothers. Dandelions are said to have been imported by our French ancestors as a salad or potherb, chicory as an adulterant for coffee, red clover and white clover as pasture and hay crops, and the beautiful blue teasel for use in mills, where its stoutly spined seedheads raise the nap of woolen cloth.

Somewhere along the line, these pleasant flowers kicked up their heels at confinement and spread themselves across the land, to the delight of naturalists and casual gardeners, but to the eternal dismay of meticulous ones.

Other aliens that the United States might well deport: hoary alyssum, henbit, poison hemlock, and that novel weed of vacant lots known as cheeses. At least half the thistles are fugitives, too.

As a child on my first visit outside the United States, I saw broad fields of yellow mustard below Winnipeg, Manitoba. A filling station attendant commented, "That's States mustard. You say we sent you Canada thistle. If so, we'll gladly trade back." As a loyal child of America, I was appalled that anything from the United States could be noxious or even obnoxious.

Lest the FBI be summoned to defend America's gardens from foreign influence, let me point out that without foreign plants our gardens would be pretty dreary. We'd have no cosmos, marigolds, or dahlias, all of which came from Central and South America. We'd have no citrus, banana, mums or peonies, which came from the Far East. From China came the aster, ginkgo tree, bleeding heart, forsythia, tiger lily, weeping willow, butterfly bush, and hydrangea. On balance, the United States is undoubtedly far ahead.

How to Tell a Petunia from a Pigweed

If you plant your seeds carefully, in a single straight line as I told you to, you won't have any trouble knowing which are weeds and which are flowers or vegetables. Keep whatever pushes up in a single file at the bottom of your V-shaped trench. Rogue out all bystanders. You can hoe or pull them out even before the right plants show through. If you don't do that along your carrot or onion row, you might never find your onions and carrots—they're that delicate and hairlike when they first appear.

The right position for that first weeding is on the knees, praising Allah. That close, you can quickly learn what is and what isn't a weed. You can safely pull seedlings in the row that match those outside. Before long you will notice a distinct line of something different—sometimes more vigorous, but usually less so. By the process of elimination you discover what to save.

If the right plants are slow in coming—as they often are—simply hoe between the rows and wait and hope.

How to Enjoy Weeding

As I go down a row of radishes on my knees, pulling out pigweeds, I hear a whisper of soft, fervent thank yous. I like to weed. There are so few safe ways of being a hero in today's world that I welcome the role of weeder. When I move along a row of carrots hidden in grass and lamb's-quarters I am a knight in shining armor rescuing not just fair maidens but a whole grateful populace. The dragons lie gasping and uprooted behind me as I lumber along on hands and knees. At the time it seems the battlefield has no survivors. But the day after—ah, there's the magic. The carrots are like a thin line of maidenhair ferns. Their color is good. They somehow have lifted themselves erect and suddenly the garden begins to look like a garden.

Whether or not you like to weed—as Norman Vincent Peale might tell you—depends on you and your willingness to think positively. In any event, the first time through is the slow job. After that, you can stand and hoe out latecomers.

For that first weeding, my favorite tool is really two tools, each with five claws that can probe for hidden roots, yet never need sharpening, and which, with considerable scrubbing, you can take to church the next day. A dual-purpose weeder that I like has a set of wire claws on one side and a knife blade on the other for slicing just under the surface of the ground to eliminate seedling weeds. The best hoe is a lightweight three-cornered one so small you can chop between plants. I only hope someday I can find one with a handle long enough to accommodate my frame without stooping.

Chopping down weeds with a hoe is a satisfying experience, though quite different from the face-to-face combat of hand-weeding. Give names and faces to the pigweeds—someone from the office or school or administration—and chop them down. You will return to the house tired, but drained of your hostilities.

The best time to slash down those enemies is on a bright day when the sun burns them to a crisp. On cloudy days, weeds have a way of striking down roots and surviving.

Still another way of enjoying weeding is to buy a tractor with a cultivator—but that's not living up to my promise of showing you how to garden without an expensive outlay.

A Meal of Weeds

Lazy gardeners: a reward for you. Let your lamb's-quarters grow big enough so you can harvest a mess of greens from them. They beat spinach, to my way of thinking. But don't delay long. The stems soon get wiry and tough. Another fine green is dandelions. Fast-growing ones are delicious, either raw in salads or quick-cooked like spinach. Still another: purslane, or pussley. Although somewhat gelatinous on cooking, the flavor is fine.

Plants That Are Too Aggressive

It's a pleasure to have plants that grow without bother and always look neat and trim. Violas are one such plant. Campanulas are another. So too is that ornamental grass called ribbon-grass. The trouble with such plants is that they keep on growing and pushing and crowding out the helpless glamor-flowers. It's always a temptation to let aggressive flowers keep spreading, but don't do it. Aggressive flowers have equally aggressive roots that suck moisture and sap food. So spade off the rim of new growth periodically. The pared plant will look better and grow better, too.

Keep a no-man's-land of soil around each of these plants: achillea, costmary, most campanulas, physostegia, and others that find your soil and climate too agreeable. Sure sign of an amateur gardener is a border where one of these is permitted to smother less vigorous neighbors.

Beware of Friends Bearing Gifts!

The cheapest way to get a flower garden is to accept all gifts that come your way. You'll soon have blooms all over the place—everywhere, that is, except on the walls and roof of your house, and perhaps on your concrete walks, although some gift plants do fairly well there, too.

The trouble with gift plants is that they're overpriced. Give them a week or two around your home and you'll have them—like freeloading relatives—for the rest of your life. And no amount of hoeing, hand-pulling, or herbicides will completely eradicate them.

Twenty years ago—it seems much longer—I asked a friend for a root of his bluebell-of-Scotland, a beautiful three-foot steeple of bluebells that edged his vegetable garden and ambled through the weeds behind.

"You'll have to watch it," he said.

And that's what I've done ever since, as the plant sneaks through my flower borders, smothering out young lilies. It does little good to pull it out. Far below is a thick rootstock that shoots up new growth as generously as asparagus. Even if you get that out, you can be sure that seeds will keep your bluebell-of-Scotland ringing.

The answer to gift plants is to keep them in isolation for a summer to see if they're safe. If not, either transplant them out into a wilderness of weeds at the back of your property, or else give them to some of your friends, with the injunction, "Better watch it."

A near cousin of the bluebell-of-Scotland is called Coventry bells, a beautiful flower when you see it blooming in a meadow in Switzerland below the Alps, but one you'll soon despise if you get it started in your cultivated garden.

I hope I am not already too late in warning you to avoid ground ivy, otherwise known as creeping Charlie, or some of the others I mention under the section How to Read a Seed Catalog.

Most gardeners I know would much rather not spray anything. They're concerned about birds and ecology as much as about humans and their own health. They are searching for safe ways of keeping ahead of bugs—by using ladybugs, praying mantises, and the like. Yet sometimes, to save a crop, they resort to insecticides.

The Best Way of Debugging

My gardening friend, Margaret Sletten, who comes from Scotland, has a way of controlling most insects. She squeezes them flat between her fingers. I have seen her flatten a nest of tent caterpillars without even gloves intervening between fingers and hairy bodies filled with tobacco juice. I have tried the method once, and commend it to you. It's one of the most effective and certainly the simplest method of bug control—although don't ask me to do it bare-handed. I need gloves.

It's surprising how many insects you can handle that way, providing you're on the lookout to get the first few. Watch the growing tips of your apple, cherry, or other fruit trees. The leaves aren't unrolling? Just give each uncurled tip a pinch and you'll feel the worm hiding inside. On small trees that doesn't take long. On big trees, you needn't bother because they have plenty of leaf surface already. Keep watch over your small trees to see that limbs aren't being denuded by a brood of worms—which can happen in a few days if you aren't watching. A few minutes is all it takes to rub off the lot of them and stamp them underfoot. If you make it a habit to watch for the first signs of bugs, you can generally keep them under control.

How about the worms that live inside your fruit? Do you really need every last apple? And can't you salvage those with a slight blemish? If we're going to stop pollution, we may need to bury our squeamishness, at least in part. Let's leave to commercial growers our serious fruit-growing, and let the Food and Drug Administration prescribe for them what insecticides can or cannot be used.

On cabbages and their relatives—cauliflowers, Brussels sprouts, turnips, and the like—you can handpick the cabbage worms, or you can sprinkle leaves with some form of rotenone, which is a safe insecticide.

Cutworms

Before work in the morning, you go out to look at the tomato or cabbage or pepper plants you put out the night before. What's this—they're broken off? Not broken, but chewed off, by that villain, the cutworm. Why he should chew them off and then appear to eat nothing of them is a mystery. His work seems more like vandalism than plunder and pillage.

You can nearly always find him hiding under a clod of earth or bit of refuse nearby; killing him may end your problem. But you probably will want to insure your plants against other cutworms. It's absurdly easy. You barricade each plant with a cardboard collar, pushed into the ground an inch or so, with two or three inches above ground. That's all it takes. I wish other pests of the garden were that easy to manage.

Bug Killers

I don't like insecticides any better than you do, and that includes rotenone, which somehow escapes the wrath of the purists. I am mindful that "harmless" rotenone is poisonous to fish, and is widely used by natives in the tropics in collecting fish.

Perhaps your garden may go bugless for a year or two, and you argue that pesticides aren't necessary. More likely you will have an infestation that makes you wonder if gardening is worth the anguish. Although I disposed of all my DDT years ago, I still stock and use rotenone, pyrethrum, and Chlordane, or, more generally, combinations of insecticides and fungicides in all-purpose dusts. I apply them only when I begin to see bug damage. Often, that is too late to save a crop.

Amateurs are almost sure to be organic, no-pesticide gardeners, and who wouldn't be? Nobody likes to think of imbibing poisons in his food. But if they continue gardening (which many probably won't), they come to a view that Frank J. Taylor of New Jersey expresses in his column, "The Liberated Gardener."

Taylor had heard that bugs attack only weak, emaciated plants, and detour around healthy foliage. "Great!" he thought. "I'll pull out the weaklings and save only healthy plants. No more bugs in my garden." What happened? His bugs, he says, hadn't been enrolled in Organic School, and they'd never been taught to know a weak plant from a strong one. Or else they were smart bugs with an appetite for lush, juicy plants. They kept right on sucking and chewing on healthy plants, which soon began to wither. As strong plants became weak, he pulled them out. Pretty soon there were no plants left, healthy or unhealthy.

"My hassle isn't with the organic gardening idea," he says. "I probably spread more organic stuff than any organic evangelist in our area. My quarrel is with the bleeding hearts who say we should be kind to bugs so they'll be kind to you and feast only on your sick plants. Kind my eye! What do you do if yours are smart, greedy bugs?"

His zinnias were at their peak when root aphids, transported by ants, starting gorging on zinnia juice, turning the green leaves to gray. He loaded his spray gun and soaked the soil around the roots. Soon the cottony webs around the roots disappeared, color crept back into the leaves, and his zinnias bloomed until frost.

When he planted spaghetti squash—which he figured was immune to all problems—he figured without whiteflies. A few of them found that young squash leaves are not only good eating, but are fine umbrellas and perfect incubators. Every time he touched a leaf, a cloud of whiteflies swarmed off. "Oh well, they can't hurt squash," he thought. "They're too vigorous." He says, "Never in my life did I guess wrong better. Within two weeks the vines were turning black. Too late to save them with sprays. I could cite a score of similar adventures with smart bugs. Nowadays I don't waste time trying to find out the I.Q. of destructive bugs. When they begin chewing, I get smart, too, and load up the hose spray gun."

The Safe Insecticides

There are three insecticides commonly thought of as safe:

Nicotine sulphate, generally sold as Black Leaf 40, is a tobacco derivative that kills insects on contact. It's poisonous to humans but is easily washed off vegetables and fruit. In spray or dust, nicotine sulphate kills aphids, leafhoppers, and lace bugs. One drawback is that its effects last only a few hours, and it is mainly effective in hot weather, in temperatures of 70 to 80 degrees. Naturally, this quick disappearance means no residues to worry about.

Rotenone, a powder made from derris root, and used either as a dust or spray, will kill aphids and leafhoppers, continuing its effectiveness for several days, although it leaves no dangerous residues. It kills fish, so keep it clear of your pool. It is apparently harmless to man and warm-blooded animals.

Pyrethrum powder is made from the pyrethrum, or painted daisy, and is particularly good against aphids, killing them on contact, but will kill chewing insects on contact, too. Pyrethrum is of little danger to man and animals, doesn't persist in the soil, and insects don't seem to develop resistance to it. It has been used as long ago as two thousand years.

A new synthetic pyrethrum, tested late in 1971 by Beltsville scientists, is a synthetic found to be far more effective than the natural product. In some tests, it knocked out 100 percent of DDT-resistant houseflies and Japanese beetles; in other tests it was almost that good. A week after it was applied as a residue, it killed crickets and cockroaches better than chlordane and malathion. It now sells as a "synthetic pyrethroid" or as SBP-1382. It's future looks bright.

What About DDT?

I can't condemn this extraordinary chemical. It has worked miracles—no less than that—in eradicating malaria from many areas of the world. As my Nepali driver and I were descending by jeep from the foothills of the Himalayas to the Rapti Valley, he said: "My father say never spend the night here; always go up the mountain before you lie down." The caution was a wise one, since at night malaria-bearing mosquitoes used to swarm in the lowlands. Now, after DDT had been introduced by United States technicians, the vast valley was free of malaria. We saw hundreds of hungry cattle being brought down the mountains to an area as fertile as Iowa. The valley had been unpopulated except for a couple of villages we visited where people looked wasted by disease and scrawny from inbreeding. Now new homes were going up. Older ones each bore the date of the last DDT spray on a corner of the wood foundation. DDT is saving lives and will continue to do so.

The trouble has been that so effective an insecticide has been used in practically every tree-spraying program, farm enterprise, and hobby garden, even when substitutes were at hand that didn't pose the danger of residues.

Bugs Aren't as Smart as People

The big edge that insects have is their ability to reproduce. They're not nearly as smart as people, really. With persistence, any gardener can keep ahead of them.

If gardeners were blessed with a bird's eyesight and persistence, there'd undoubtedly be less trouble with bugs. A bird's vision is probably about like ours with binoculars, which means we could see aphids and leafhoppers without half trying, and wouldn't delay dusting, spraying, or pinching. If you start dusting susceptible plants like nasturtiums with one of the safe insecticides even before you see aphids, you'll probably get by free. But if you delay until aphids or leafhoppers are thick, you won't believe you're making any headway.

Keeping weeds mowed down near the garden also keeps down the danger of infestation. During a season when I can't get to mow the jungle of lamb's-quarters, cockle, and hoary alyssum beyond my garden, I am generally overrun with leafhoppers, and no amount of dust or spray seems to knock them out.

Sanitation is a good practice both for insects and for disease. If I keep fallen fruit and leaves policed during summer, I can generally get by without scabby or wormy apples. If I trim out and burn the galls (bug houses) on my rugosa roses, I can keep them under control fairly easily.

This means keeping a keen eye on my garden, though, and learning to detect abnormalities. Why is the columbine wilting? I get down on my knees and find out. The trouble starts halfway down the stalk; below that it seems healthy. The stem above that is discolored. There are bits of sawdust. A borer is inside. Sometimes I can squeeze the life out of him and save the rest of the stalk. Otherwise I break off the stalk and dispose of it, after first slitting it and finding the borer. Often he has already bored down into the taproot. In that case, I probe for him.

It's important that he doesn't go on to propagate more borers. I find that with just a little attention I can keep stem borers under control.

In the same way I find I can keep borers out of my young apple and crabapple trees. Now and then I check their trunks, looking for wetness of the bark or flecks of sawdust on the main stem, generally on the southwest side of the tree. When I find where one is working, I cut him out with a knife. I haven't found any in several years now, even though borers seem to prefer the red-barked ornamental crabs, which I am planting in increasing numbers.

A neighbor tells me, "My trees are blighting," and asks what he should do. His trouble: not disease but aphids, which he has allowed to multiply until they are curling and distorting all the young leaves at the branch tips.

Nasturtiums diseased? Again the problem is probably aphids. Spray or dust with nicotine sulphate or rotenone.

Your seed dahlias won't bloom? Perhaps slugs are eating the buds. Look for them under bits of rubbish or matted leaves. Put out slug bait to get those you don't find. If you prefer, set out beer for them in cups or saucers. They crawl in, drink, and drown. Sounds like a piece of folklore, but it's true.

For the Future

Keep an eye on bug control via insect diseases that affect only a single species. Already the cabbage looper is being kept in check by a virus that can be stored as a dry powder and dusted on plants at the first sign of trouble, and that persists over winter in the soil. The beauty of this approach is that other insects are safe, as well as man and other animals. That safeguard means, though, that separate diseases will probably need to be cultured for each of our major insect pests, and this will take time and a lot of expensive research.

Another approach is through finding naturally occurring chemicals that guide bugs to food, water, the opposite sex, to egg-laying sites, and to safe overwintering spots. Conversely, scientists are discovering antiattractants that repel insects from food, water, predators, and the like. They're also isolating chemicals that predatory spiders, ants, and wasps use to kill their prey. Other chemicals work to sterilize insects. The last count I heard was that there are more than forty chemicals that sterilize houseflies.

6
then there are other troubles . . .

There may be help for you here in this chapter. I hope so. At least, in sharing our assorted garden problems, we are bound to find solace.

The Neighbors' Kids

Of course they'll make shortcuts through your hedge and across the lawn. Every red-blooded American cuts corners when he's in a hurry, and what kid isn't in a hurry when the bus is waiting?

You have already considered the obvious solutions: a German shepherd veteran of the K9 corps, barbed wire entanglements, land mines, or the police. Let me suggest a subtler form of control: indoctrination, or call it just plain brainwashing.

On the day you start planting, ask the neighbors' kids over and let them plant a row of beans or glads or something. Give them a corner as their own to plant whatever they want. Your life will be richer for having them around. Remember the excitement you felt as a child on first seeing bean plants shouldering the soil aside to raise their heads erect? There is a way of recapturing that excitement in part—by sharing it with a child.

Don't expect your neighbors' children to keep their garden or row weeded. That will come later. But let them pick bouquets to take home, and a mess of peas or beans.

If your fruit tree has been raided year after year and its branches broken off, try this strategy devised by my cousin Mae, who, more than anyone else in the world knows how to deal with children. She assembles her many small friends each summer and explains that there will be plenty of apples for them all, but that they must be harvested carefully or the limbs will break. She asks each of them to explain as much to other children who might come to get apples a little early. If the trees are untouched by harvest time, she throws a watermelon party for them with all the watermelons they can eat. Year after year the idea works. Self-appointed guardians of her apple tree keeps it cordoned off, and even a suspicious glance in its direction brings them running over.

Gardens can grow a pretty nice crop of kids as well as beans.

How to Dog-Proof Your Garden

If you were trapped inside a heavy fur coat, couldn't sweat, and it was ninety degrees in the shade, you'd dig, too, in the coolest dirt you could find. So don't blame your dog for digging in the cool of your best perennials. Help him find another cool spot beside the garage, and dig out a few shovelfuls as a tip.

It's easy enough to stop a dog from digging among your best plants. Simply saw off short pieces of broom handle or other small sticks and pound them a foot or so apart in the area you're trying to save. He'll get the point.

If his aims are uplifting rather than digging, you've got more of a problem. A barricade of stakes or old chicken wire around your evergreens should discourage him. I haven't used the commercial preparations, but my friends say they work. Puppies are another matter. Either fence them in or fence your garden in, or else forget your plants for the season until the pups are grown.

Pocket Gophers

Once in my callow youth I thought I could eradicate all the pocket gophers on our place. "Let's get through with them once and for all," I told my dad. He only smiled and said that pocket gophers are like sin—something you need to work at, but that never gives way. After long years of battling them, I know what he means.

The Lord seems to have a role for everything—weeds, early frost, drought, even Japanese beetles—and I understand that. But pocket gophers are something else: they must be an invention of the devil. They have their apologists who claim that gopher tunnels open up the soil and aerate it. But in our sandy soil, those runways start erosion. Their mounds are an eyesore, pockmarks on meadows and fields and lawns. Farmers hook into the mounds with their mowers, dulling blades. But it's the gophers' underground vandalism that stirs me to fury.

In my ten-acre plantation of red pine, the pocket gophers carefully detour around the roots of willows and other weed trees to zero in on splendid young pine that may be ten feet tall. I have long ago learned that the wind isn't to blame for healthy trees that suddenly lean or even fall flat on their needles. A pocket gopher has gnawed off the big tough roots, and I can lift the trees out like bouquets of dead flowers from a bowl.

Perhaps if pocket gophers were less discriminating in their taste, I would feel less threatened. But they like the very things that I like best, so my dislike of them is a highly personal thing. They pass up the roots of my wild plums to feast on my fancy tame ones. They are connoisseurs of apples, and they find my best varieties within weeks of the time I put them out. They know the flavor of my Fireside and Prairie Spy and Honeygold long before I do. My Oriole was fast growing into a beautifully rounded tree when it fell on its side and wilted. A small root or two must have been missed because the Oriole still survives, but barely, sending up a feeble handful of sprouts year after year. Once the taproot of an apple is gone, the tree seldom recovers, I find.

A pocket gopher's ability to find my goodies is uncanny. I thought my Stockton double-flowering cherry was safe in a corner of the lawn where no mounds had appeared for years. I treasured that tree. I had seen one in bloom once and was delighted when I learned where I could buy one. But though I lavished the tree with water and plant food and affection, it languished. Moving it might help, I thought. From the first thrust of my spade, I knew the trouble. It had no roots of any consequence. How a pocket gopher had found it in an acre of ground, in the pitch-dark below ground I don't know. Was it smell or radar or what? In someone else I would have admired that ability, but not in this wretched creature. For years I planted tulips and daffodils and lilies each fall during my week in Minnesota. They seldom stood the winter—or so I thought. Now I know better. Without a mound to betray their presence, the pocket gophers had burrowed around the house, chomping up every bulb.

Pocket gophers are solitary-dwelling members of the rodent family, so foul-tempered that whenever two meet, they fight furiously—well, nearly every time, that is. A female bears a litter of one to five young, and how she does this is an interesting obstetrical note. Her pelvis is so narrow that she can't give birth naturally. If it were wide enough, she wouldn't be able to squeeze through the narrow labyrinth of tunnels. Shortly before she has her young, the pelvic bones soften to something as pliable as gristle. Afterward they harden again to bone.

A gopher's pockets are external, attached to its cheeks, and they inflate to enormous capacity. I would guess each one could comfortably hold a golf ball. A single gopher in a night can throw up a chain of mounds across your lawn or orchard. Since those mounds mark his location precisely, it should be easy to find him and either trap or poison him. And it is, but, within a week or a month, another gopher takes his place.

Let me pass along my father's techniques against this "sin." To find the main tunnel from which the short spurs emerge, my father made a probe that is much the best I have ever used. It is the handle and shaft of a tire pump with the end filed to a point, and a small nut screwed on about a half inch from the end. When you probe, the nut resists the soil until it bursts into the tunnel. In summer when gophers are using runways just a few inches below ground, it's relatively easy to find the main tunnel. Then all you need do is insert a few kernels of poisoned grain or else enlarge the opening and set a trap. It's as simple as that. (You can get poisoned grain at a feedstore or garden supply store.)

One summer long ago, after a week of intensive trapping, I returned from my rounds and announced to my parents that I had exterminated the last pocket gopher from the place. My mother hesitated a moment and then chuckled softly. "Look in the basement," she said. There in a corner where we had struck through the concrete to let water drain out was a foot-high mound of earth. A gopher with ghoulish prescience had tunneled straight down to the only chink in the whole basement!

The worst thing about my vendetta with pocket gophers is that they arise anywhere to haunt me and to spoil my appreciation of an otherwise flawless view.

Like my cousin Mae, who can't see Mount McKinley for the beer cans beside the road, I found myself counting the gopher mounds at Lake Louise.

At Christmas a few years back I was in Jerusalem, walking up the rocky path on the Mount of Olives. Here was the very path the Lord had used, and it looked probably much as it had in his time. I was moved beyond words. Until there, ahead of me, was a string of pocket gopher mounds going on up toward the Garden of Gethsemane! Nothing, no nothing, is sacred to them.

Even in my traps they defeat me because they wring my heart with their courage, lunging out at me and clicking their long teeth. I feel no sense of righteousness when I dispatch them with a shovel.

Last fall, on my trapping rounds, I spotted a striking blue flower in the meadow, and as I came closer, I saw it was a delphinium that had taken root in a gopher mound. Here was my answer to the pocket gopher's role in world affairs! How else could a plant or weed get started in the solid sod of a prairie? Gopher mounds are seedbeds of wind-borne seeds, and thereby bring diversity and variety and interest to wild meadows.

I was almost enthusiastic about pocket gophers until heavy rains just before freeze-up started following the main thruways of gopher traffic that apparently surround my house, funneling water that seeped through the walls and floor. Normally such water drains out that corner and into a drain—but the drain was clogged. With winter approaching, I dug furiously, at intervals, from the house all the way to the end of the drain field—to find that a pocket gopher had packed the end with two feet of soil.

Sin, taxes, and pocket gophers—by now I know they are inevitable.

A Way to Keep Your Tools from Walking Off

Paint every tool you own with your own distinctive color, and they'll eventually come home to you. Until I painted mine bright red, I was forever missing my favorite hoe and ax and rake. No longer. The bright red must be accusatory: a sharp-nosed spade that almost never used to return is back in a week, ready for someone else to borrow.

For those who don't like the feel of a painted surface in their grimy hands, just extend the paint partway. If I were to start all over again, I'd paint my tools in contrasting bands of blue and yellow—colors my red-green color-blind eyes could spot more readily when the tools fall in the grass. That way, too, I wouldn't claim any and all tools dipped by the manufacturer in red paint or, at least, eye them suspiciously.

7

all about soils and fertilizers

Soil that's either sticky like bread dough or sandy like sugar is in bad shape. It should be porous and crumbly like cookie batter or bread or cake. There are few words that describe texture, and that's too·bad because texture or soil crumb is more important to gardens than fertilizers.

Bear in mind, then, that texture and chemical makeup aren't the same.

What's Wrong with Your Soil?

If your place is a sandpile, you already know it; if it's heavy and poorly drained, you may not be aware of it.

To tell whether or not your soil is soggy, dig a hole a foot or two deep and fill with water. If the water doesn't soak out of sight in a couple of hours or less, you need better drainage. Your plants will show you poor drainage, too. They'll be tall and spindly. Portulaca instead of flat will grow upright.

Correcting poor drainage isn't easy. You'll have to mix in enough peat moss to make it fluff up. Mix it well, too, and as deep as you want your plant roots to grow. Generally this is a foot at least—and that means starting at one corner of your plot and digging down two spade depths, adding the peat and replacing the mixture in the hole. Work? You bet it is, but in the process you'll learn a great deal about your soil, about the roots of trees and how far they range, and about the character of your subsoil, the earth below your good growing soil. You might even run into a concretelike layer called hardpan, which may be what keeps excess water from draining away. Few roots can penetrate hardpan.

The remedy for too-sandy soil is the same as for clay soil. Add peat moss. This amounts to putting a sponge in the soil to soak up moisture and hold it. As moisture-retentive as peat is, it sheds water if you leave it on the surface, so get it mixed in well.

Manure, straw, and other organic materials will loosen up soil and increase its water-holding capacity. They're also good for improving fertility, but they rot quickly and need to be renewed. Peat, on the other hand, resists decay, and a thorough mixing of your soil should last many years.

A good soil texture is generally more important than its fertility. It's easier to add plant food than to improve soil structure. The right soil texture is one that you can form into a ball when moist, yet crumbles easily. It might be a bit sticky after a rain, but not for long. The right texture will go far toward making your garden and grounds the best in the block.

What's This About pH?

If you want to appear informed, be sure to learn that soil ranges from a very acid pH 4, generally found only in peat bogs and under dense evergreens, to a pH 8, found in alkaline flats out West, on heavily limed soils and in salt marshes. A pH 6 is slightly acid and pH 7 is neutral. Armed with that knowledge, you can make most of your gardening friends uncomfortable.

I haven't found that adding lime has helped anywhere in my gardening. Nearly all vegetables and flowers do fine in a slightly acid or neutral soil. I used to add a handful of lime to the soil around each clematis vine, but they do just as well without it. I add ammonium sulfate to my lady's slippers and they thrive, but they have done equally well now that I have discontinued using it.

Most garden plants tolerate wide ranges in soil acidity.

Soil-Testing Kits

Buy one if you like, as a toy. You'll probably try it once and then store it in the garage for a few years before you throw it away. Soil testing is for real experts. Even gathering the samples takes precise attention to getting a mix of soils and keeping them free from contamination, let alone the actual testing. I recall one friend who got a clear-cut reading from her kit: her soil was strongly acid. Demonstrating the test to friends, she got another clear-cut reading: her soil was alkaline! She threw out the whole kit.

You can easily tell whether your soil is acid or alkaline. What wild plants grow near you? On acid soils you'll find evergreens thriving: pine, cedar, fir, plus associated plants like wintergreen and arbutus. Wild strawberries will be growing there and ferns and birch trees. On neutral or slightly alkaline soils you'll see these plants thriving: dandelions, clovers of most kinds, bluegrass, elms, willows, wild plums, and most garden vegetables and flowers.

A nearby farmer can tell you how to improve your soil and whether or not you need lime. In fact, he can tell you what you need to do to put your soil in shape. He's more of an expert than you probably ever will be, with or without soil-testing kits. Another man to give you an analysis of your soil is the County Extension Agricultural Agent.

Fertilizers

On a back road near the Amsterdam airport you travel along canals and small homes so picturesque with flowers and tiny footbridges that tourists can't help but stop to admire and take pictures. Behind the houses are commercial gardens and greenhouses that all but float on the water, and here I stopped to talk and to admire flowers, some of them strange to me and others so far superior to our best that I hardly recognized them. There were cyclamens, I remember, like none I had ever seen before.

"How do you do it?" I asked a man who spoke English.

"It is a secret of the family, passed on from father to son for several generations," he said.

He was a graduate chemist, no member of the family, and although he was general manager, even he had not learned all the secret techniques.

Along a side canal beside the plot was a building housing a giant hopper where soils were mixed to exact formulas, a different formula for each of the half dozen plants that this firm specialized in. Piles of earth awaited mixing. One came from the Black Forest of Germany and seemed to be largely decomposed pine needles. Another pile was sand from the oceanside; another, silt from another source, besides smaller heaps of materials, each calculated and weighed and mixed with laboratory precision. Every week the soils are chemically analyzed. At other firms I visited along the canal I found other graduate chemists with the same devotion to soil. Obviously, soil is of crucial importance to optimum gardening.

What then can an amateur do about his soil? Feed often and lightly. And to make sure you don't burn plants with it, dissolve your fertilizer and water it in, then soak it in with more water. A feeding at recommended strengths every two weeks or so is best. What kind? Look to the label, and when you see figures like 4-12-4, remember this phrase: No Poor Kid (NPK). The first figure is the amount of nitrogen per hundred pounds, the next the phosphorus, and the third the potash. Nitrogen is the expensive part, the one most often lacking, and the one that is washed away quickest by rain. It's especially needed by leafy crops like cabbage, Swiss chard, and asparagus. Bone meal gives off nitrogen more slowly than most forms and is less likely to burn from overdosing. Phosphoric acid, which costs a third as much as nitrogen, comes from rock phosphates and bone meal. Potash is the easiest to get—wood ash is about five percent potash—but essential too for proper growth.

If fertilizers all leached away by the end of the season, adding them would be a simple matter. The trouble is that residues build up, some making the soil more acid, others more alkaline. And they all have a tendency to burn up the organic matter that gives your soil a good texture. To keep your texture up, you need to keep adding organic matter in the form of peat, compost, straw, or what-have-you that you buy or scrounge from the countryside.

Manure is best of all as a soil conditioner, but hard to get hold of and hard to transport. Its main value is in keeping up soil texture. Its value as a source of plant food is much less. In fact, it's expensive as a nutrient, and a ton of it is worth only about two dollars in chemicals. (More about this later.) Don't think of it as fertilizer but rather as soil conditioner, one that breaks down fast and needs replenishing at least every couple of years.

Compost does almost exactly the same job as manure, but unless you put it on in great amounts every year, it needs the help of fertilizers. These can be added to the compost as you build it or else applied directly.

My favorite fertilizer is one trademarked MagAmp, marketed by the Jiffy-Pot people. It's concentrated, yet formulated so it can be spread safely without danger of burning anywhere. I buy mine through my local nursery, and keep a jar of it in the garden, sprinkling it in the bottom of my seed-row, covering it slightly before I plant. I use a handful or two in the bottom of transplanting holes for shrubs, too. I have never had any burning, and my plants have a healthier, greener look than before.

P.S. I own no stock in Jiffy-Pot, nor do I get any free samples.

What About Organic Gardening?

I have a friend who is suing the United States government for atomic fallout. For several years now, he has been suffering from it. As proof, he offers these symptoms: He has occasional insomnia, his hair is falling out, he can't remember the way he used to, he doesn't like to get up in the morning, he doesn't feel up to par, and he can't seem to get things done.

You can't laugh away symptoms like that. They're real. I should know because I have every one of them too, to a greater or lesser degree. But I had attributed them to less actionable causes.

Perhaps someday we'll discover the cause of falling hair and failing memory, and a remedy for those conditions. If so, I'll be the first to use it, and espouse it.

Things don't taste the way they used to when I was a child, either. Could it be that scientists have the answer, that taste buds disappear as we grow older? A baby at birth has taste buds not just on his tongue, but covering the lining of his cheeks and mouth, and these gradually shrink in area until confined largely to the top surface of the tongue.

I don't like those facts. I'd much rather blame someone else—the people who produce today's foods. And while I'm at it, I'll blame them for all the symptoms my fallout friend describes.

And so I take up organic foods and nibble whole grain cereals and rose hips in the pathetic hope that I can feel once again as I did at eighteen. Not content with that, I try to convert others to the Organic Creed, hoping somehow that in numbers there is truth, that if enough people buy organically grown vegetables, the scientists with all their controlled experiments will be proven wrong. It's like putting truth up to a public referendum.

What I forget to realize is that health foods and organically grown foods have become a billion-dollar industry, whose entrepreneurs are delighted with the way aging Americans are making a religion of organic foods. A religion with a billion dollars a year going for it has no lack of high priests dipping into the collection plates, pouring out tracts that keep the money rolling in.

Nutritionists—who have no business interest in the outcome of their experiments—say that vegetables do indeed differ in their food value. Tomatoes grown during the sunny days of summer not only taste better, but may have twice the vitamin C content of those grown under glass in winter. Tomatoes in the South grown in soil will vary widely from tomatoes in the North grown in the same soil. But in the same climate—even in widely different soils—there is no difference. The amount and intensity of sunlight makes the difference.

The food value of crops and vegetables is influenced by several things: how much light they get, the temperatures of both soil and air, the amount of moisture in soil and air, the plant variety, and soil fertility. There is no reputable evidence that crops grown only with manure, compost, or other organic nutrients are superior to those grown with inorganic chemicals. In fact, before plants are able to absorb any organic matter, it must be decomposed into simple chemicals—exactly the same as those in inorganic fertilizers.

I am reminded of an American who was introducing commercial fertilizers to the farmers of a village in central India. A truckload of fertilizer came too late in the day to be distributed, and it stood outdoors. That night rain poured down, and the fertilizer lay thick around the truck. When farmers saw how it burned the vegetation, they backed off. They couldn't afford to experiment with something that might ruin their food supply. A single crop failure would mean starvation for themselves and families. Word of the dangerous chemicals traveled far and fast through central India.

What ignorance, I thought, as my friend first told me the story. But today, he says, those same farmers are using fertilizer on all their land, having seen its dramatic results in government demonstration plots. Yields have doubled. Their children, once undernourished and diseased, are healthy. Those Indians may be ignorant, but they have the capacity for learning. Fertilizer plants are being built in India as fast as the government can find the money.

What is there left to worship, then, if not organic foods? Regular exercise, perhaps, although this isn't much fun, quickly gets boring, and provides no devils to inveigh against. Why not look outward—away from your own wearies—toward other people? Harvest a row of snap beans and walk a sack of them over to a friend's house across town. You'll be amazed at how good it makes you feel. And though I can't claim that such a program will stop falling hair or failing memory, I believe it will reward you with a good night's sleep.

Manure—What Is It Worth?

Certain days of trauma I will never forget. Learning the facts of life wasn't one of them; I absorbed them unconsciously, I guess, from watching the seasonal antics of our cats and dogs, cows and poultry.

But I shall never forget the day I learned that manure is barely worth the hauling. My friend, Ralph D. Wennblom, agronomist and soils expert, had come back from a nationwide symposium with that disturbing assessment. It was almost like having him deny the Divinity.

Why then have we hoarded manure in pits to prevent loss, spread it carefully on fields all these years, these generations, these millennia? To get it out of the way, Ralph said coldly. A ton of barnyard manure has ten pounds of nitrogen, five pounds of phosphate, and ten pounds of potash. At twelve cents a pound for nitrogen, seven cents a pound for phosphoric acid, and five cents for potash, it's worth about two dollars and five cents a ton. But how about the humus it delivers? You can get more of that by turning under a crop of rye. Yes, but how about all those soil microbes? You'll have just as many from the rye or any other "green manure" crops. With a lot less work and worry, too, he concluded as he left, walking over the shards of my ignorance.

He paused at the door. "We can build good soil out of raw subsoil in a few years by fertilizing and plowing down vegetation. Manure has nothing to do with it."

How about the commercial dehydrated products? Just check the contents and see what you're paying per pound of nitrogen, phosphoric acid, and potash. Whether or not it's a good buy depends on that.

Compost

"Thou shalt have no other gods before me," saith the Lord. Organic gardeners, do you hear? If I were going to build me a graven image to worship, I think I'd look for something more inspiring than a manure pile—artificial at that. My tools might get a little messy. Yet magazine articles and even books have been written about how you build compost heaps, water them, feed them, get up in them every week and turn them—by writers who probably got no closer to them than their public library. And there is awe, reverence, even worship in their flowery phrases.

Come on, gentle writer, where on a city lot do you hide a pile of manure, out of sight yet in full sun as required? And where do you get all the "garden refuse" and topsoil and cornstalks to fill one? Do you actually lift and turn your compost every week? In fact, do you yourself have a compost pile? Do you even own a pitchfork?

Without the chemicals added to compost, it's worth no more, no less in fertility than manure, or about two dollars a ton. Not counting delivery from pile to garden by wheelbarrow.

My compost heap is eight feet across, encircled by wire netting stiff enough to need no supports. Into it I have put grapefruit rinds, eggshells and comparable garbage, straw, old tomato vines, coffee grounds. A year ago when I moved it, I found it just beginning to decompose. Interspersed were pieces of broken glass, aluminum foil, and walnuts secreted by a resident squirrel. I am not exactly proud of my compost, as I am told I should be. I much prefer plowing down a crop of rye in late fall, or of vetch, or adding a few bales of peat moss. I am a trifle proud of that fence idea, though. It's not unsightly, and all I need do to extract a few pails is peel back the wire.

A far better idea, though, is what Ruth Stout espouses in her delightful book, *How to Have a Green Thumb Without an Aching Back*. She puts her refuse directly onto the garden, so, in effect, her whole garden is her compost, performing the excellent job of mulching and weed control, eliminating the extra transportation to and from a distant compost.

In all my experience I have encountered only one person who genuinely uses a compost, and that is my gardening friend, Margaret Sletten, who learned gardening in Scotland from her mother. Her compost pile (she has four of them, actually) is made up of kitchen refuse, "everything except glass and tin cans," she says, together with weeds and leaves. To keep the heaps from smelling, she adds lime. Aside from watering occasionally, she does nothing else. After two years, she begins mining what she calls her black gold from the bottom of the pile, and it is marvelous stuff that she brings with her as a gift when she comes to visit. It is only the thought of Margaret Sletten's compost that keeps me at my dismal task of turning refuse into soil.

Better Yet—A City Compost!

Like many a good idea: why didn't somebody think of this one sooner? Have a city compost heap. In Scarsdale, New York, homeowners pile their leaves at the curb for the city's leaf-picking machines, which shred, compact, and haul them to a city compost area where they are transformed in a year to excellent humus that is given away to gardeners in small amounts or sold at about six dollars a yard.

Other places are beginning the same city compost heap and everybody seems happy about it. The city saves money. Homeowners can replenish their soil. And a big source of air pollution is ended. In some towns, preparing compost is a Boy Scout project.

A Middle Ground on Fertilizers

My friend Bob Smith of Minnetonka, Minnesota, has the most beautiful and most productive vegetable garden I have ever seen. Bob's system of fertilizing is to provide all the plant food he can by using manure, compost, and other organic matter applied directly or as a mulch. In addition, he supplements these fertilizers with more concentrated natural fertilizers like fish emulsion, cottonseed meal, soybean meal, or hydrolyzed turkey feathers (for nitrogen); phosphate rock or bone meal (for phosphorus); and granite dust, greensand, or wood ash (for potash). These, he says, aren't much more expensive than their chemical counterparts.

Bob says he is an organic no-pesticide gardener, but he's not a nut about it as many of that ilk are. His garden reminds me of the Dutch ones that use soil from various parts of Europe, fortified where necessary with appropriate chemicals.

8
vegetables— the kind money can't buy

The mighty Inca, who ruled a sprawling kingdom in the Andes, long ago knew the value of freshness. Every day swift runners—at relay points a mile and a half apart—raced watertight baskets of fish, swimming in salt water, all the way from the Pacific to the Inca's table in Cuzco, arriving little more than a day from the time they left the ocean. Most vegetables aren't as perishable as fish, although nutritionists say that vitamin content drops markedly as vegetables wilt. As far as detecting flavor goes, I am more of an eater than a savorer, but my discriminating, taste-conscious friends swear that vegetables fresh from the garden are infinitely better than those that are store bought.

Perhaps, they say, it would be better if vegetables announced their age the way fish do. Then we'd know that home-grown produce—minutes away from the garden—is something that money can't buy.

Does It Pay You to Grow Vegetables?

A seed catalog proclaims: "This is the year to FIGHT INFLATION AND THE HIGH COST OF LIVING." It winds up, again in giant type: "GROW YOUR OWN GROCERIES! The average garden can save you $300 to $500 a year!" Nearly half of America's families (47 percent or 33 million families) grew their own vegetables in 1974, and according to a Gallup poll, 46 percent of them did it to help the budget.

That's a fine idea if you're the nickel-budgeting type, although, in all candor, I think you could do better by growing your own rabbits for food, knitting your own socks, or fermenting your own wine. With these, your hourly return might be ten cents an hour rather than the five cents an hour, which is the going rate for home vegetable growers. If you're gardening to save money, you're going to have some weak moments.

More flavor from your own? Maybe.

More vitamins? Very likely.

More fun? You bet!

So much more fun that you wouldn't believe it. You'll be so engrossed in your garden that you won't have time or inclination to shop for new draperies, a new carpet, a fancier car, or worry about where to go on vacation.

The result? You FIGHT INFLATION AND THE HIGH COST OF LIVING.

But, more important, you sleep well (no pills), eat well, learn to know the neighbors, and—with vegetables that would otherwise spoil—achieve a reputation for generosity. That early morning walk in the garden gives you a reason for getting up. At home, after work, you exercise without knowing it. You stoop and squat and bend with a purpose. Watching plants sprout and stretch and grow makes you feel a rebirth of vigor and strength—yes, and purpose, too.

There are a dozen reasons for growing vegetables, but saving money is not the primary one. Cornell University has computed how much you can cut food costs through canning. The figures are interesting.

Product	Source of Jars	Source of Produce	Cost of Home Canned Per Quart	Cost of Store Bought Per Quart
TOMATOES	On hand	Home grown	**4.3c**	
	On hand	Bought	**29.3c**	**64c to**
	Purchased	Home grown	**25.9c**	**90c**
	Purchased	Bought	**50.9c**	
GREEN BEANS	On hand	Home grown	**3.9c**	
	On hand	Bought	**41.4c**	**62c to**
	Purchased	Home grown	**25.5c**	**78c**
	Purchased	Bought	**63.0c**	

The university's researchers concluded that freezing vegetables was more of a convenience than an economy.

A Kitchen Garden

Maybe you think you don't have room for vegetables. I feel sure you do. Just open the back door and have a look. All you need is a patch of ground *in the sun* no bigger than a tabletop. If you don't have sun on your back step, how about out front beside the driveway? Or south of the garage? The nicest vegetable gardens are those only a few steps from the kitchen sink. Even people with big gardens ought to try a kitchen garden.

Just plant five feet of lettuce and five feet of radishes and, if you have room left over, that many carrots and onions. A single tomato plant will do. But have it right at your back door or elsewhere nearby so that you can watch it daily. That's the fun of a kitchen garden. You can tend it in your slippers and robe.

The pleasantest kitchen gardens I've seen were in Holland and Switzerland, where yards are postage-stamp size. Meticulously tended, without a weed, they are jewels. Until you see them, you don't realize how decorative the fresh green of vegetables can look.

Besides annual vegetables that you use all summer, most back-door gardens have a clump of chives, for flavoring cottage cheese and soup, and a plant of parsley.

Vegetable Gardens That Bloom All Summer

If you are lucky enough to have considerable room for vegetables, let me suggest a delightful variation for your garden this year. My brother's wife, Anna —one of the best gardeners I know—indulges in a strange custom derived from her German ancestry. She plants rows of flowers here and there throughout her vegetable garden. A solid column of zinnias blazes through the greenery of carrots and peas, and calendulas shine between beets and beans. Marigolds and cosmos alternate with cabbage and cucumbers and dill. To tradition-bound gardeners, the idea is ludicrous. Yet Anna's gardens are more exciting than almost anyone else's. And when she returns with a basket of cucumbers and peppers and beets, on top are dazzling stalks of glads or zinnias. You realize that on every trip to the garden she returns with food for the spirit as well as the body.

There are strong practical reasons for growing flowers in rows in the garden. Whenever you can cultivate by machine rather than by hand, you cut weeding time to a small fraction. I can weed my entire garden by Rototiller in less time than it takes to hand-weed six feet of mixed annual and perennial border. Besides that, most flowers grow and flower better in full sun with plenty of room between rows. Rank-growing flowers like cosmos tend to sprawl across the openings, making cultivation by machine difficult, but by that time weeds generally aren't much of a problem.

Gardens with flowers interspersed in them look good even when the peas are finished, the radishes pulled, and the beans covered with rust. And with rows of zinnias to cut from instead of a few plants, you can supply your friends, church, and hospital bountifully. I know that garden books suggest "cutting gardens"—an idea that scares me off, connoting an age long dead, of estates with pergolas, gazebos, and full-time gardeners. But, all I suggest—no, strongly urge—is that you mix flowers and vegetables in a ratio depending on the importance you attach to stomach versus eye.

Certain flowers seem made for this garden mix. Above all are zinnias, in any and all types and sizes. The little pompon is apt to be lost where it grows, but gather it in bouquets and you have a fistful of jewels, which don't fade appreciably even after a couple of weeks. A row of glads, with bulbs three or four inches apart, gives an unbelievable amount of bloom. Methodical people plant glads at weekly intervals to have continuing flowers, but I am content with the several weeks of bloom that a single planting gives. Other naturals for the garden are asters, calendulas, marigolds, larkspur, dianthus, and the superb double sunflowers.

Certain tall biennials and perennials look great marching in a line across the garden. The favorite of visitors to my garden is the double hollyhock Powderpuff (from the Park Seed Company). Foxgloves are equally striking. Such big flowers often overpower a perennial border, but they can reach and spread to their heart's content in the vegetable garden. Of course, if you have the garden plowed every year, these overwintering plants would get in the way.

My sister-in-law has started a trend in neighboring gardens. Men who wouldn't otherwise be bothered with flowers are now growing rows of them, and though they don't quite have the courage to harvest them the way they do beets or cucumbers, they're glad to show them off and let the ladies cut bouquets.

Now then, to your planting.

Mark When You Plant

On the day I plant my garden, I have a sense of making history. I am drunk with the powers of decision making: carrots go here, radishes there, tomatoes and zinnias next. I feel the need of keeping notes. Sometimes I record in a book the variety names and dates of planting. At other times I make notes on wooden stakes at the end of each row (as every book on gardening says you must).

A month later, I couldn't care less. Of course, this row is carrots, and if none show through the weeds, who cares what variety they are or when they were planted? Naturally, the next row is lettuce, and I can tell at a glance that it's the beautiful oak-leaf variety.

When the cucumbers start bearing—each of six different hybrids—that's when I start scrambling about, looking for the eight-inch stakes. They're gone. I can't believe they've been stolen. I give up looking and continue thrashing about through the leaves for more cucumbers. Some are monstrous and would easily be two feet long if they hadn't decided to grow in a circle like some giant doughnut. (The cucumber was a hybrid "burpless," which the catalog describes as "inclined to curve unless it grows from a trellis.") Beside one cucumber is a wooden stake that turns out to be my record, but, alas for history, it is weather-beaten and blurred. So it is with all my staking. If I do find the stakes, they are washed clean or have a few ghostly tracks that my best detective efforts cannot decipher. My record book, likewise, is lost.

Sometimes I put the seed package itself on a stake, encased in a plastic bag, which—dogs and kids willing—should work. My latest effort is using wire coat-hangers bent to their tallest, with tags supplied by my nurseryman, of the type used to mark fruit trees. This particular plastic is the only kind I know that retains pencil marking.

Take It Easy with That Cultivator!

If you have succumbed to that delightful machine, the power cultivator, better ration the gas you put into it. Or else let it ride shallow. It's a temptation to sock it in deep and close to the row. But try to curb yourself. You're killing the weeds, but you may be half-killing the crop, too, by pruning the roots. To get the weeds between the plants and close to them, take out your hoe.

Tools

Gardening, like many of mankind's most basic pleasures, needs little in the way of equipment and tools for success. The best weeders I own are ten fingers. The best tool is a hoe.

But that's too simple. What else can gardeners talk about if they don't favor certain refinements? I like a small triangular hoe sharpened on all sides so I can hack in tight places. I would like one with a handle a foot longer, as I have already mentioned, so I wouldn't need to bend over as I do now, but such a hoe apparently doesn't exist.

Besides a spade and a spading fork, the only indispensable tool for me is a wheelbarrow. Mine has been crippled by a car bumper, overloaded with stones, and used as a vat for mixing concrete, but it still serves me faithfully in countless ways. It has a place in my heart that no car can ever hold.

The Rewards of Vegetable Growing

All summer you have feasted on fresh vegetables, but it is in winter, when vegetables are sky-high at the market, that you'll value your garden most. Go into the basement and gloat a bit. The freezer is still full of peas and green beans, broccoli, corn, strawberries, and raspberries; shelves are gleaming with jars of beets, pickles, tomatoes, and applesauce. Perhaps you still have a row of squash, and in a cool basement you may have carrots, rutabagas, parsnips, and potatoes. Outside there may be a blizzard, but you feel snug, knowing you have ample food to survive.

For your sake, though, I hope your basement is too warm to store potatoes properly because then you'll be justified in building one of the most pleasant little hideouts you ever knew. Now then, build yourself a root cellar.

Outside my study window a little red squirrel is sitting atop a hollow chunk of fireplace wood that he has stuffed full of pinecones. He reaches inside for a cone, then sits stripping the long cone of its husk, supremely content.

I know something of the contentment he feels. I speak not as a squirrel but as one who has just built his own root cellar, and already has it filled with many of the essentials of survival: a sack of potatoes, a pile of rutabagas, another of beets, still another of cabbages, a ten-gallon crock of dill pickles, and a sack each of carrots and parsnips. The fragrance of parsnips and potatoes mingles with that of moist earth into a heavenly concoction. Opening the door and walking in bring me back to my childhood and the earthen cellar below our house.

Build a Root Cellar

Every gardener with room for a root cellar should have one. It's perfect for storing bulbs and tender plants. I have two sacks full of canna roots for our garden club, some fancy chrysanthemums that don't usually live through Minnesota winters, and a dishpan full of geraniums overwintering.

Root cellars are great for forcing bulbs. I potted up a dozen Enchantment lilies that ought to make a splendid show in midwinter. Today I'm potting up a couple of dozen hyacinths, too.

Every week my cellar has visitors who plan on building one like it. Mine is modeled after an ancient one in my neighborhood, which was dug into the side of a pine-covered hillside so that only the entrance—faced with fieldstone—shows. It is a beautiful thing, with the charm of usefulness and stability. Every time I drove past it, I coveted it, the more because it was something money couldn't buy. You can't lift and load and transport a cave, or a hill, either. "Thou shalt not covet" rang in my ears. So I built my own.

Lacking a hill, I simply sank a shovel into a spot convenient to the house and started digging. It took me an hour to lift the sod from a space eight by ten feet, and another four hours to throw out the sand down to about four feet. Lining the hole with concrete blocks and mortar took a couple of evenings more. Near the top I fitted shelf brackets between blocks.

How about the top? I wanted the same curved ceiling as the ancient one, which started at four and a half feet at the walls and arced to six and a half feet at the center. A friend suggested I saw half-moon rafters out of half-inch plywood, drawing the curve I wanted and cutting with a power saw. With five such rafters laid on top of the walls, I nailed strips of plywood lengthwise on them and chinked up the ends. Then I covered the top with reinforcing wire and stuck a three-foot plastic pipe in the roof for ventilation.

Believe me, I held my breath when a truck came out and started pouring on the ready-mix concrete. My knowledge of carpentry, let alone stresses and strains, is not so hot. But the plywood held and my cellar took shape. After it dried a bit, I added inch-thick sheets of foam insulation, then covered with a foot of my excavated sand. The final touch: carpeting the top with sod saved during the digging. The result is what looks like a pioneer's sod shanty, complete with chimney. It's really very nice, and next year after I face the front with fieldstone, I suspect it will be even nicer. Each time I see it, I know the feeling of my friend the red squirrel, secure in the knowledge of his hidden bank accounts.

9

vegetables— do you really know your old friends?

My Indian friends in Cochin, state of Kerala, are Jain believers who not only eat no meat but eat no potatoes either, lest they destroy anything living inside. Yet when I sat down to dinner with them, I marveled at the flavor and substance of the squash and greens and pulses (leguminous seeds) they set before me. I am not espousing vegetarianism, but I do believe that Americans have much to learn about growing and preparing vegetables.

Isn't there wonderful variety in our garden crops? Some are rich in protein, others in sugars, many of them in vitamins and minerals. Several come already flavored and ready to eat. What need have carrots or celery or radishes for any spices? For that matter, isn't it hard to improve on the unadorned flavors of sweet peppers or tomatoes or turnips or onions or kohlrabi or lettuce or cauliflower or asparagus? Many other kinds need only a pinch of salt and a little cooking to bring them to perfection.

What beauty in vegetables, too! The glow of tomatoes, the sheen of eggplants, the gold of carrots, and the gleam of sweet corn are all magnificent. Isn't it providential that most vegetables should be as handsome as they are nutritious?

Artichokes, Jerusalem

The Jerusalem artichoke—which isn't an artichoke and doesn't come from Jerusalem and isn't even related to the Waldorf-Astoria vegetable—ought really to be called Indian potato because it's a tuber and, along with corn, was first cultivated by the Indians and probably originated with them. It's a vigorous cousin of the sunflower, reaching a height of eight to twelve feet and growing wild in the East. A smaller kind with comparably smaller tubers is a Midwest wild flower, and we, as children, dug for its tubers, which were seldom bigger than a peanut.

The garden type is a generous yielder of tubers egg-size and bigger, which are as crisp and juicy as potatoes, and taste perhaps more like water chestnuts. They are best sliced thin and used fresh in salad or to replace water chestnuts in cooking. Some use them for pickles, but we have had no experience with that.

You can get a start of artichokes from Park's, among others. They're easy to grow. You plant in the spring, then stand back and watch them shoot up. They make a hedge dense enough to stop wind. Either dig in late fall and store or else mulch with straw to keep the ground from freezing and dig and use them throughout the winter. In any case, be sure you keep them under control. Stray tubers pop up with real vigor and could become a temporary pest.

Whether or not you plant artichokes a second year will depend on your taste for them. But let me add that if you have a place in the country, you'll find that artichokes during winter are a favorite food of deer. They will devour every dead stalk all the way to the ground.

Asparagus

One of the golden moments of gardening comes when someone shouts, "The asparagus is up!" Year after year the spears come like some gift of God, which they certainly are. If you haven't yet known the excitement of your own asparagus, don't wait another year. Unlike beans or peas or most vegetables, asparagus seldom floods you with a crop so big you can't handle it. The spears don't come faster than you can eat them, so you're seldom surfeited. On top of that, they're ready for the pot practically direct from the garden. What other vegetable is like that? Then, along about late June or early July, when you have had enough and ought to stop harvesting anyhow, the stalks can be left to grow into handsome, airy shrubs that eventually deck themselves with red berries.

The problem with asparagus, your friends may tell you, is weeds. You can't use your power cultivator close to the row lest you hurt the roots. But I find that a few strokes with the hoe as you pass by is all it takes to keep the asparagus weed-free—unless you let grass grow into the row from the edge of the garden. Your friends may tell you to sprinkle salt along the row to keep out weeds, and it's true that asparagus tolerates salt. But why not clean-cultivate instead? It's great for your middle. My friend Bob Smith says that his heavy mulch keeps out weeds like a charm. For early shoots, he rakes some of the mulch away in the spring to help the ground warm up.

The only hard part about planting asparagus is deciding where to put the plants. They are perennial and will yield for years. They need sun, although they are fairly tolerant of shade. The more fertile the soil the better. But where do you plant a crop that won't be in the way of plow or cultivator for the next twenty or twenty-five years? That's one you alone can figure out.

Plant asparagus roots one to two feet apart, ten inches deep, and cover with a few inches of soil, adding mulch or soil as they grow, until by autumn the trench is full. Don't harvest until the second spring thereafter.

Beans

I can't whip up much enthusiasm for growing beans, I'll have to confess. The big shiny seeds are fun to plant, gliding between your fingers like rosary beads into the waiting trough of soil. Unlike most seeds that you barely dust to cover

over, you pull in a good inch of soil to blanket these. You really feel as if you had planted something.

What prettier sight is there, a little later, than that of the young plants "mole-hilling"—as southern farmers call it—through the soil. As a child, I used to help them along—this included pulling off the seed that kept their twin leaves clamped together (and which fed them before the rootlets began to deliver).

Beans are great to grow—until they start bearing. The first tiny snap beans, barely brought to a boil in whole milk with a little salt and pepper, make you resolve to plant an extra row next year. Store-bought frozen or canned beans can't hold a candle to your home-grown. After you have picked, stemmed, and chopped the second meal, you are somewhat less determined. And after you harvest and prepare the third, fourth, fifth, and sixth pickings, your enthusiasm plunges as your back pains increase.

"Help yourself to our beans," you tell your neighbor brightly. "We have more than we can use." He thanks you, a bit perfunctorily, it seems, just as he does later when you carry over a paper sack full.

It's so much easier to prepare them by ripping off the paper from a frozen package or by opening up a can. And it is really amazing, you conclude, how good the commercial pack is.

But, for many, a garden without beans would be unthinkable. Plant string beans when the ground is warm, fertilize, and keep weeding. Stay away from them when the leaves are dew-covered or rain-wet, since brushing against them spreads diseases from leaf to leaf. Lima beans are harder to grow and, in a cold spring, often rot. As a safety measure, sprinkle a little Arasan or Semesan dust over them before you plant.

If you haven't grown peas or beans on the ground you're using, you will probably find that your beans start faster if you dust them with a legume inoculator like bacterin. Beans, peas, clovers, and other legumes have colonies of bacteria attached to their roots in warty clumps, which permit the plants to use nitrogen directly from the air. Soil in which legumes have grown generally has all the bacteria spores they need.

For those of you with backs that complain when you stoop, try growing pole beans. They bear longer than bush beans and are generally considered to be more flavorful. Plant half a dozen seeds to a hill and erect a tepee of three sticks lashed together at the top with twine or stout cord. Pole beans are generally so prolific that a single hill may be all you need. I have an old unnamed variety so rich in flavor that it tastes as if it had been laced with butter. If you want to freeze any beans, do so when they are at a very young stage.

A couple of tips for lima growers: for better germination, plant them with the eye down. Harvest them when the beans are only babies. It will seem like infanticide, but you'll discover flavor and texture like nothing else you've tried.

Pole beans and limas need much richer soil than other beans. Plant them in your best soil, and enrich it with compost, manure, and fertilizer.

Beets

Why do you always have to thin beets?

Because that rough little ball that you plant as a seed is really a fruit with several seeds, and generally three or four seeds germinate and crowd one another for space. So no matter how sparsely you plant seed, you'll have clusters at each spot. This is the reason that commercial growers of sugar beets hire migrant workers to thin their fields, to chop out all but one plant at each cluster. Plant breeders, after years of work, have finally begun producing single-seeded varieties, and when these are improved, sugar beet growers will no longer use migrant labor.

Luckily for home gardeners, beet thinning brings rewards—the most succulent greens in the world, to my way of thinking. You wash and cut up the whole plant, including the infant beet bottom, barely cook, season with salt, pepper, and a few lumps of butter, and you'll have a potherb for kings. I always sow beets thick, partly because they're uncertain germinators and partly because I want to make sure there will be thinnings.

Some gardeners plant a few radishes to mark the beet row, since beets are slower to germinate and take off. It works well. The radishes are gone by the time the beets need room.

Broccoli

Like cabbage, broccoli is a cool-weather plant. In the South it's a winter vegetable. Elsewhere, you harvest it in late summer and fall. Whether or not it prospers depends mostly on your climate. Where it does thrive, it's an easy vegetable to grow and it's beautiful, too. Its healthy leaves are crisp and deep green—to the delight of cabbage worms.

Webworms, though, are at times the big problem. If you don't control them with rotenone, you may have heads so laced with webs that you can't eat any of them. In some years you may get by without dusting.

Remember that broccoli, like all members of its family—brussels sprouts, cabbage, and cauliflower—is shallow-rooted and therefore needs rich soil and continuous moisture. Pick the heads before they "break," that is, before individual flower stalks break away from the main head. For best flavor, gather them in the morning and store in an inch or so of water in a pot or pan. If you keep them well picked, side shoots will develop and keep yielding until frost knocks them out. Try freezing any excess. Frozen broccoli is just about the equal of fresh.

Brussels Sprouts

You'll probably want to grow these sometime, just to see if they really do look like their picture in the seed catalog.

Sow seeds in good rich soil, cultivate and water in dry weather, and keep dusted, just as you do cabbage. The plants grow handsomely, and one day, sure enough, the little sprouts begin forming. Later, when the sprouts are the size of walnuts, you snap off the lower leaves. The whole row actually looks like the pictures you see.

But unless it's late in the fall and the sprouts are mature, you're in for trouble when you try to harvest them. You expect to snap them off as you did the leaves. They won't snap. Even if you use a knife, the sprouts are as hard to dislodge as the corn on your little toe. After whittling away at a few plants, you begin to wonder whether or not nature ever intended those little heads to come free. You wonder, too, how the supermarkets can sell frozen brussels sprouts as reasonably as they do. But the flavor of your own is obviously superior. It must be—with all that work of harvesting.

Cabbages

Don't grow cabbages unless (1) your climate is cool; (2) you have plenty of space; (3) you don't mind dusting with insecticide. Cabbages take room, they suffer in the heat, and they attract worms. But in the right cool, moist areas—like along the New England coast, in patches astraddle the Blue Ridge, and in the Upper Midwest—they are magnificent. A cousin of mine in Norway grows cabbages for market along a fjord in a setting right out of Hans Christian Andersen. At harvest time, when I visited him, he drove his fat little horse and two-wheeled cart between the rows as we heaped the crisp green heads high above the sideboards. Neither of us spoke, but we communicated as only two people do who work side by side at something they enjoy. By the end of the afternoon it seemed that the little horse and I were friends, too.

Cabbages have a way of bringing people together. At harvest time on my brother's farm, a few friends come over and we make sauerkraut together, after having twisted off the heads of cabbage in the garden, pared off their outer leaves, and slashed the heads in two. Our cabbage slicer, which looks something like an old scrub board, sits astride a five- or a ten-gallon earthen jar. Periodically we stop slicing to stomp the shredded cabbage down until the juice covers it. We can never agree on how much salt to add. When we follow old recipes, the result is too salty for most of us, so we sprinkle a few tablespoons between six-inch layers. Some folks bury an occasional head of cabbage in the kraut so they can have "pigs in blankets"—a savory German dish of ground beef and rice and spices, blanketed in cabbage leaves and cooked in sauerkraut. When the crocks are filled and the shredded cabbage weighted down below the surface, we store them in a warm place.

Where can you find a place that keeps at seventy-five to eighty degrees? Basement or garage? Not warm enough. Bedroom? Kitchen? Bath? Study? All fine, as far as temperature goes. Fastidious people will find the fragrance of fermenting kraut a little high. But in ten to twenty days or so, it will be all over, and you'll have the finest kraut you ever tasted, partly if not wholly because it's your very own.

To discourage cabbageworms—the constant companion of all cabbages—I dust with a little rotenone. A neighbor sprinkles a little salt on the leaves when the dew is on, and my friend Bob Smith uses diatomaceous earth, which seems to invade the breathing spiracles of insects and which eventually returns to the soil to enrich it. In any case, cabbageworms aren't generally much of a problem.

Carrots

If it weren't that carrots always need thinning and a first fine-tooth weeding, they'd be the perfect vegetable for beginners. They're reasonably dependable, once they make up their minds to sprout, and they seldom get into trouble with bugs or diseases. But because they're poor germinators, you need to sow them thick, and by the time their feathery little leaves wisp their way through the soil, a hundred or so aggressive weeds stand shoulder to shoulder above them.

There is no other solution than dropping to your knees and scrutinizing every sprig of vegetation until you find the carrot, then pulling out the competitors without grabbing the carrots, too. As you waddle down the row, casting out demon weeds and a few carrots, you leave behind a few survivors so pallid from their long confinement that you wonder if the rescue was worth the battle. Carrots lie on their sides, spent and yellow. But a week later, the row is a vision of loveliness.

And that's when you face the second and final ordeal. Only one of every dozen or so plants can remain, and you—a Solomon on his knees—must decide which lives and which perishes. This is where I usually fail. I can't thin the plants to the three- to four-inch spacing they need. And so, if you see my carrots, they'll be long and lean and often misshapen. Good, though. The very best.

If you have trouble with carrots, try growing them in a different location, and add a balanced fertilizer.

Let your child keep watch on the carrots to see when they're ready to be pulled. Do you remember your surprise at the first one you pulled? Scandinavians call the carrot *gulrot,* which means "gold root"—a much more appropriate name, I think.

My friend Bob Smith suggests that you match your carrots to your soil: Chantenay varieties for heavy soil, long Imperator types for lighter soil. You can't go wrong with Nantes for flavor and sweetness in any soil. For summer use, plant carrots as early as you can work the soil, thinning for delectable baby carrots. You can plant carrots in the fall for early harvest. To keep carrots through the winter, leave them in the ground until late in fall, then wash them and store them in plastic bags in the refrigerator. If you have a cool basement or a root cellar, top the carrots and store them in a closed container, inspecting occasionally for sprouting or rot.

Cauliflower

Cauliflower is harder to grow than its cousins: cabbages, brussels sprouts and broccoli. It won't stand frost the way the others do, and it won't form a head if the weather stays warm. More than that, when the first young flower buds begin to show, you need to tie together enough of the central leaves to enclose the developing buds and bleach them white.

Growing cauliflower is truly an adventure. And when all goes well, the rewards are ample. Cauliflower is beautiful. It's good to eat raw and is practically devoid of calories. On a tray of hors d'oeuvres, it beats crackers as a vehicle for gouging up the creamy sauces—thereby defeating itself as a friend of dieters.

Corn

If you have grown corn even once, you are an expert, and there is nothing more I can tell you. Corn is so rewarding, so appreciative of every small effort on its behalf, that it bestows on every grower an honorary MD (Doctor of Maize) degree. Weed it, water it, bury a fish under it—anything you do will make it spurt.

Not only is the beginner suddenly an expert. He also has the world's best and sweetest variety. My brother Thomas is convinced of this and keeps the name of his variety a secret. It is no wonder that in South America, where corn probably originated, Indians have kept distinct strains, some two hundred of them, among which is a giant kind with stalks like bamboo over twenty feet high. It is still grown in Guatemala for fences and house building.

Ancient tombs in Peru have yielded popcorn—corn so well preserved it would pop—which has been determined by radioactive carbon dating to be a thousand years old. A Harvard archaeologist, digging down through the rubbish of a cave in New Mexico, found corncobs at every level. At the very bottom, six feet deep, were primitive ears of corn barely an inch long, on which man was munching at least fifty-six hundred years ago. Drilling operations below Mexico City have brought up corn pollen grains at least ninety thousand years old.

Columbus wrote in his diary that in Cuba, in 1492, two members of his crew found "a gran they call maize which was well tasted, bak'd, dry'd and made into flour." But if corn is a New World product, how and when did it leap to southernmost Africa, where Vasco da Gama found it in 1498? In a boat he captured he wrote "we found 17 men, besides gold, silver and an abundance of maize" (an Indian word for "mother").

Corn played mother to our Founding Fathers as it had to the Indians. It grew in luxuriant patches of shining green along the seacoast when they arrived, and it so impressed Captain John Smith that he decreed that every family in Jamestown must grow it. Up the coast, at Plymouth, Pilgrims stumbled on (and stole) buried caches of corn just in time to save the colony from starving. The first Thanksgiving, some historians say, had its origin in an ancient Indian ceremony expressing gratitude to God for the corn harvest. How delighted the Pilgrims must have been when a brother of Massasoit surprised them with big baskets of snowy popcorn!

Corn quickly took its place, alongside buckskin breeches and flintlocks, in the lives and hearts of early Americans. Corn pone and hominy and steaming bowls of Indian pudding began warming the body even as corn liquor began to warm the spirit. A bushel of good corn made three quarts of whiskey, and soon just about everybody, including Washington and Jefferson, was brewing his own.

Corn set the colonists free from their dependence on the fisheries of the seacoast. Travelers in the wilderness, with a few squares of journey cake (now johnnycake) stuffed in a pocket or packsack, could eat for a week. Once again corn began traveling, as it had all its life with man. Settlers streamed westward with bags of corn that were both food and seed. Even without oxen or horses to plow, a pioneer family could hoe in a few hills and within twelve weeks have a harvest of food that didn't even need threshing. Before long a verdant belt of green stretched for more than eight hundred miles across the heart of America—the so-called corn belt—a lifeline of plenty for the thousands that followed. America's agricultural strength grew more than anything else from its prodigal fields of corn that fed ever-growing numbers of cattle and hogs and poultry.

Grow sweet corn this year—on your city lot, in your penthouse garden—and join the nation's twenty million corn experts. And if you harvest more than you need, rest assured that this is one vegetable you can always give away.

Cucumbers

Wait a minute. Is your seed package marked Hybrid? If it isn't, trade it in for one of the truly remarkable hybrids that have been bred for your region. You wouldn't believe how much more productive they are than the old kinds. I thought I was seeing a freak variety when my first hybrids started blooming no more than an inch from where the young plants emerged from the soil. Most flowers were female, too, with sizable fruit already formed before the bloom opened. There were cucumbers ready to use even before the vine had done much traveling, and the vines continued to bear until frost.

And the fruit—well, for the first time I was growing cucumbers that looked as uniform and beautiful as those in the seed catalogs. By all means, plant a few hybrid cucumbers this year. No need to hurry. If the gound is cold, the seed may rot. Oak trees are a good planting-time indicator. They seldom get caught by a freeze with their leaves out. I aim to plant when oak leaves are the size of squirrels' ears, but usually lag behind a week or so. It doesn't seem to matter. Cucumbers grow so fast that before you know it you're up to your ears in fruit.

Only two problems with cucumbers. On our sandy soil, they quickly wilt without heavy watering and wilted leaves often mean fruit with bitter stem ends. The other problem is getting rid of surpluses. My solution to this one is of vine-shaking significance: compact with your neighbor to grow cucumbers in alternate years, and share the patch with each other.

The best idea I know for using up excess cucumbers is to keep them sliced in jars of brine in the refrigerator or a cool basement, where they will generally keep all winter, giving you cukes almost garden-fresh whenever you want them. We started out the winter with twenty-five quarts of them, and we use them several times a week.

Here is the recipe, which, I think you will agree, is worth the price of this book:

Fill jars with thinly sliced cucumbers, and over them pour this syrup: 4 cups sugar, 4 cups vinegar, 1/2 cup salt, 1/3 teaspoon turmeric, 1 1/3 teaspoons celery seed, 1 1/2 teaspoons white mustard seed. Cover and store in refrigerator or cool basement. Ready to use after five days.

The result is more vegetable than pickle, but it will liven up any midwinter meal.

For a couple of years now I have experimented with putting down cucumbers the way our forefathers did, in a crock or wooden barrel in the garden, in a brine of one part salt to thirteen parts soft water, plus plenty of dill and grape leaves and garlic if you wish, with a plate and a rock to hold the cucumbers below the brine. This is the classic pioneer method. You leave the crock in a sunny part of the garden or some other warm place until the cucumbers undergo a fermentation such as sauerkraut undergoes. You skim off the foam occasionally and wash the rock and plate. After about ten days, depending on temperature, the pickles become translucent. Store them in a cool place. As you use them you rinse off excess salt. You also can convert them into sweet pickles. I wish I could report complete success with this method, but I can't. The top cucumbers spoil. But I keep trying.

A word about planting the new hybrids. Among certain hybrid seeds you may find colored seeds. These are of a strain that produces a great deal of pollen, and they should be spaced evenly along the row.

Here's a gardening trick I think you ought to try this year. Get a length of the wire mesh used in reinforcing concrete, prop it up at a forty-five-degree angle all along the row and let the vines climb it as if it were an inclined trellis. The cucumbers hang below the mesh and you can pick them like grapes from an arbor. Your cucumbers will be as pretty as a picture, the fruit will be clean, and you can pick them at any size without worrying about missing the jumbos.

Eggplants

Pick up a few young eggplants at the market and plant them in your flower border. The intricate, feltlike leaves are handsome, and the fruit seems always perfect, without blemish, almost too beautiful to eat.

A good crop of eggplants in the garden is fine for a gardener's ego, but don't expect a big crop unless you live where the summers are long and hot. Last summer I watched my dozen plants daily, and though they bloomed, nothing more happened. And then *voilà*, there it was, a full-grown egg hanging blue-black and glistening and perfect. It was like finding a ten-dollar bill in an old pants pocket. That was my only "egg," however.

The first time you'll grow eggplants for the novelty of it. Whether you continue to grow them will depend on whether you have the recipe for *ratatouille (rat-a-tú-ee)*, a Mediterranean casserole of tomatoes, eggplant, zucchini, green peppers, thinly sliced onions, each quickly browned in hot olive oil, and laced with garlic and basil and parsley and then baked in a casserole. It's a scrumptious dish, but takes considerable time to prepare. However you fix eggplant, in general you need to slice it, salt it lightly, and allow the salt half an hour or so to draw the moisture out of it, then dry the slices with paper towels. Like zucchini, eggplant doesn't have much flavor of its own, but it is a great receptacle for all the subtle flavors of exotic herbs.

My brother and his wife, Anna, during the years they lived in the mountains of northwest Greece, learned to love *militzanes* the way the Greeks prepared it. Here's how Anna fries them. She cuts the eggplant in thin French-fry slices, sprinkles them with salt, and leaves them for an hour in the sun, if at all possible, then dries and dips each slice into a flour-egg batter and fries them in hot oil (preferably olive) until crisp and golden. Don't say you don't like eggplant until you fix it the Greek way.

Gourds

For the young and young in spirit, by all means plant a package of mixed gourds. If you can't decide whether to use the large-fruited or small-fruited kind, get both packages. No need to plant the whole package. A few of each kind will do—in fact, they'll spread all over your garden if you let them.

Gourds produce fruit easily. Unfortunately for many of us on the northern fringe of the United States, the season isn't long enough for them to mature properly, and sometimes the beautiful fruit we gather in fall begins decaying a few weeks later. I have tried several times to grow bottle gourds, the kind you encounter through South America that are hung on crosspieces attached to a high pole as homes for purple martins. Right now I have a dozen bottle gourds in the basement, too good to throw away, too weak to put up. And yet I like gourds. Even with a bumper crop, there's no need to hurry up and pickle, preserve, freeze, or can. You need only harvest them to enjoy their beauty.

Horseradish

Don't plant this one unless you're a nut about living off the land. Horseradish is fun to grow and easy to start, and once started, it's with you for life. Yet it's not a weed that spreads. It sends up its fresh green leaves from exactly the same place, year after year.

It's when you start harvesting this plant that the trouble begins. In spring or fall when the weather is cool and the flavor of the horseradish is strongest, you dig up part of the clump and wash the big white roots. Don't worry if you appear to take them all. Horseradish comes again from deep fragments of roots that remain.

You scrape the roots preparatory to putting them through the meat grinder. It's a laborious job, but it's something more, you soon discover. Before long you're weeping as copiously as a Miss America contest winner. Do onions bother you? Then you've never known horseradish. It will help a lot if you hook up a fan to blow air past your operations.

Go on bravely. Bottle the grindings in vinegar, add a little sugar, and refrigerate. My brother Thomas prides himself on the potency of his home-ground horseradish. The trouble is that it's almost impossible to spoon out a speck of this liquid fire small enough to surround with the mouth and survive.

Kale

Go ahead and try it, especially if you like cooked greens. It's as easy as growing cabbage (of which family it's a member), and, with its crinkled leaves, it is pretty to look at.

At a friend's place outside Washington, D.C., I found kale growing at Easter time; it had been planted the previous year and forgotten. Now it stood beautifully green and ready for picking, even after a late snowfall. Boiled briefly with bits of bacon, it was superb.

My own kale has sometimes been bitter. Perhaps it grew too slowly or needed cold weather to transform it. Kale does improve after frost. Harvest the bottom leaves first, before they get big and tough.

Kohlrabi

Even if you don't like turnips or rutabagas, plant this one. It's a show-off turnip that grows aboveground, and develops so quickly and easily that it will delight you. Its clean blue-green foliage and stems are pretty enough for a flower garden. I like them best raw, cut into half-inch cubes to munch on like peanuts or popcorn, or as sticks for dipping in cheese spreads and mixing in tossed salads. Cooked or fried in a smidgeon of butter, they're fine, too—but then what isn't with that treatment?

That superb cook Myrna Johnston, former Foods Editor of *Better Homes and Gardens* magazine, says that kohlrabi should be pulled and used when it is less than two inches in diameter, though she admits that getting this vegetable pulled at that tender age may involve the gardening half of her family in some arguments.

Lettuce

Too bad we don't grow lettuce as an ornamental. Then we could gather a mess of leaves as a bonus, and we wouldn't need to feel that lettuce is a loss unless we keep it mowed as clean as a lawn.

Lettuce is beautiful enough for any flower garden, from the time its bright leaves break through the soil until it pushes up a flower stalk. In Nepal, where the climate is cool, I have seen lettuce used in formal gardens as part of the design.

If you're in a rut about lettuce, try some different types this year. The oak-leaf type is beautiful, tender, and tasty. So too is the Bibb variety called Buttercrunch. With such a name, how could it help being good?

Whether you succeed with head lettuce will depend far more on your climate than on your ability. That's what I like to believe, anyhow, never having been able to grow a respectable head. Good lettuce weather is both cool and moist.

Whatever you do, plant leaf lettuce close to the kitchen. One year I tried sowing lettuce in midsummer. It didn't amount to much that fall, but next spring it was still there—after a winter of fifty below zero. A big buck deer was as delighted to find it as I, and kept it well trimmed.

Muskmelons

I have long been in awe of people who spoon their breakfast melon and call it cantaloupe. To me, it's muskmelon. Cantaloupes on a fancy menu seem to justify the stiff price; muskmelons are something for backyards. If I wanted to be stuffy about it, I could show you that true cantaloupes aren't grown anywhere in North America, and that's a fact. But go ahead and call them cantaloupes; I'll say muskmelon.

Like all melons, they like hot weather and sun and a long growing season. The fruits of the newer varieties are supposed to ripen within seventy or even sixty days after planting, but that's assuming day temperatures above eighty degrees and night temperatures above seventy degrees. In the north, unless we start them indoors and then set them out under Hotkaps, growing muskmelons is a gamble. Muskmelons that mature while the weather is still warm are always sweeter, so early varieties are important.

Honeydew and casaba melons have been out of bounds both in Minnesota and in the Philadelphia area. Perhaps I'll try them next year again—one seed catalog sings to me of a kind that has done well as far north as Morden, Manitoba, with "fruit 6 to 8 lbs. at maturity and quality exceptional." Ah, siren song!

Even in a bumper muskmelon year, you generally have little trouble giving these fruits away. But why not convert a few into balls for freezing? With a melon baller, it's rather fun.

My melon project for next year comes from my cousin in Norway, who nails four boards together in a rectangle topped with window glass that he leaves in his garden all summer. He starts melons under the glass, and when the weather is warm simply lets the vines scramble out over the edges. This way he grows fine muskmelons and watermelons much farther north than any part of the United States. The idea is so simple that there must be something wrong with it. Want to experiment, along with me?

Okra

Why anyone should plant okra confounds me. If it tasted as good as the fragrant white paste I remember eating in kindergarten, it would be different. Some soups get their "body" from okra, I understand, but I am told you can get the same effect from faded squash blossoms or old day-lily blooms. This is information I hope you need never have to use.

Okra is a handsome plant, however, with pleasant flowers and leaves. It is prolific, too. The time to harvest the fruit is when it is very young and small. The flavor is better then, and there's another advantage—you won't have so much of it to swallow.

My southern friends, who swear by okra, say it should be washed, dried, cut into quarter-inch slices, then floured and fried in hot fat. Give it another try, they plead, in tomato stews, hot dishes, and soups.

Onions

Don't buy onion seed. I repeat: don't buy onion seed. If you do, you'll spend the summer weeding and waiting for the wispy blades to look like onions. Buy onion sets and plants (in bunches) instead. They're foolproof, and they're ready to use in a few weeks.

I used to think that planting onion sets or plants wasn't really gardening, any more than putting a frozen dinner into the oven is cooking. But I'm no longer a purist about either. A bunch of about a hundred little onions costs a dollar or less and will keep you in onions all summer. Bermuda types don't keep, so use them as they ripen. Spanish kinds are the keepers.

Growing onions the first few times is generally easy. But thrips and maggots often move in after a while. That's when you'll need to change ground or else start spraying or dusting with rotenone. Perhaps a better idea is one that Bob Smith uses. He plants a "trap crop" of radishes in his row of onions. The maggots prefer the radishes and Bob rarely loses an onion.

For best results, plant onions in rich soil and keep them well watered. Their roots are so shallow that they can't endure dry weather without suffering.

Parsley

It's either feast or famine with parsley. Plant a row and you'll be garnishing all the plates at the next Lions Club banquet. But if you plant only a few seeds, you may be skunked because parsley is not only slow but also uncertain. Don't expect last year's plants to live any longer than it takes to shoot up a stalk and die.

One way to use up excess leaves is to preserve them by drying them in the oven for winter. Another way is to pot up a dozen or so plants for winter and give them as Christmas gifts to good cooks for garnishes and for incorporating into gravies, dressings, chopped-meat dishes, and *bouquets garnis*.

I know of no sure way of getting potted parsley to thrive. Perhaps the answer is to plant it in a deep pot to accommodate the taproot, along with plenty of fertilizer. At best, though, only about half of my plants thrive, even under fluorescent lights. Those that do make fine houseplants. The variety with curled leaves is especially handsome.

Parsnips

Parsnips are so easy to grow that every garden should have a few. Plant them thick and early. They're poor germinators and need a long season. To mark the row while the parsnips are germinating, sow in radishes and have a crop of them while you're waiting. All summer the parsnip foliage will decorate your garden, its fresh green leaves surviving after hard frost. But the real payoff is in spring, when you survey the dead, wet garden and find bright green fronds emerging from the parsnip crowns. Pull up a few and surprise the family. What other vegetable can you gather at that gray time of year?

Parsnips improve greatly after frost. Sliced thinly and fried in butter, they're great. Even if you're sure you don't like parsnips, try them once again this year.

Peas

Just because you have decided to garden, don't think you must plant peas. That amazing idea never came to me until last year, and, believe me, I feel liberated. Not that I don't like to eat them; in salad or soup (anywhere except rolling around on a plate) they're great. But growing them is no pleasure. First you need to put up a fence or brush for them to climb on. And in order that they come up early enough to escape the summer heat, you really ought to plant in the fall or else in the spring just as the ground thaws. Picking them is hard work. Shelling is laborious. And though their leaves and flowers are beautiful for a few short days, their youth is quickly spent, and they soon look downright ratty. Heat prostration hits them after the first few days of warm weather, and they stop bearing. Sometimes I wonder if I get my seed back, pea for pea.

Lest you think I am completely antipea, let me suggest that you grow the kind you eat pod and all. Your catalog will list them as sugar peas. They seem to stand the heat better than regular peas, and the purple flowers are pleasant. The cooked pods or raw peas in salad are both splendid. And, best of all, you don't need to shell them.

For some reason known only to the interpreters of our free enterprise system, I have paid as much as a dollar and fifty cents for a side order of sugar peas. Now then, I guess you'll like them. If you don't, I have only one other suggestion about growing peas. Watch your supermarket for special prices on canned vegetables.

From the wings comes an antiphonal chorus in defense of peas. Peas fresh from the garden are a treat very few people have experienced, the chant goes. They're not the same vegetable that you eat frozen or canned. If you don't know any better, you won't miss the delicate flavor. Raw peas from the vine, they say, are something no one should miss.

Peppers, Sweet

Of all vegetables, this is my favorite to grow. On the hottest days of summer, the fruits are crisp and juicy and almost cool when I pick one to eat. The plants with their deep-green leaves are beautiful enough for a flower garden. There is something exotic and unreal about the way the big shining fruits hang—like Christmas tree ornaments—on the plant.

Like many people, my Swedish sister-in-law stubbornly refused to taste a sweet pepper—so sure was she that it was hot. I tried to assure her that peppers belong to the potato family, and aren't related at all to the vine that produces the seasoning. And though some kinds of pepper plants bear hot fruit, sweet peppers are as mild as tomatoes or cucumbers. Stubborn as only a Swede can be, she still maintains that peppers are strong, even though she has learned to like them as much as I do.

During a six-week stay in the Arab world, I was served peppers a dozen ways—all of them fine. Mixed with meat and fresh mint leaves, peppers are used to stuff zucchini, grape leaves, and even carrots.

Peppers are as much fun to grow as to eat. They thrive in poor soil and can even stand dry, buffeting winds. I buy the plants already started and set them out. During cool weather they stand still, but with warm weather, they take off fast. Except for cutworms, I haven't found an insect or disease that bothers them. For me, that's something of a record.

Try ornamental peppers. They are beautiful in the flower border and good to eat, too. Pinocchio is a small red ornamental sweet pepper about two inches long and pointed, fruits pointing straight up. Other kinds are interesting and useful in salads.

Potatoes

Centuries ago, on a hill above Cuzco, Peru, the Inca Indians built a fortress that is a marvel of rockwork, with giant stones in geometric patterns fitted so carefully together that you can't slip a knife blade between them.

I can't tell you any more about it than that because, at the foot of it, I found a plant no more than a foot high with leaves and blossoms exactly like a potato's. The resemblance dumbfounded me. Could it be some kind of potato? I scratched among the rocks to look for tubers, unsuccessfully, but as I dug, I slowly remembered that potatoes came from the Andes and that these indeed were true potatoes. Gardening has a way of getting in the way of travel.

Later, on the way to the long-lost mountaintop village of Machu Picchu, while others were admiring the lofty views, I confess I was craning my neck to look through the railway car windows for other kinds of wild potatoes. And though I didn't see others, there were patches of cultivated potatoes on the hillsides. A native told me he preferred small round potatoes, which he brought home at harvest by rolling them downhill. Whether he sensed a sucker in me I am not sure, but I did see some interesting varieties. One kind, in an experimental garden, grew as high as my head and its full purple flower was a magnificent sight. The principal variety grown in Peru seems to be one that, when cooked, is creamy yellow and, to my taste, seemed better than our white-fleshed kinds.

Grow potatoes this year. The flowers are pleasant, the seedpods that sometimes form are amusing, and from the seeds you might develop new varieties. As you would expect in view of the ancestry of potatoes, they grow best in cool areas.

As an experiment this year, try planting potatoes on top of the ground, and cover them with a foot of wet or rotting straw or hay. The roots strike into the soil, but most of the potatoes grow in the straw where they can expand at ease. All you need do at harvest is pull away the straw and there—like a nest of eggs—are the potatoes, clean and without a blemish. A friend of mine let me help harvest his crop. The potatoes grew on peat soil underlaid with sand and had plenty of moisture. I have never seen more perfect or prolific spuds: a dozen big ones under each vine and a dozen more the size of golf balls, and still growing. The technique is no time or labor saver, I hasten to add. Have you ever tried handling half-rotten hay or straw? It's bulky and it's heavy. It would, though, add lots of organic matter to your garden. Be sure the mulch covers well. Tubers exposed to sun turn green.

The term *spud* is no recent bit of slang, but goes back well over a hundred years; it derives either from the British *spud (spade)* used in digging potatoes or the Scottish term for a short, stumpy person.

Pumpkins

The way to grow the biggest pumpkin in town is to send a quarter to Henry Field of Shenandoah, Iowa, for his Jumbo variety. Some of them grow to be a hundred pounds, he says. You might even get your picture, along with Henry's (dead these many years), in the newest Field catalog. Jumbo is a good yielder: four or five pumpkins to the vine. The flesh is a trifle coarse, though, so he suggests you feed it to your livestock, for which it is "extra fine." However, buying enough livestock to eat all those pumpkins might cost you somewhat more than you have bargained for.

Let your child grow his own jack-o'-lanterns. They're great fun and almost never disappoint. I have found that any pumpkins will grow big enough for fine jack-o'-lanterns, especially if you plant them in good earth and fertilize them.

Like most plants that originate in the tropics, pumpkins need little more than hot weather to thrive and, in their native home, probably keep growing and maturing, with new young plants arising and striking out continuously from the moist security of the ripened fruit. Plants native to temperate (which means our own intemperate) climates, on the other hand, have built-in safeguards against sprouting in midsummer or fall, many requiring cold or even freezing weather for several weeks before they budge.

Radishes

The trouble with growing radishes is having to eat them or having to find people who will. I am convinced that if radishes were scarce and hard to grow, they'd be in demand for their beauty, their crispness, their pungency. But who wants to gather and wash and stem something as common as toast? And when the relish plate makes the rounds, why bother with low-calorie radishes when there are olives?

This raises another psychological if not philosophical question: how popular would a radish be if it were loaded down with calories? Tradition doesn't even allow us radishes in cream sauce or butter or gravy!

Growing a radish is purest pleasure, and no child of three or up should miss it. The seed sprouts in four days or so, in the coldest of weather, and is ready to offer itself to mankind before the month is out. I know people who grow radishes for the fun of it. I'm one of them, although I say I use them as row markers for slow-starting perennials. When they're not in the way, I like to let them flower. I think they're pleasant.

My friend Leon Snyder, eminent horticulturist, says he always lets a few plants go to seed. After seeds mature, he plows the entire plants back into the soil with his garden tiller. Seedlings soon come up broadcast fashion and produce radishes for a long while into the fall. The fall crop is free of the maggots that often plague the spring crop.

Years ago in Japan, my host prepared shrimp tempura, which we dipped into piquant sauce made of ground radishes. So when I saw Japanese radishes listed in a catalog, I promptly ordered a package. They grew prodigiously, to the size of footballs. They were pure fire. Even a cautious nibble would leave you gasping.

Last year I planted black winter radishes, the kind my grandfather used to tell about. They, too, were a joy to watch as their jet-black roots swelled to the size of your two fists. And though they were mild and crisp, we have never found the occasion to use them. I am sure they would be pleasant in a salad or in a stew, but our kitchen just isn't tooled up for winter radishes.

Rhubarb

A young woman newly arrived from Chicago came with her husband to live next door. I asked her to help herself to my rhubarb. She looked shocked. "What's that?" she asked. Suddenly a generation·separated us. Or was it geography or simply city-country differences? I'm afraid not.

Only once before had I experienced the same abyss of time between human beings. A precocious ten-year-old had asked me to identify a strange birdcall.

"That's the pump-handle call of the bluejay," I said.

"What's that?"

"Don't you know a bluejay?"

"Yes, but what's a pump handle?"

If he hadn't known the president of the United States, I could have understood. But not to know what a pump handle sounded like! He had never in his whole life seen a pump.

For those unfortunates of a newer generation, let me say that rhubarb is a gift of the Almighty. Small children can play hide-and-seek in its shadows and fashion a wondrous hat from a single leaf. Its towering seed stalk makes a striking dried arrangement for winter. And its crisp acid stalk makes a tremendous sauce. As kids, we loved the sauce even though we were reminded that it was a "spring tonic." Rhubarb pie, to me, ranks only alongside gooseberry, and I would be hard-pressed to say which is better. Someone long before me tipped his hat to the rhubarb and gave it the common name of pieplant. If Ben Franklin did introduce rhubarb to America, as some say, what further proof do we need of his wisdom?

Whether you plant the giant green-stemmed variety or the smaller red-stemmed kind doesn't matter as far as flavor goes. A couple of plants is all a family needs to keep well supplied, provided the roots are planted in deep rich soil and well supplied with humus or manure. Give them a corner of the yard or garden where they can grow undisturbed. Or use them as a foundation planting for your home; they're certainly handsome enough for that. Wherever you put them, rhubarb plants will become members of your family, greeting you each spring with fresh new stalks.

Be sure to freeze a few bags for winter. And if you want a clear wine, try this recipe.

To 2 3/4 gallons of water add 10 pounds and 2 cups of sugar; stir to dissolve. Water should be more than lukewarm. Then add baker's yeast in the amount of 1 inch; dissolve. Next add 5 quarts of cut-up raw rhubarb and place in a warm room out of drafts. Stir every three or four days for three weeks, then strain and bottle, without sealing tight. The wine will keep indefinitely this way, and it improves with age.

There are other fine ways of fixing rhubarb, among them rhubarb crunch, but this is a gardening, not a recipe book.

A final word: a child can grow up without a dog or cat or even a fond aunt or uncle, but don't deprive him of a plant of rhubarb.

Rutabagas

These are the slow growers of the turnip-rutabaga family and, unlike turnips, have light yellow flesh that cooks to a bright orange. With only a little seasoning, the dish is ready for the table, where its bland, soft texture is a nice accompaniment to any meal.

Plant them in early summer. A good idea is to put several seeds together at eight-inch intervals, then thin them to one plant at each spot. This ensures that your roots grow large. Where maggots are a problem, seed radishes in between as a trap crop or else plow up new ground and seed there. For the best flavor, leave them in the ground until just before freeze-up. The Macomber variety, a white with a slight greenish tinge, is available from the Harris Seed Company.

If your crop is too big to eat up by early winter, dip a few roots in wax and they'll keep until spring in a cool place.

Many people like rutabagas raw in cubes for the dieter's snack rack. Mashed and mixed in soup, they are pleasant, but I like them best in a "boiled dinner," with cabbage, onions, celery, parsnips, or other vegetables briefly boiled or braised with an inexpensive cut of meat. Their orange color brightens the platter of steaming vegetables.

If any deer are co-owners of your property, you can be sure they'll extract a little rent from your rutabaga ground.

Salsify

Plant this one if you want to show me up. I've never got it to produce. Year after year our whole family tried it—we were intrigued with the catalog description of a vegetable that tasted like oysters—and every year we got no more than a few wisps of grassy tops. Again in New Jersey I tried it with less than spectacular results. I have seen them for sale in markets, though, so I know that at least one person in America can grow them.

Apparently there is only one variety—Mammoth Sandwich Island. Isn't that a beaut? What a combination of three delicious, romantic words!

Spinach

Why anybody would grow spinach when he knows about Swiss chard I can't for the life of me figure out. Spinach is easy to grow and quick—you can start eating it in little more than a month from the time you plant it. But, at the hint of hot weather, it runs up a flower stalk like a flag of surrender, and that's all. No more spinach. Swiss chard, on the other hand, keeps sending up big tender leaves all summer. Another excellent substitute is New Zealand spinach. Although not a true spinach, it tastes and looks like spinach when cooked. It grows best in hot weather and keeps producing till frost. After you pick the first shoots, new ones form. Several plants will give you all the spinach you need for eating fresh and for freezing. It appears to have no disease or insect pests. Better try some this year.

However, if you must grow spinach, plant it just as early as you can hoe in the seeds. And see that it has plenty of plant food. For a fall crop, try planting it in early August. I haven't done so myself, but I am told that it grows vigorously until frost. In some areas, the best crops are in winter or early spring from plants that are seeded in September and survive the winter.

Certain weeds are good substitutes for spinach. Lamb's-quarters that have grown fast make fine eating, and they are a bonus to many a procrastinating gardener. They're as good as spinach, I tell my friends. And that miserable weed, purslane, or pussley, imported from France where it is used like spinach, makes a good if slightly gelatinous dish. It's almost as tasty as spinach.

How does it happen that all these herbs are compared with spinach? Could it mean that spinach is the ultimate? It well might be, and laced with a touch of vinegar and butter, it probably is.

Squash

Most gardeners I know would sooner switch their politics than the brand of squash they grow. One of my brothers swears by a pear-shaped kind called Butternut, while another is convinced that nothing comes up to his own gray, warty kind whose name he long ago lost. For the sake of family harmony, squash is a topic they avoid.

There's something American about squash in the tremendous number of shapes, sizes, and colors they come in. Their ancestry is as diverse as our own, too. It's even hard to say sometimes what is pumpkin and what squash.

If you're crowded for garden space, don't try to grow squash. Except for summer squash, which grows like a bush rather than a vine, and one bush-type winter squash, most squash take over and smother everything in their path. They'll grow on a fence, but the weight of their fruit often pulls the vines down. I shall never forget how an old Greek couple in the mountains of northern Epirus grew squash in their tiny courtyard. The vines grew on a short piece of fence, and carefully supporting each fruit was a pie tin held up by wires attached to the fence. I felt an immediate kinship with those people.

I have only one other practical suggestion for growing squash in limited space, and I learned that in a valley at the foot of the Himalayas in Nepal, where I saw big white squash covering the roofs of a tiny village. It was a pretty sight. The plants grew alongside the houses, and the vines were trained to the roof where the squash grew and matured, safe from marauding water buffaloes and an occasional rhinoceros. Even if those don't often trouble you, you might adapt the idea for your ranch-style house.

If you still can't find room for squash, and even if you don't care about eating them, buy some at the market just the same. To me there is no other vegetable quite as beautiful, in form and color and feel, from the whimsical scalloped Pattypans to the sleek, green Table Queens, the prim Buttercups, and the hearty, nubby old Hubbards. Unlike most gardeners, I love them all.

Swiss Chard

Swiss chard is a fine vegetable, and the red-leaved version is as beautiful as it is tasty. It grows lush and tall and—except for a long bout of hot weather—will stay that way until frost. Its stems are such a vivid red that my color-blind eyes can pick it up. Even the smallest veins of the leaf are red.

I have often wondered why more people don't grow Swiss chard. It's the equal of beet tops for flavorful greens. In fact, it is a beet that simply doesn't make a bottom. It's easy to grow, except that, like beets, each seed is a capsule of several seeds, and therefore needs thinning no matter how you plant it. You can harvest Swiss chard all summer and the stalks keep coming up, tender and tall.

Southerners are the principal users of cooked greens, and they seem to like their potherbs bitter, like their popular mustard greens. Swiss chard never gets bitter. Could this be the answer?

Tomatoes

That inimitable newspaper editor, William Allen White of Emporia, Kansas, liked to quote an old saw to the effect that there are three things every man knew he could do better than any other—build a fire, make love, and run a newspaper. How his eyes lit up when he said it!

I'd like to add a fourth—and that is grow tomatoes. Even if a person has no more than a summer's worth of experience, he's suddenly an expert. Probably that's because tomatoes—like corn—are so absurdly easy to grow that almost anything you do with them succeeds.

Start them early under lights: they grow like wild. Sow them in the garden: they race with the early house-started ones. Plant the stalk on its side and bury most of the stem so that roots form along it, and it prospers. Or plant it upright and eventually the plant falls on its side and roots take hold along the stem. Either way works fine. Stake them and they grow fine. Let them sprawl and they do fine.

However, in a year when the fruit rots, almost nothing seems to work. And in years when the fruit splits, nothing helps, although modern varieties are far less subject to splitting.

A real expert (like me) will tell you that what tomatoes need most of all is plenty of water. In fact, the more water you pour onto your patch, the more tomatoes you get. Plenty of sun is essential, too, but that's something you can't do much about. In heavy, poorly drained soils, obviously you couldn't follow that advice.

Early varieties are generally "determinate"—that is, they set their fruit and the vine stops growing. Later varieties are "indeterminate" and keep right on growing and flowering until frost.

To all of you experts: try some new kind of tomato this year. I like the orange ones that are low in acid, yet tasty. So too are the yellow ones. Patio tomatoes do actually flourish on the patio, and they are as handsome as any flowering shrub.

You can keep tomatoes in the basement after frost and have them ripening for weeks, generally until Thanksgiving or even Christmas. We keep ours on newspapers on the floor—unwrapped—so we can watch them as they ripen.

Turnips

Here is the first vegetable ready to cook in the spring, and it is a delight to grow because it matures so fast—in something like forty days. Its flesh is pure white and juicy. By midsummer, though, it is tough and woody. Plant turnips as early as you can in spring. I am told that fall-sown turnips are also good, but, by then, so many other vegetables are ready that I haven't tried them.

Watermelons

If you're the kind who wants guaranteed results, without any gamble, don't plant watermelons. They're risky. If the spring is cold, the seeds rot. If the summer is cold, the vines stand still and frost catches them with only a hint of the riches they could shower on you. But if you're a gambler—you'll get your reward all summer long, just watching.

My five brothers and I ordered watermelon seed every spring, arguing the virtues of Klondyke and Rattlesnake and Cole's Early, generally settling instead on Kleckly Sweet—a name you almost eat with a spoon. The vines grew rampant and beautiful; leaves were more intricate than maple or oak. When the fruits began to appear, we marked each plant with a stick, and before long there were well marked trails to each one through the patch. Were the melons ready to pick? We held a caucus over each one, thumping, smelling, and eventually cutting out a plug to peek inside.

When frost hung heavy in the hollows, we spread bed sheets and burlap bags and newspapers across the patch, and we gathered all we couldn't blanket and stored them in the barn, hoping they would ripen there. They didn't. Watermelons don't improve after picking. Finally the frost blackened the vines and softened the fruit, and we said we'd never try again. But in January, when the seed catalogs came, we flipped back to those enchanted pages of mammoth melons. And once again we'd be off in a fantasy land of Kleckly Sweet and Dixie Bell.

It was one day during harvest that the cows got out and romped across the garden, me after them. The sound of melons popping made me sick, but even at a distance I could see that they were no longer white, but red. I shouted to no one in particular, "The watermelons are ripe! The watermelons are ripe!" And inside of minutes, the threshing machine shut down and all hands—family and friends—converged on the patch to feast on the shattered Irish Greys. There were wheelbarrow loads of watermelon that year. We gave them away, and long after we ceased caring for them, we kept on eating them just to keep them from spoiling.

Today, the new early varieties take much of the gamble out of watermelons. In a hot summer, some kinds actually do produce ripe fruit within sixty-five days.

The first year I tried Minnesota's Golden Midget, I returned from an extensive trip to find leaves and fruit turning yellow. I soaked the ground and sprayed the leaves with fertilizer because they seemed to be starving. And still the vines yellowed and died. The melons were the size of grapefruits and as yellow as lemons. Here and there wasps were beginning to bore holes inside. My niece inspected the garden. "Your watermelons are ripe," she said, matter-of-factly. "Are they any good?" And when I scoffed, she said, "Look, they're red inside."

Sure enough, just below the yellow skin was a thin layer of rind and under that the pale red, juicy flesh. I'm sure they weren't the equal of Kleckly Sweet, but they were good anyhow.

Here's an idea to boost the growth of your melons and the appearance of your patch. Lay down a thin film of plastic around the melons after they're up, or a layer of straw, which keeps down weeds and conserves moisture.

How do you tell when a watermelon is ripe? Andy Duncan, horticulturist, is something of an expert on watermelons. If the underside where the melon touches the soil is yellow, he says, the melon's ready. The big varieties that you find in stores have skins that feel slightly sandy when fully ripe. If the melon is completely smooth and very glossy, pass it up. Some testers prefer to lean on a melon with both hands; if they hear it crack inside, they know it's crisp and ready It's strange, but even when they are given this treatment, decay is almost never bothersome. But plugging a melon is something else. Once you've plugged a green melon, you might just as well toss it.

My favorite way of telling when a melon is ripe is to thump the toe of my shoe. When I get the same sound from my melon, I know it's ready.

Zucchinis

If you plant no more than one hill, you'll have more than you need. Zucchini is the Uncle Sam of vegetables, providing enough fruit for all the neighbors, and is generally about as well received as our gifts abroad.

The trouble is that few Americans know how to use them, and they are afraid to try. Last summer when my brother picked one the size of a hot dog and asked me to eat it—raw and unpeeled—I thought he had flipped. But when I sampled it, following his example, I found it surprisingly good. Its texture was crisp and rich, almost buttery, its flavor pleasant and without a hint of the green taste I find so objectionable in some raw vegetables, like peas. I am sure that if I hadn't already made up my mind about raw zucchini, I would admire it that way.

Few gardeners—up to their knees in excess zucchinis—realize that the young fruits are equal to cucumbers both for slicing and pickling, with or without peeling.

An average or unimaginative cook who tries zucchini will never again bother with it. Boiled in water by itself, it's a mess, as inviting as dishwater. It takes a good cook to make zucchini come into its own. Creamed with onions and herbs, it's a dish fit for Sardi's on a Saturday night. Sliced and baked in cheddar cheese soup, it's excellent. Laced with green peppers, tomatoes, onions, meat, a little oil, a bay leaf or two, and oregano, it's as good a vegetable as you can grow—if you can still call it zucchini after all the seasoning.

There's no need to tell you how to grow zucchini. It cares for itself. About all you need to do is to pick it. Unlike members of the winter squash family, zucchini and other summer squash don't need a whole yard to romp in. They're too busy fruiting to do much traveling. Good cooks say you should harvest the fruit when it's young.

10
how to
have a
beautiful border

Your yard needs a picture frame to set the whole place off. So around the edges you plant a border, generally of perennials. Between your neighbors' back lots and your own, if you live in town, you might like an informal, friendly boundary marker. Here again is where you might put in a border. Maybe you don't need a border at all, but just the excuse to grow some of the picturesque flowers that have been ogling you from the catalogs.

Starting the Border

The easiest borders to keep weeded are narrow ones, not more than three feet wide, that you can reach by hand or hoe from either side. Narrow borders show off most plants to better advantage than wide borders. A dictamnus, or gas plant, for instance, is at its best with nothing behind or in front of it. So too are the tall sedums, euphorbias, hostas, and many others for which plant form is as important as bloom. (Don't worry over all those names. I'll explain and catalog them later.) Narrow borders are easier to keep spruce-looking; you'll need to pull off dead leaves and pick off old blooms, and the like.

In spite of all the advantages of narrow borders, most of us squeeze in new plants, widen the border, and what was once orderly now becomes a mass—and often a mess—of blooms.

Lay out your borders so you have maximum sun. Few plants do well in the shade. Put in the best soil you can lay hold of and dig it down deep, at least a couple of spade depths. Mix in compost, rotted manure, peat moss, or whatever you can beg, borrow, or steal in the way of organic matter. In places where you feel your soil is still too soggy, raise the bed six inches or more above ground level. In light soil, leave a depression to hold rain.

When Your Order Arrives

Open the packages immediately and let shrubs (and tree roots) soak in a tub of water for twelve hours before you plant, or twenty-four hours if the buds seem dry. If you can't plant them at once after that, then dig them down temporarily in some shady spot and cover the roots with soil. A better idea is to cancel that poker or bridge date and put them out at once after soaking.

It is even more important that packages of perennials be opened at once so the plants don't suffocate. Plants with a thick rosette of leaves are especially prone to rot. Unwrap them completely, remove any rubber band you might find. (Groups of plants are sometimes lashed together that way.) Remove all dead leaves, and plant. Rather than let perennial roots soak before planting, I prefer watering them after planting, but not enough to cover any leaves or crown, then shading them a few days with shingles. Remember that plant roots are like fish. Exposed to dry air, they soon die.

Now the Fun Begins—Planting the Old Standbys

There are a few plants that ought to be in every border, old standbys around which you plant the newer ones. The first plants to install are those that dominate the border by their size, and are generally slow in getting started.

If any one flower can be called the backbone of a border, I would say it is the day lily. Once planted, it's there to stay, is handsome all season and generous in bloom. Leave plenty of room for it—at least three feet for the tall kinds.

Perhaps your border is too small for peonies, and you'd rather have perennials that bloom during a longer season. That's all right, but you still ought to have at least one plant. Try a new hybrid, like Red Charm. Again leave three feet to the plant.

Put in a dictamnus, or gas plant, in a permanent place. It won't tolerate transplanting. In a shady space, put in a bleeding heart. In a sunny spot, plant a butterfly weed. In light shade, plant whatever hostas you especially like. You now have the framework of old dependables.

These Shorter-Lived Perennials Are Splashy

Now that you have the standbys in place, put in the heavy-blooming perennials, starting perhaps with delphiniums, in climates where they thrive. Again leave room—a good two feet or even more per plant. Add phlox, again leaving room around each for air circulation. You now have the mainstays of the perennial border.

Irises are all right for the border, but I prefer them by themselves in rows in the garden, since when they are out of bloom they detract somewhat from the border; also, they need air and sun to keep healthy.

If you have room, consider these excellent perennials: scarlet lychnis, lythrum, shasta daisies, trollius, evening primroses, platycodon, globe thistle, lupines, and monkshood. Except for platycodon and lupines, all of these plants transplant fairly easily, and you can shift them around as your plans change.

Now for the finishing touches. Do plant a few clumps of Silver Mound artemisia as accents. Put in a plant of doronicum next to your spring bulbs, and tuck in a perennial flax wherever you have a little space.

With these plants, I guarantee you'll have a spectacular border.

What Do You Mean—Accent Plants?

In a magazine, editors avoid monotony by what they call a change of pace—a page that is all type follows a page of pictures, a serious article follows an entertaining one, and so on. To avoid monotony in a perennial border, you plant a tall, stiff plant here and there or one with light gray foliage. These are accent plants, the exclamation marks of the garden that halt the monochrome of green abruptly.

Good tall plants: Siberian iris, lythrum, and some day lilies.

Plants with gray foliage: Silver Mound artemisia, santolina, *Dianthus plumarius.*

One that is both tall and gray-leaved is bocconia, but it is so big that it would overwhelm any but the biggest borders.

All these plants are discussed elsewhere.

Nothing But White

Perhaps you've seen such a synthetic flower garden at the spring garden show—nothing but white petunias, lilies, stocks, carnations, snapdragons, geraniums, ageratum, candytuft, Shasta daisies, and the like. It's a breathtaking sight.

A genuine all-white garden is almost that nice, too. You get a feeling of coolness, and when freed from the competition of colors, the white flowers can show off the beauty of their line and form and texture. It is in the evening that the all-white garden comes into its own; even after dark, the white flowers stand out. And it's after dark, too, when those white flowers turn on their fragrance. I have an idea that white flowers in general are much stronger-scented than colored ones. Perhaps that's the come-hither they need in lieu of color to lure pollinating insects.

I know that a few regal lilies can perfume the whole yard. A friend of mine had a clump at the back door of her rural retreat. The fragrance wafted through the whole house, and the whiteness of the lilies seemed to light up the back steps. As one went down the hill at night, it was the white flowers that lit the way, terrace after terrace, down to the garden, which was bright and fragrant with white nicotiana.

White flowers, to some people, mean funerals, but if you don't have that hangup, you might try an all-white garden one year. Even if you don't do that, use them here and there to brighten your place by night and to accentuate vivid-colored clumps of flowers.

My favorite white flowers are delphiniums (with white, brown, or black centers knows as bees), Shasta daisies, Siberian iris, single white peonies. Among annuals, my favorites are Iceberg candytuft and white nicotiana, new varieties of which remain fully open all day even in bright sun.

A Trick to Keep the Edges Looking Trim

If you are blessed with a lawn of nothing but bluegrass, you can skip this section. All you need to do to keep the edges of the border trim is slice them with a rotary blade, and rake or hoe away the bits of sod. But if you are cursed with that old renegade, quack grass, or witchgrass, it's another matter.

I have tried half a dozen techniques for keeping quack grass from infiltrating my perennials. Up until this year, none of them worked. I put down railway ties as combination seat and edging; the quack quickly grew underneath. I laid down sheets of black plastic so ugly that I felt compelled to sprinkle soil over it; old quack pierced it happily from below, annual weeds sprouted above. I put down aluminum edging; where it was flush with the soil, the quack leaped over, and if the edging protruded, the lawn mower macerated it. I tried limestone flagging; the cool soil below the rocks was ideal for quack runners. In desperation I even tried soil sterilants, but the dead brown earth looked frightful.

A solution that has worked for some of my friends in quack-grass country is to buy a heavy plastic, dig it down six to eight inches as a root baffle, then lap four to six inches of it aboveground as a mowing strip, either around the perennials or outward onto the lawn. Cover the strip with tanbark, peat, sand, buckwheat hulls, or (as I have done) with railroad ties, building up the soil inside the bed to the level of the ties. On other borders I use 3/4-inch rocks from our gravel and cement plant. The heavy plastic should last for many years, since none of it is exposed to sunlight. I find that the lawn mower clears the rocks safely. My borders for the first time in their life look well groomed.

Best Thing You Can Do for Your Perennials

Lift them with a spade, cut or pull them apart, and replant the best small, vigorous clump, preferably in a different spot. This is positively the kindest deed you can do for most perennials, especially mums, phlox, asters, iris, and members of the daisy family. Fast-growing plants simply need to be lifted free of their own refuse of dead and aging roots.

The only hard part of the job is discarding the extra plants you find yourself with. I've never yet found the gardener who is hardhearted enough to toss them away. Most gardeners use them in unsatisfactory ways: they widen the border, lengthen it, try talking friends into taking plants they don't really want. Or if they have waste ground, they plant them there to fend for themselves.

I have worked out a system that isn't bad. I plant my new divisions in a ''give-away'' row in the garden. That way people don't need to watch the major surgery of splitting off a piece of the main plant—something that disturbs most people. And with the young plant already growing in the garden, they know it isn't part of your landscape plan.

Bald Spots in Your Border

The best-laid plans of mice—and especially of men—end up in bald spots. Often a rose dies out, a pet perennial peters out, or annuals turn brown. What do you do with that empty space?

First of all, consider putting in one of those unadorned pottery birdbaths. What was a desert now becomes a focus of attention. Your border takes on glamour.

Early in the season you might pick up such things as Canterbury bells at your nursery. They can be moved when they're practically in bloom. You can do the same with columbine, too. A delphinium plant will fill an enormous vacancy. In fact, a good many perennials transplant easily, including Shasta daisy, painted daisy, phlox, and even lilies. Obviously, if your nursery still has flats of annuals, you can fill in with them, too.

To bolster your border late in the season, nothing does better than chrysanthemums, which go on growing and blooming without even wilting.

Consider a final idea, which was suggested to me by a visit to small gardens in Switzerland. Simply leave the ground bare, and let the surrounding plants draw more attention. To the Swiss, it seems, nothing sets off a flower more dramatically than bare, weedless black earth.

Cure for the Late-Summer Wearies

It's hot. Weeds have sprung up, well, like weeds. Some have the nerve to be in full bloom. Wisps of delphiniums still bloom down around the scrawny neck of the plant. Poppies are still blooming, but the plants look half dead. Hollyhocks are still blooming, but they are heavy, pregnant-looking, with seed. Peas and beans are still bearing, but look bedraggled. The place looks a mess. You wonder if you'll ever again plant a garden.

Peace! Take the cure for tired garden blood. Get out shears, slash off fading perennials just above the ground, and haul them off to the compost (or burn if diseased). Most flowering plants don't age very gracefully, and once they start going to seed, well they go to seed.

So pull out those poppies, rip out the peas and beans and aging lettuce. As soon as you do, your spirits will soar. And after you run through with the tiller and the earth lies clean and smooth again, the rest of your garden will look downright beautiful. In fact, with all that good ground lying free of weeds, you might even be tempted to put in late-summer radishes and lettuce and a few packets of biennials like Canterbury bells and foxglove.

A bonus for sprucing up your perennials. Before you know it, you'll have a fresh batch of hollyhocks and another of delphiniums, not as tall as before but just as fresh and colorful.

Now let me take you on a garden odyssey of perennials. Except for a few that survive in tropical America, I have tried them all, both in the Midwest and the East. Consequently, I feel a compulsion to offer you this scorecard of perennials.

11
perennials: the year-after-year flowers

Perennials—as if you didn't know—are plants that come up from the roots year after year. They don't, however, live forever. Most of them have a few good years, then dwindle—unless they are dug up and rejuvenated. Biennials are those that come up one year, live through winter, bloom the following year, and then die. For purposes of simplification I have included them under annuals. Annuals germinate, bloom, and die all in one season.

This scorecard of perennials is the result of my experience with every perennial that just about every catalog offers. My candid ratings have this purpose: if I can save you the grief and expense of buying a poor perennial, you'll have space and money for a good one. Obviously you won't agree if I downgrade a flower that was Grandma's pride and joy, or one that comes to perfection in your unique climate. Nevertheless, I offer you this highly opinionated guide to perennials I think you'll enjoy.

Achilleas

Like many a human family, the achillea clan has one good member and another you'd rather not talk about.

The yellow, flat-topped achillea is worth having. It grows waist-high, needs no staking, and gives bold horizontal lines to its corner of the garden. For small gardens, there is a variety half that high. Both make fine cut flowers, especially for winter arrangements. After flowering, the plants look somewhat ratty, though, and need trimming back.

The black sheep of the achilleas is white; it's called the Pearl, and it's pawned off on more unsuspecting neighbors than almost any other flower I know of. Actually, for a week or so at its best, it is very nice, but soon it falls over, smothering its neighbors. Its white roots race out in all directions and engulf everything within reach. By the time you decide that the Pearl is no gem and you reach for the shovel, it's too late. For the next year you'll be digging. Plant it in poor soil so it doesn't grow so rank? I've done that, too, and then it always looks weedy.

There's still another achillea, which looks like the wild white yarrow of the meadows except that its flowers are rosy red. My neighbors discovered it growing at the edge of their lawn, and they rescued it from being mowed. They like it. To my color-blind vision, it is totally without merit.

Ajuga

If you must plant this one—and I can't see why you would—let it be a ground cover in light shade. The first year you have it, you'll say I'm wrong, that it's a beautiful plant (especially the purple-leaved kind) with its tiny delphinium spikes coming up all over from the prostrate plants—and it is. But the second year, about the time you're tired of weeding it, you'll begin to change your mind. Poor little ajuga isn't dense enough to battle weeds, and before long you'll decide to let it go on its own. Ajuga tolerates the lawn mower, but if you mow off its spring flower spikes, what's the point of having it? When mowed, it resembles nothing more than a patch of weeds.

There is a good ajuga, one that grows taller and has bright green leaves and handsome spikes a foot high. It does well in shade and carpets the ground as the junior members of its family do. Last fall, mine was blooming at freezeup.

Alliums

The giant flowering onion is a spectacular plant. At the Brooklyn Botanic Garden, the big sparkling flower clusters grow as high as your head and draw all eyes to them. You plant the bulb—it's as big as your fist—whenever you can find it for sale. The following spring you'll have the first bloom. Slowly the clump increases until you have a dramatic showing.

In my own gardens, both in the Midwest and in the East, I haven't had such results. Thrips might be at fault. My soil perhaps isn't rich enough. Out of three bulbs I own, just one is blooming, but that is enough. Giant alliums are among the finest new plants of this decade.

Smaller alliums are worth some space—not much, but some. One that grows in a tight cluster with stiff stalks of white or rose flowers about two feet high makes a pleasant tufted spot in the border, and its seedheads are fine by themselves or mixed in with winter bouquets. Don't let this one get out of bounds, though.

The tiny yellow moly is a novelty for the rock garden, as is a rose-purple foot-high one from the Rockies.

Alyssum

In a rock garden, the golden splash of this perennial alyssum is superb. Sprawling across the top of a rock ledge, it is elegant. It blooms for a long while about tulip time, carpeting the ground. The pale yellow variety is generally preferred to the deeper-colored one.

In perfectly drained soil, in sunlight, alyssum grows and survives and spreads both by crawling and seeds, although it is in no sense weedy. Mine had sun for only half the day and eventually died out. I haven't reinstalled it, partly because I have no rock garden and partly because its prostrate stems go bare during summer.

Anchusa

For a couple of weeks in June, this plant is a knockout, its brilliant blue the most dominant spot of color in the garden. But its glory passes quickly, and for the rest of summer the plant does little more than sprawl, its hairy stems falling to the ground unless they are staked. I have tried keeping off all seedpods, but unlike delphiniums, anchusas can't be persuaded to put on much of a second act. Try anchusas if you like. They're fun because they grow like weeds, sometimes blooming the first year.

A smaller biennial anchusa, with its cloud of blue flowers above big, stalkless leaves, is pleasant. You will have trouble finding a start of this one, though.

Anemones, Japanese

This is a fine fall-blooming anemone with fibrous roots, and though it is not nearly as striking as the florist's tuberous-rooted ones, it is eminently worth planting. The plant comes up late in spring, and unless you have the place marked, you're likely to hoe it out. All summer its clump of handsome leaves expands, and by September a flowering stalk emerges and stands two or three feet tall. There is a lush, woodsy look to the blooms, which may be pale silvery pink, a deeper rose pink, or pure white (the catalog's words—not mine). My variety, September Morn, only begins to bloom before frost strikes it down. But in the East and in most of central United States, it brings a fresh, clean beauty to a landscape when generally little more than mums and asters are afoot.

Anemone clumps grow bigger and finer with the years, and they should be left untouched except for mulching and fertilizing.

A hardy anemone from China, available from Wayside Gardens, Hodges, South Carolina, blooms a month earlier than the Japanese anemone and is said to be just as pleasant. I have not tried this one, however.

Anemones, Tuberous-Rooted

These are the exotic poppylike anemones that overwhelm visitors at every garden show, and whose tubers are sold indiscriminately to practically everyone who sees them.

What a giant fraud! Nobody is ever told that these are greenhouse flowers. Taylor's *Enyclopedia of Gardening,* that standby of garden honesty, says, "The outdoor cultivation of all of them is confined to California or the South." They can be set out, like dahlias or cannas, but I have never known anyone who grew them outdoors with anything approaching success. Most of the time, the tubers never start growing.

Another flower, resembling this anemone and also sold at flower shows, is the ranunculus. This, too, is a greenhouse flower. I have tried growing it repeatedly in both the East and the Midwest. Only once did it even start to grow, and then it died in midsummer.

These two flowers have probably soured more would-be gardeners than anything else in the plant world. It's a shame that nurserymen and seedsmen don't realize it.

Artemisia

If you never before cared about foliage plants, the artemisia called Silver Mound is bound to break you down. Hardly another plant on my place is surer to cause comment. It is truly a silver mound, no more than eight inches high, handsome and trim all season long, adding a splash of white wherever you put it. More than that, its prim form accentuates the carefree character of adjoining plants. Silver Mound would make a fine edging, I am sure. It never creeps or spreads.

Artemisias are wormwoods, aromatic herbs that have been cultivated since antiquity for their fragrance and their taste. I have one other favorite artemisia —*Artemisia Abrotanum,* or what we call the Old Man—which has been a part of our family since long before I was born. It is a shrub that is two and a half to four feet high and has filmy green foliage that is aromatic, as all the wormwoods are. Our Old Man came as a sprig tucked in an envelope, from the plant in Wisconsin that our grandmother, as a girl of sixteen, had brought with her when she came by sailing ship from Norway, a thirteen-week voyage.

There is no reason for you to plant Old Man except as proof that you have read my book and that you, too, are a sentimental oaf.

Asters

Long ago I had every aster that Wayside Gardens pictured: the tall New England kinds, the dwarf ones, and the semidwarfs. After years of neglect, I have only the New England asters left. A few of the dwarf variety struggle to escape aphids and some kind of disease that stunts and distorts the foliage.

For a year or two after planting, all of the asters were resplendent, I am told. (I was not around to see them.) One by one they began to peter out, probably from not being lifted and divided as they ought to be at least every second year.

A giant blue and a giant pink continue to grow into bushes that bloom every year just before heavy frost. They require a sharp spade or an ax to divide them. For the small garden, better try the dwarf varieties.

The species *Frikarti* has never done anything in either my midwestern or eastern gardens. It barely survives the winter, doesn't begin blooming until late summer, and even then looks no better than a wild aster. I am certain, though, that in other climates it must be excellent, since Wayside Gardens calls it the finest garden plant introduced during the past twenty years.

Astilbes

If astilbes grew as they do in Holland, every garden would have them. In Minnesota, mine were killed by winter; in Pennsylvania, without frequent watering they went into a slow decline. I feel sure, though, that with careful attention, astilbes are worth growing in shady, moist places.

They grow from two to three feet high, their plumy flower heads come in shades of pink, red, or white, and their foliage is handsome and clean. Give them a try, if you like, but I offer no guarantee on performance.

Bergenias

There's no reason why you ought to grow bergenias. They're like a bunch of crisp cabbage leaves covering the ground. In early spring a few clusters of rose-pink flowers barely show among the leaves. Since the leaves do carpet the ground, bergenias ought to make a good cover, and one that is practically ever-green. It always surprises me to see such big, crisp, juicy-looking leaves come through the winter, green and healthy under the snowbank beside the house. In a shady border, bergenias would be pleasant. I hate to knock any plant so willing and dependable. Try it.

Betony

If this pleasant flower grew wild—as one of its cousins does on the path to my lake—you'd call it beautiful, which it is. But it gets lost in a crowd of almost any three other perennials. Betony grows two feet tall, and its rose-purple flowers top a minty-looking stem. It can take extremes of heat and drought, sun or part-shade, and it keeps coming up year after year.

Why do I grow it? Because I'll give room to just about anything that wants to grow, as betony does. And because I enjoy a garden zoo more than I do overall visual smash.

Bleeding Hearts

Beg a root of this one from your aunt, country cousin, or grandmother. You can buy a start at a nursery store, but why not get one that already belongs in the family? This is a magnificent perennial—maybe you should call it a centennial, rather, because it lives so long, growing and blooming without any attention. It is one plant that rarely needs dividing the way most husky perennials do. Fall is the best time to get a start. Plant it in a shady, rich place protected from winds.

You would think that anything with such lush foliage would succumb to the first hint of frost, but it doesn't. In early spring, strong shoots push up, and very shortly there are wonderful arching sprays of pink and red blooms that last for days in an arrangement—if you have the heart to cut them. In much of the United States bleeding heart dies down in summer, but in the North it keeps on blooming much of the summer.

Perhaps if bleeding heart weren't so easy to grow and so willing to return every spring, more gardeners would sing its praises. To me, it's one of Japan's greatest gifts to gardening pleasure.

The plumy bleeding hearts are getting a play because they fit into a smaller garden, bloom almost continuously, and are easily grown. They are fine for semishade, although their pink or white flower sprays aren't especially showy. Each plant is handsome, though, with its ferny foliage and graceful stalks.

Bocconia, or Plumepoppy

What a plant this one is! In a few weeks from the time it emerges, it shoots up to six and eight feet, with handsome cabbagelike leaves that are eight inches across, white on the underside and bluish-green on top. The flowers are small creamy-white ones and grow in clusters at the top of the stem, not much to look at. It's the crisp, striking foliage that gives bocconia (plumepoppy, or tree celandine) its distinction.

Naturally, you need plenty of room for plumepoppy at the back of the border or as a shrublike plant all by itself. Although it is a lusty grower, you needn't worry that it will take over a border. It's easy to keep in bounds. I started mine from seed, which was easy. Side shoots in spring are easy to lift and give neighbors a start.

Butterfly Weed

A clump of butterfly weed, blazing away in a dry sandy field in July or August, is so vivid that once you spot it you're almost sure to stop the car to investigate. This is one of the finest wild flowers in North America—an orange that cries out to butterflies as well as humans. It blooms for a long time, is always clean and well dressed, and its milkweedlike pods are decorative.

Butterfly weed is a floral masterpiece, with no help from seedsmen or hybridizers. What has held it back from wider use in perennial borders is the difficulty of transplanting it. The root is a thickened tuber that strikes deep in the light, sandy soil where it is most at home. Once you do get it started, nothing seems to faze it.

I found it easy to start from seed, but gardening *in absentia,* as I did for several years, I lost all but one of the seedlings. That one grows alongside our bright red log house, where its orange fights a losing battle. I have considered moving the plant away, but I have decided, instead, to give in and paint the house a more compatible color.

Do start butterfly weed this year. It is a superb plant. Let it have full sun and good drainage, and you'll have a perennial that will never fail you, never needs lifting or dividing, and doesn't spread, but grows more luxuriant every year. It's slow at emerging in spring, though, so mark it well.

Some butterfly weeds bloom several weeks ahead of others, for what reason nobody has discovered. Might it be the depth of the thickened tuber, or is it a genetic difference?

Campanulas

The Campanulaceae family embraces some of the best—and worst—perennials in the garden. So before accepting a single one of them as a gift, ask to check this book.

Beware of blue-bells-of-Scotland, or *Campanula rotundifolia,* a handsome plant with a steeple of bells two to three feet tall, heart-shaped leaves, and with roots that grow underground into a Mafia determined to take over your whole garden. The best you can ever do, once they are planted, is to keep waging a constant battle with them. Perhaps with chemicals and weed killers you can eradicate them, but I am reluctant to use those, and so I keep pulling and digging, trying wherever possible to find the chunky, thickened root from which new sprouts continue to arise.

Beware, too, of Coventry bells, which runs wild and is practically ineradicable. This one also grows two to three feet tall, and it has bigger, pendulous bells of pale bluish-purple.

The leaves of both varieties so much resemble the good campanulas that to be safe, you had better not gamble with anything like them.

Now for the good campanulas. Perhaps my favorite is the little *Campanula carpatica,* which grows in a single tuft not much taller than a foot and, for most of the summer, is absolutely covered with big sky-blue flowers a couple of inches across. It keeps on blooming a little until frost, always looks neat, and positively doesn't spread. A white variety is good, too. My plants after twenty years are still healthy and hearty. Few perennials are as hardy and long-lived as that.

Peach bells, *Campanula persicifolia,* is another good perennial, and it comes both in bright blue and white, grows about two feet high, and blooms much of the summer. In my experience, this one isn't long-lasting, but seedlings come up and, if thinned, carry on for their parents.

Even taller is *Campanula latifolia,* a vigorous, upstanding three-footer with deep purplish-blue flowers. Unlike most of the good campanulas, this one needs no staking.

There are many others, most of them of value in a rock garden because of their small flowers and tendency to sprawl.

Centaurea

This coarse, ragged-looking flower has very little in its favor. It can't hold a candle to the beauty of its annual cousin, the cornflower, and it is a poor substitute for globe thistle—no relative, but reminiscent of it. Any of the campanulas are pleasanter and give the same violet-blue that brightens the centaurea during summer and fall.

Chinese Lanterns

There's hardly any reason for planting this stout perennial unless—like me —you revel in every strange new member of the plant world. Chinese lanterns, however, do make nice bouquets for winter. I am told that they are dangerous to introduce into a border and that their long, wandering roots are hard to control. This hasn't been true for me. I'd even welcome their spreading more than they have. To get the biggest lanterns, give them rich soil and considerable moisture.

Christmas Roses, Helleborus Niger

If you have ever breakfasted at the Shoreham Hotel in Washington during midwinter or early spring, you must have noticed the big, dramatic white flowers just outside the coffee shop windows. Many people probably dismiss them as artificial because they are in bloom for weeks, even during snow and prolonged cold.

The Christmas Rose, or hellebore, is certainly one of the delightful oddities of the plant world, and one that every plant adventurer must try.

Your climate is too cold for anything to bloom at Christmas? These plants survive in Minnesota, after winters of forty-five to fifty degrees below zero. Their evergreen leaves come through without harm and bloom shortly after the snow has disappeared, which is generally late March or April.

The main trouble is getting the Christmas rose started. Twice, my mail-order plants have failed to start growing, although small side plants that accompanied them have lived, to succumb later to cutworms. Others here, however, have succeeded, including one in the garden of my friend and neophyte gardener, L. J. Lee, who is as proud of his first blossoms as of the twenty-one-pound northern pike I saw him land.

The best way to start Christmas roses, according to Marie Aull of the Aullwood Nature Center outside of Dayton, Ohio, is to sow them from seed or else to move the plant with large amounts of earth when still very small. Hellebores grow like weeds in her splendid garden. The young plants look almost exactly like the annual plant called cleome, or spiderflower, and that's what I thought I had in my garden once, except that the leaves didn't freeze down over winter. When I identified them and moved them into the proper shady, moist, protected area beside the house, they promptly died.

I shall certainly keep on trying. I hope you do, too. They are something to heighten the excitement of earliest spring.

Chrysanthemums

Mums are the farewell to summer, and its brilliant finale. Even after the final curtain of killing frost, they keep on performing. Obviously, every yard and garden needs them. They shorten a winter as much as any February vacation does.

Mums are among the easiest plants you can grow, provided you do one thing: *lift and divide them at least every two years and preferably every year*. When you dig them up, you'll notice how dense and old the roots are. Often you can simply pull the whole plant up by the stem, since the roots have pushed the plant up from the soil. The fresh, live roots are at the outside, and when you pull them loose, only a few roots adhere, but these are enough to get the plant going. In many varieties, only one such stem is all you need for a sizable clump. Generally, I plant four or five in a tight circle and toss out the rest of the clump. That same season, a mum is generally at its best. Unless divided this way, it quickly declines.

Most gardeners I know grow their mums in a row in the garden, two feet or so apart, in the best soil they can muster; they keep the plants well watered and dust them with rotenone to keep off aphids. Then, as the buds start opening, they lift the plants and dig them down in bare spots in the border or elsewhere about the house. With a little care, you can transplant mums any time, even when they are in full bloom. That fact makes them even more useful than most people realize.

My favorite place for mums is the patio, in big pots that display their fine form to advantage, and bring them up closer for a better look. Big pots are expensive. I find that gallon plastic buckets—the kind ice cream comes in—work fine.

Look to your nurserymen for the varieties you ought to be growing. Some of the most glamorous ones—like the spider type and exhibition size—don't bloom early enough to beat the season outdoors. But there are plenty of others, regardless of how far north you live. Some kinds die with winter, but why let that worry you? For only a few cents you can pick up new ones at the supermarket or nursery.

One mum is so universal and easily grown that it merits special mention. That one is Clara Curtis, member of a hardy subspecies. It begins to bloom in late summer and keeps on growing all fall, covering itself with single salmon-pink flowers until it's a mound of bloom. If you haven't been able to grow any other mums, try this one. It is certainly one of the finest perennials in any garden, and if it weren't so willing to grow everywhere, it would be considered a prize. It not only winters through fifty below zero, but flowers in the wild, untended.

I keep waiting for hybridizers to offer Clara Curtis in different colors, since pink to color-blind me looks little better than dirty gray. Royal Command is her counterpart in wine-red, but I haven't tried this one.

Columbines

Here's a great perennial that will rarely fail you. It blooms in full sun in my sandy garden, yet comes to perfection in part shade in good soil. It seldom needs staking, and if you keep the seed pods picked off, it will bloom intermittently until frost.

The wild columbine is a flower all rural children know and love. We used to bite off the tip of its spur and suck the nectar. We called it honeysuckle. I moved a few plants into the border where they grew luxuriantly, all of six feet high. I could hardly wait for them to bloom; the blossoms, I figured, would be enormous. Only they weren't—not a whit bigger than normal. And on those giant stalks they looked even smaller, like dainty jewelry on a fat woman. The effect was ludicrous.

I began to realize that to improve on nature, you can't simply increase the size of the plant; the flowers must be proportionately bigger, too. My respect for hybridizers keeps growing. The new columbines they have developed have flowers two and three times as big as the wild ones, yet are as graceful as the small ones. Their long spurs make them seem like flying birds. Besides the McKana hybrids, try the blue ones and the doubles. They're all beautiful.

Easy as they are to grow, columbines have their troubles. A leaf miner gets beneath the skin of the leaf and tunnels about in intricate patterns, protected against sprays and dust. If I start picking off infested leaves early enough in the season, I can usually keep them under control

Much more troublesome are the stem borers, which hatch from eggs laid in the main stalk. Keep a sharp eye out for a stalk that suddenly wilts. This is borer damage. As the worm feeds, it burrows downward and into the crown, often killing the plant. However you get rid of the borer—by systemics, pinching the stem to kill it, or cutting off the stalk—it's a good idea to plant a few replacements every year. Columbines aren't generally long-lasting. They're worth the effort of replanting.

Coralbells

For those who like a dainty, well-mannered flower, this is it. Coralbells has a rosette of pleasant leaves surrounding a few wiry stalks strung with flowers that are more a mist of pink or red than actual blooms. It generally blooms all summer and never looks weedy. The place for it is in rich, moist soil in semishade, where it stays put and needs no other care than lifting and dividing every two or three years. This flower is too subtle for my color-blind eyes, but most visitors exclaim mildly over it before passing on to showier garden sights. Growing in tufts as it does, it looks pleasant in a rock or railroad-tie wall.

Coreopsis

On Cape Cod some years ago, I was faking photographs with the gardening expert Fred Rockwell for a national magazine. (I'm sorry—you didn't suppose that those glamorous gardens didn't need an assist now and then?) We had used up all the potted geraniums we had brought with us to fill in bare spots along a house. All over the Cape were golden coreopsis growing waist-high in the fields and along the roadsides, so we dug up a few and moved them in. But before we could set up and shoot, they would droop. I should have known that plants that grow as fast as coreopsis generally wilt fast.

Coreopsis is a fine perennial that blooms even during the hottest months. As a cut flower, it has the long-lasting qualities usual in the daisy family. In the perennial border, it comes and goes, seeding itself but dying out after a year or two. It seems to thrive best in adversity, and that's a delightful virtue in any flower.

Delphiniums

The farther north you go, the bigger the delphiniums grow. At Fairbanks, Alaska, you see them twelve feet tall and even more, with flowering stalks a foot across, yet so perfectly proportioned that instead of looking big, they make the houses beside them look small. The air terminal building, for instance, seemed like a shed until I came closer and saw that the delphiniums that towered above the roof's edge were giants of their kind. Delphs are complex hybrids, but most of their ancestors must have hailed from far northern places.

It's not surprising then that delphs winter over better in the North. Here in Minnesota we consider them a permanent kind of perennial, needing no winter covering other than snow. In Pennsylvania and farther south, they are short-lived and something of a gamble.

Just the same, most people in the United States grow and love delphs. They're easily grown from seed, flower over a long period, and give a smash of color to any garden. Cut them down to the ground when the stalk is largely spent, and they'll give you a benefit fall performance.

Delphs are such prodigious growers that old plants send up dozens of sprouts—far too many for their own good. It's a good idea to pull out all but about six or eight stems, to allow more air and room for the remaining ones, which naturally will grow taller and finer. But it's an unpleasant job, deciding which fine stalks to pull out and which to leave.

Watch for wilting of lower leaves and any black rot at the bottom of the stalk. Pull out the bad stems and hope the disease won't spread through the plant. It doesn't happen often, but you ought to look now and then. And watch the tip of the stalk for any distortion that might mean aphids or red spider. A little dusting with rotenone in the early stages will clean them up. These problems are generally minor.

The big drawback to delphs is that they grow too big, too tall, and their glorious flower stalks snap in the wind, or when the flowers are waterlogged in a rain. Delphs must be staked, and there's no good way to do it. With a small clump, it's not so hard. You poke a six-foot bamboo stake down beside the crown and lash the stalk to it. But big clumps need several stakes to prop them up. The only good thing about staking delphs is that it gives you the chance to use up those cast-off nylons. You can cut each stocking into several strips, so the nylons will go further and be less noticeable. But if you don't extend your support just about to the tip, the end is almost sure to snap over. Maybe you can figure a better way of staking than this. I can't, but I keep trying.

Last year I bought a small roll of wire reinforcing, the kind that's used in concrete floors; I planned to encircle each clump with the tall stiff support, but the wire was so rusty and unpleasant that I didn't put it up. Next year I may try nine-foot lengths of extremely stiff wire, one per stalk, which should be unobtrusive.

A word about starting delphiniums.

Seed must be fresh. If you can't plant them at once, store the seed in a plastic bag in the refrigerator. Sow them in a flat under your fluorescent light or in a cool, lightly shaded spot in your border or garden. Protect each seedling from cutworms. Fertilize with commercial fertilizer rather than manure. In a short time you'll be knee-deep in delphiniums, and by fall you'll have the first spikes, short but beautiful.

Dianthus

At the front of my perennial garden are several mounds of bluish-gray leaves that erupt in June into hundreds of pink blossoms so fragrant they perfume the whole yard. I am never sure just what to call them: grass pinks, clove pinks, Scotch pinks, or dianthus. I believe any or all apply to one of the finest perennials you can own. They require no care, look neat at any season, and don't desert you. Most mat-forming plants are hard to weed, but not this one, since it rarely pegs down roots and is dense enough to shade out most weed seedlings.

All my pinks are singles, in pale colors. I have tried planting a few fancier ones, but they seem to die out before putting on a show.

Another dianthus that keeps on growing despite the lawn mower and my hoe is the minute bright red one called maiden pink. This one is impossible to keep weeded. In fact, it has become something of a weed. The big carnation-type dianthus are too temperamental for me, whether in the East or in the Midwest. I much prefer my smaller, fragrant, dependable kind.

Dictamnus, or Gas Plant

Beginning gardeners often feel gypped when a perennial dies out. They haven't yet learned that few perennials live on year after year. Dictamnus—the old-fashioned gas plant—is an exception. You plant this one, and it's there for good.

Dictamnus is one of my favorite plants. Spring after spring its rich green leaves push up as the plant expands into a charming bush, surmounted by flowers and, later, handsome seedpods. No staking, no spraying, no lifting or dividing, even no weeding. Dictamnus is a self-sufficient individual.

I have only one quarrel with it. Whenever I want it to perform for visitors, it generally fails me. On a still summer night I rough up the foliage, and the rich oily fragrance surrounds me. I strike a match—and nothing happens. But I keep on trying because two or three times, there's been a pale blue glow around the flowers as the gas ignited for an instant (without harm to the plant).

Except for that, I'll recommend Dictamnus wholeheartedly. Get a start of it from a slipshod gardener who is lax with the hoe. Young seedlings will be coming up all around the old plant. I always have plenty of them. Once the plant has established itself, it won't tolerate moving, so decide where you want it, as if it were a tree.

Doronicum

As snow melts, this little daisy pushes up alongside emerging tulips, racing them into bloom. It's a beauty, I think, and one you ought to have. Its bright yellow blossoms seem to sparkle. Its leaves are perfect hearts. It is orderly without being prim, friendly without being riotous. After a month of bloom, as it declines, you wonder what you liked so much about it—the blossoms, you conclude, aren't really any nicer than a sow thistle's or a dandelion's. And yet each spring that it opens, I am as enthusiastic as ever.

Plant doronicum alongside tulips in good soil in sun or partial shade. In summer in warm areas it dies down completely. That's the time to lift and divide it and spread it to other areas. It stays where you plant it and doesn't crowd.

Eremurus, or Foxtail Lily

Foxtail lily is a good name for this one, mostly because it's as elusive and seldom seen as a fox's tail. I have planted it three or four times in Minnesota, and though it sometimes pushes up a paltry rosette of leaves, it has never blossomed here or ever lived a third year. In my Pennsylvania garden it has bloomed weakly once before dying. Most garden catalogs do admit that it's not hardy in the North, yet I keep on trying because my sister Adeline's garden in Montana, foxtail lilies not only thrive and bloom, but multiply, even though the winters there are among the coldest in the United States and often there is little or no snow cover.

So I keep trying, supplied each year with new roots from my sister's willing volunteer plants. She maintains that they are magnificent, the equal of the best color reproductions in the catalogs. The spikes of orange, yellow, white, or salmon stand eight feet tall and put on a show for several weeks.

Roots are expensive and fragile. I'm not about to tell you how I try growing them. If the climate isn't at fault, I certainly must be.

Eryngium Maritimum, or Sea Holly

This plant is for those who love novelties, and that includes me. Eryngium is a thistlelike plant with metallic blue spiny flowers and even blue stems. There's nothing spectacular about it, yet to a gardening buff, it's great. You wouldn't guess that it's a member of the carrot family until you try digging one up to give to a neighbor. Its meaty stem goes straight down. If you plant eryngium in a sunny, well-drained spot, you'll probably have it for life. New plants will spring up from its seed, but they're easily eradicated.

Plant eryngium out of the normal traffic lanes through your garden. The spiny flowers can snag hose.

Euphorbia

Some of the euphorbias are weeds that are a scourge. Knowledgeable gardeners may warn you against the one called cushion spurge (Euphorbia epithymoides). Probably that's the reason you won't be able to find it in catalogs or at many nurseries. But, believe me, it's worth searching for, and it won't spread.

My cushion spurge in spring is a perfect little globe of yellow, no more than a foot high, reminiscent of a cushion mum. Its outermost leaves just below the flower cluster are what give it the color. Even after the color fades and the plant turns to green, it is neat and orderly.

The best place for it is in the front of the border by itself, where its stiff form will show off. Wherever you put it, this spurge will stay without spreading. The only difficult thing about it is trying to divide it for your friends. The root is as hard as that of a tree, and it may require an ax to break it up. Never a visitor here in spring but wants a start of it.

Evening Primrose

This primrose—technically Oenothera (ee-no-theé-ra)—is a pleasant one for any perennial border. It is easily grown, it blooms in early summer at about two feet tall, and its lemon-yellow flowers are bright and clean. It grows best in light soil, and yet needs considerable moisture. In fact, nothing I grow seems to wilt as fast in hot weather or to respond as quickly to watering.

Evening primrose is neat, doesn't crowd out its neighbors, and seldom needs staking. It's neat when out of bloom, too, and its winter rosettes are among the pleasantest I know. About all you need do to keep it coming is lift and divide it in early spring and toss out the old center stalks. Like many hardy perennials, its best year is the year you divide and replant.

Feverfew

Beware of this one. Give it back, with thanks. Don't let it get started on your place. Sure, it's a pleasant flower, but it's altogether too willing to grow and reproduce and turn your whole garden into a feverfew. There's nothing few about feverfew. Rather call it f'evermore.

How do you recognize it? It's a daisylike plant of the mum family, two or three feet tall, and it has light green, feathery leaves and nondescript flowers. Its leaves are more aromatic than those of other mums.

Flax

I have no more useful perennial in my garden than perennial flax. It blooms all summer, its silky blue petals flattering just about anything beside it. It never crowds, since the sparse leaves and slender stems hardly cast a shadow. Yet when the sun shines, it's suddenly there, with hundreds of blossoms. On top of that, it never needs staking.

You won't find it in many nurseries, though, because it's somewhat hard to move and it dies out pretty fast. But there are always young plants coming up to replace the old, so that once you start them, the casual live-and-let-live gardener will always have them. A clump of flax is one of the many bonuses of casual gardening. Order a package of perennial flax seed right now. You will have cause forever to thank me.

Gaillardias

Why this temperamental flower should be otherwise known as blanket-flower, I'll never understand. Perhaps in parts of the West where it grows wild, it blankets the ground, but for me it simply falls on the ground, asking to be put out of its misery. I have seen fine banks of it in the Brooklyn Botanic Garden, however, so I—rather than the flower—must be at fault.

Plant it in full sun, in light soil. My only surviving plants won't tolerate being moved away from the shade of a vigorous day lily. Could it be that gaillardia doesn't like full sun, despite what the experts say?

Geranium, Hardy Type

Sure, go ahead and buy *Geranium grandiflorum* if you like. For about one week in early summer, you'll say it's a fine perennial and wonder why it isn't more popular. But soon it becomes heavy with seed so that you hardly notice the remaining vivid blue flowers. The clump grows to be mammoth and begs for dividing. In rich soil, the stems have a strong tendency to double and grow up together like Siamese twins.

Geranium is for the man who already has everything, including plenty of room. I much prefer the native wild geranium, which has much of the beauty of the domestic and blooms generously for a long time.

Geums

Several years ago my garden befriended an "improved" geum. I am delighted that I haven't known the unimproved plant. Mine lives over winter all right, but it squats on the ground all summer long. In midsummer it sends up a cautious flower stalk that bears one or two and sometimes three one-inch blooms that are bright scarlet. Exhausted from the effort, it spends the rest of the year squatting. *Geum* hybridizers: better go back to your pollen brushes again.

Globe Thistles

This big, prolific flower suffers from an unfortunate name. It has the brilliant blue of wild thistle, but not its fierce spines or spreading nature. This is a fine flower for the back of the border. It grows so lustily, even in rather poor soil, that it helps make any garden look lush. The metallic blue of the big round heads is arresting.

When the flower heads are completely ripe—but not old—cut off the bracts at the base of the head, taking two or three at a time so as to leave the stem bare but intact. Then start pulling out the faded florets, a few at a time, leaving the fine thistlelike fur behind. Work carefully or you may pull out pieces of crown. When all florets are removed, hang the stalks upside down in a dry warm place until the fibers arrange themselves into a silvery ball.

Gloriosa

If you are the average flower-show goer, you come home with anemones, ranunculus, and one other plant that seldom if ever grows: Gloriosa. A person wouldn't feel so cheated if any of these plants put forth just a little effort, even tried to come up and grow. But almost always there isn't a sign. That hurts, especially in the case of Gloriosa, whose long, thick root is expensive. I have tried. it outdoors, started it indoors, and just once did it emerge. Then it grew and bloomed as beautifully as the greenhouse-grown ones you see at the flower shows.

There's no doubt that Gloriosa is a charming plant, its blooms fine in both color and form. The tips of its leaves look and act like tendrils, allowing the plant to grab hold of things and climb.

In all fairness I must say that I have not always been at hand to give Gloriosa the constant attention, warmth, and watering that it may need. If you don't mind gambling, go ahead and buy a root. It's a shame, though, that nurserymen continue to turn off would-be gardeners with Gloriosa. They should be labeled: grow at your own risk.

Goldenrod

With five acres of goldenrod blooming in the fields on all sides of me, I am not about to order any more, even if they are improvements on the wild. Goldenrods are beautiful, and if you aren't pollen-allergic, do plant them. They never fail and would probably be in thousands of gardens if they weren't so abundant in the wild.

On the way into Copenhagen from the airport, I saw goldenrods used as narrow hedges to divide one small garden plot from a neighbor's. In September, it was a beautiful sight.

Gypsophila, or Baby's Breath

Unless you are an ardent flower-arranger, don't bother with baby's breath. It sprawls, adds nothing to the landscape, and quickly dies out. Rather, plant the annual kind for bouquets. It's the equal in bouquets and it takes far less room.

All right, if you must have it, strew seeds of it along a sandy road near you. Once the plants take hold, they keep seeding themselves and are constantly on tap for bouquets. The side roads near us here are misty with baby's breath, especially near the cemetery, where seeds must have dropped from some wreath years ago.

I like a flower that will fend for itself rather than content itself with the easy life of a well-tended garden. Baby's breath is certainly one of this kind.

Hemerocallis, or Day Lily

Planting a day lily is much like planting a shrub or even a tree. Once it is planted, you have it for as long as you want. Each clump of the taller plants is a prominent part of your landscaping. Except for a little weeding or mowing under the drip of the leaves, day lilies need little attention. Best of all, they're handsome in or out of bloom. Their fountain of fresh green leaves is free from diseases and insects all season long.

For ease of growing, there just aren't any better perennials than day lilies. And now hybridizers, bless them, have come up with new varieties that add new colors, from palest yellow to deep gold, light pink apricot, red, and black-purple. I'm using other people's words for all those colors. What I can best appreciate are the glossy sheens, the crepe-paper surfaces, the fluted edges. Some of the new tall plants have stalks that soar into space. And there are dwarf ones barely two feet tall that look fine at the front of a border, and they bloom for a good six weeks. Several kinds are fragrant, too.

Day lilies grow on you. You're seldom satisfied with only one or two. If you don't look out, you'll keep ordering every new one that comes along, and eventually you'll join the growing membership in the American Hemerocallis Society.

Some of my day lilies grow in full sun, others in light shade. I can't seem to see any difference in their health and flowering ability. The nicest spots for them are at the edge of the lawn, where their magnificent form isn't obscured by other plants. They are good beside a fence, or in front of evergreens, or in a narrow border. Don't plant them near one another because low-growing ones then look stunted by comparison.

Most day lily specialists suggest that you dig and divide and fertilize the plants every five years or so, in order to keep them blooming profusely. In practice, you will probably find yourself spading off roots for your friends and neighbors in enough quantity so that you won't need to lift and divide, especially if you replace the missing roots with rich new soil.

Some especially fast-growing kinds need even more hewing than this, I find, in order to keep the clump from expanding and losing that fountainlike form that is such a handsome feature of day lilies.

It is a pleasure to grow a flower that is a dependable friend you need never apologize for, who never gets seedy-looking, who brightens summer during long periods of heat and drought, and who can give you the reputation for generosity without costing you a penny.

All hail, Hemerocallis!

Hibiscus

Here's a fine one to try. The 1971 all-America silver medal winner, Southern Belle, is supposed to bloom from seed the first year, and is said to survive the winter in most climates. Mine didn't bloom the first year, although I started the seed inside. It did live, though, and that seemed like accomplishment enough for anything generally considered a southern flower. The plants got started late in spring, however, and were just beginning to bud when frost hit. Perhaps the season is just too short in the North. I hope not.

The wild plants from which it was developed are beautiful flowers that brighten the brackish marshes of the East in August. Those wild hibiscus grow higher than your head, rising right out of the marsh, and they bloom for months, with flowers at least six inches wide. Around Hancock's Bridge, my favorite haunt in south Jersey, folks call them hollyhocks. If you have Southern Belle blooming in your garden, I feel sure it is something you are proud of.

Hostas

Neat, orderly people will delight in hostas (also called *Funkia* and plantain lilies). Each plant is a fountain of fresh green or blue-gray leaves, depending on the variety. They stay that way, too, adding tall flower stalks in midsummer that are orderly and neat. Some kinds have leaves edged in white, others have wavy-edged leaves. Flower stalks range from a foot to two feet high, and they carry pleasant small lilylike blooms.

Although most hostas will thrive under any treatment, they do best in light shade, with considerable moisture. They look their best in a spot alone, where their handsome form isn't obscured by plants elbowing them.

If you can't find hostas in your nearby arboretum, nursery, or park, look for them in the Wayside Garden catalog available at small cost from Hodges, South Carolina. Hostas are just as beautiful as they appear there.

Iberis Sempervirens

Call it candytuft, if you prefer; this one is an ideal plant to grow in a rock wall or railway-tie wall. It's long-lived, evergreen, and in spring it's a knockout, covering itself with white bloom. You can start it from seed rather easily or by dividing up an established clump.

Iris, Bearded

You think you have fine irises. Have you ever seen one with twelve or even more giant blossoms and buds on a single stalk? That's Blue Baron, and like most of the new irises, it makes yesterday's varieties look puny.

There's no sense in giving garden space to anything but the best. So dig up and toss away your dependable old-timers and plant something else. Then, in a new sunny spot in your garden or yard, plant a dozen or so of the best new ones.

Experts around the country have voted on the prizewinners—one a year—and awarded them the Dykes Medal. Here are the Dykes Medal winners in my garden, all of them fine:

1952	Argus Pheasant, a golden brown one with a coppery sheen
1953	Truly Yours, an enormous yellow and white one
1954	Mary Randall, a rose-pink with tangerine red beard
1955	Sable Night, a velvety red-black
1956	First Violet, a big, ruffled beauty
1957	Violet Harmony, another big, ruffled one
1958	Blue Sapphire, a giant heavenly blue one
1959	Swan Ballet, a ruffled snow-white giant
1960	None awarded
1961	Eleanor's Pride, all-over powder blue
1962	Whole cloth, with uprights (called standards) with clean blue descending petals (called falls)
1963	Amethyst Flame, a lilac lavender with a soft pink overlay
1964	Allegiance, a ruffled navy-blue with broad petals
1965	Pacific Panorama, a deeply ruffled sea blue
1966	Rippling Waters, blue-orchid with a tangerine beard
1967	Winter Olympics, pure white with branching stalks
1968	Stepping Out, brilliant pansy-violet stitching on snow-white petals—so striking it makes people gasp.

That's as far as I have gone with my Dykes Medal winners. The recent ones are a little too expensive for me. I can wait.

It is difficult to advise on iris culture for the entire country. Much depends on climate and soil. In general, plant irises in August in well-fertilized, well-drained soil, spreading the roots out, leaving the thickened rhizome just at the surface of the soil. Water well.

Watch iris closely for signs of disease or insects, and remove unhealthy-looking leaves. Pull weeds by hand or else by very shallow hoeing, since iris roots lie just under the surface. In most parts of the country, irises need some winter protection. Snow is probably the best insulation, and I make sure that it will stay in spring by covering the snow with straw or evergreen branches and removing them a little at a time as the ground thaws out. Most years irises come through winters here without any damage, but occasionally the best ones freeze out.

When growth starts, I like to give plants a shot of liquid fertilizer to boost the size of the flowers a bit. I use a mild solution, soaking the ground on both sides of the row. The irises I prize most I grow in a row in the garden, with lots of room for air circulation and for visitors who come to admire them. I seldom allow large clumps to form because the flower size decreases and because I trade with other growers. More than that, the fancy new ones don't increase the way old-timers did. A small bunch of irises is much easier to keep weeded and fertilized than a big clump. It's easier to keep watch for disease and insects.

So far I have had little scorch in my irises. This is a disease that hits the new young leaves in midsummer; little is known about it. Borers, too, haven't troubled me much, although I keep a sharp eye out for any sign of chewed leaves and dying stems. One year I had crown rot. I thought someone had been stepping on the new shoots until I found that a fungus had attacked them, causing them to fall over. I soaked the affected plants with Terrachlor, and the trouble ended. After irises bloom, their leaves have a tendency to spot and dry and look a trifle ratty. The worst ones I pull off. On the few occasions when I found that rot had penetrated a rhizome, I lifted the plant and either threw it away, or scraped off the rotted portions, then dipped it in an all-purpose fungicide and replanted it in an isolated spot in the garden. Most plants pulled through. I shouldn't prolong this talk of troubles. If you are reasonably antiseptic and painstaking in policing unhealthy leaves, you will probably have as little trouble as I have had.

Be sure to order a few of the new varieties this year if you don't already have them. There are few finer gardening adventures than iris growing.

Iris Cristata

For a shady spot among the rocks, this one is a little gem. Its rich amethyst flowers—only a few inches high—have some of the same sparkle as *reticulata* (see page 102). Cristata grows wild in the Blue Ridge, perching atop a rock in the shade. Grow it in the same sort of place, in a prominent position where other flowers won't steal the attention. Cristata spreads by creeping rootstalks.

Iris, Japanese

In the East, Japanese irises often put on a remarkable show. I remember especially a half-acre of them west of Philadelphia where they grew in rows of majestic plants topped with flat blooms a foot across, in colors from white through lavender to deep-violet and crimson-purples.

At their best, Japanese irises are spectacular. What they seem to need most, besides rich soil, is a flood of water until they come into bloom. Yet they don't thrive for me when I plant them along my lake where the soil is always moist. They need a somewhat acid soil. In my garden among other perennials they simply exist, putting up a solitary bloom now and then. Perhaps they have too hard a time surviving our winters to have energy left for flowering. Perhaps they need more acidity. Give them a try in your climate, though. To those who can grow them, they must be rewarding.

Iris Reticulata

Imagine a miniature orchid in bloom outside your window just after the snow melts. That's *iris reticulata,* a deep-purple tiny flower set off with bright yellow that makes it sparkle. This choice little novelty plant lops off the ragged edges of winter. It's a real favorite of mine, partly because it's one plant I never need to wait for. In fact, I forget all about it until suddenly there it is, perched on the dead shank of a day lily where it has grown for years. Others bloom through a prostrate juniper. The only fault of this minute iris is that its foliage is like so much grass, and it's hard not to pull the plants out when you're weeding nearby.

Iris, Siberian

Most gardeners already have a clump of Siberian irises. They are easy plants to divide, and they grow without effort or care. During their brief flowering period in early summer they bear splendid flowers. For the rest of the season the dense clump of tall, healthy leaves makes a handsome background for other summer flowers.

Siberian irises are so easily grown that little needs to be said about their care. But if yours are old and mammoth, try splitting off most of the clump and discarding it (or if you can't bear to discard it, persuade a neighbor to take some). A clump a foot across or less gives you the fountain effect that you liked so much about the Siberian when you first planted it. Blooms are more numerous, too, and bigger. At a distance, such a plant looks as if a cloud of butterflies has come to rest on it.

Iris Spuria

These irises, too, are worth trying, especially because, like the Japanese iris, they extend the iris season well into July. Spuria blossoms resemble the florist's iris, and they will keep for a week in water. They need plenty of water. After six years in my garden, the first plant flowered this year—a rich yellow bloom called Golden Nugget. In the Minneapolis area, spurias are booming. The arboretum has a collection of over fifty kinds, and all bloom readily.

Larkspur

How can I recommend a perennial larkspur that I haven't been able to find in any of the dozen or so seed catalogs currently smothering my desk? I have looked for it under dwarf delphinium but can't find it. It is not the new Connecticut Yankee, although this comes close. Technically, it is probably *Delphinium grand-*

iflorum. At any rate, mine came from an ancient garden where it had been seeding itself for at least two generations. It grows two feet tall and its flowers are intensely blue. It's extraordinarily hard to transplant, but once it decides to live, it will cast enough seed around it gradually to form not a clump but a loose colony—except in the gardens of compulsive hoers. Any of the small delphs (or call them perennial larkspurs) are fine plants.

Liatris

To all people transplanted from the prairies where they grew up, this is a plant to bring back the open sweep of sky and grass. Another name for the common type of liatris is Kansas gay-feather. It's not a must for every garden, yet I like the way it draws bees and butterflies, as well as its willingness to grow and flower, and the memories it calls up of walks through the sunny prairie grasses. Some varieties are two feet high; others grow to six feet. The tall ones, including a white one, get caught by early fall frosts before blooming, but the plant should make it in most parts of the United States.

The most beautiful liatris I have seen grow in a field of mammoth prairie grasses at the Aullwood Nature Center.

Lilies

Thrifty, sensible people should never start growing lilies. Dollar for dollar, you can get much more decoration for yard or garden from almost any other flower. Mice chew up lily bulbs; sometimes disease hits them, and you have to pull them all up and throw them away. The bulbs aren't cheap, either. Worse than that, once you start trying out new varieties, you're hooked. The old ones are beautiful; newer ones are even more so. And there's no insurance that a lily will put in an appearance year after year. And yet man probably began growing lilies before any other flower. I think I know why. They're so tall and stately that they command respect everywhere. They just can't be ignored.

It's the lure of far-off places that draws me to lilies. Here is a giant from the lofty Himalayas, growing eight, ten, and even twelve feet tall. Another, barely a foot and a half high, is from the Philippines. One comes from Korea, another from Persia. The madonna lily and at least one other lily come from Greece. Perhaps the most glamorous of all are from Japan, where for ages they have been hybridized, crossed, and recrossed until the flowers are enormous, ranging in color from white through yellows and pinks and crimson.

Of the hundred or so kinds that grow wild, only a few have been happy to grow in gardens. One of the first was the tiger lily, which the Chinese have grown from antiquity for its edible bulb.

At first, explorers who found glamorous lilies growing wild in far-off places had no success in bringing them home. The bulbs never go completely asleep the way bulbs of tulips do. Eventually, plant explorers learned to pack the bulbs in peat moss to slow down the drying, and many exotic kinds survived the long trip back from the steppes of Russia and from Burma, Nepal, and China.

Those early plant hunters had some glorious moments. Think of the excitement E. H. Wilson felt at finding the regal lily in western China in 1903. He wrote:

> There, in narrow, semi-arid valleys, down which thunder torrents, and surrounded by mountains ... whose peaks are clothed with snow eternal, the Regal Lily has its home. In summer the heat is terrific, in winter the cold is intense. ... There, in June, by the wayside, in rock-crevices by the torrent's edge, and high up on the mountainside and precipice, this Lily in full bloom greets the wayfarer. Not in twos and threes, but in hundreds, in thousands, aye in tens of thousands. Its slender stems, each from two to four feet tall, flexible and tense as steel ... crowned with ... flowers pure white and lustrous on the face, clear canary yellow within the tube and each stamen tipped with a golden anther.

In more recent times, a plant explorer named J. F. Rock found other wonderfully hardy lilies in the high mountains of China, where he camped out with Tibetans in tents just below the snowline. Tigers sometimes attacked his pack horses at night. "Several times my horses had chunks of flesh bitten out of their hind flanks," he wrote. In 1948, writing from Yunnan Province to Sam Emsweller of the USDA Plant Industry Station, Beltsville, Maryland, he explained why some of his lily shipments might be late. "We are surrounded by bandits but they dare not come in as we are surrounded by the Yangtze which flows 2500 feet below us on each side." Later, a village where he encamped for the night was captured and his trunks carefully searched for guns and ammunition. Out of such courageous explorations have come many coveted species.

Many lilies, however, are hard to grow in American gardens. It has been necessary for hybridizers to cross, back-cross, and recross many species to get the dramatic, easily grown hybrids that are the mainstays in today's gardens. Dr. Rock and many others, both in home gardens and experiment stations, have produced fine new lilies. But it remained for a friendly young Dutchman to bring hybrid lilies to their current state. Jan de Graaff combines a scientist's dedication and care with a businessman's acumen to provide America with some gems of the flower world. His first patented lily, a nasturtium-red named Enchantment, makes any gardener feel like a professional. Perhaps because I like de Graaff's sincerity and warmth, I like all of his introductions.

Now to get you off and running with lilies. Go ahead and plant the tiger lilies your neighbor offers you. They're beautiful flowers, and I can just imagine Thomas Jefferson's excitement when he first saw them coming into bloom in his garden after they arrived from the Orient in ships of the East India Company. The flowers are big and colorful, and a well-grown plant may be head-high. Only a few other flowers are as dependable without becoming weedy. The trouble with tiger lilies, for one thing, is that they're so easily grown that they confer no distinction on the gardener, and for another, they're a Typhoid Mary for lily mosaic, an aphid-borne virus disease that knocks out many of the fancy new lilies.

The other easily grown lily—*elegans,* sometimes called Flame or Red Russian—has the same two faults. *Elegans* was growing quietly and resplendently in Japan up to several hundred years ago when it found its way into American gardens. Blooming in June, its vivid orange flowers look up at you, in contrast to the outward-facing tiger lily.

Once you have either tiger lilies or Red Russians growing in your garden, I doubt you'll have the heart to root them out. They're too willing to grow and flower. Luckily, I have a patch of meadow where I can keep them in splendid isolation.

If you feel sure you'd like to try growing lilies, why not go directly to the glamorous ones? The most spectacular one I have grown is *auratum platyphyllum,* which stood seven feet high in my Pennsylvania garden. One stalk had twenty big blooms a good five inches across, with a bold yellow strip down the center of each petal, and so fragrant they perfumed the whole garden. I don't believe I have ever seen a more glorious flower. Apparently the mellow, rotted tree stump in which I planted it was exactly to its liking, and the rocks that were clustered tightly around it kept the ground cool and reasonably moist. I had planted the bulbs perhaps eight inches deep, and had encased them in hardware cloth to keep mice from eating them, but my precautions weren't enough. Mice crawled up and over the jagged rim of wire that extended above ground a few inches. They followed the stems downward, eating as they went until they reached the bulbs, leaving only a few scattered scales. I gathered up the remnants for my Minnesota garden, and some scales have formed bulbs. A friend of mine, who bought bulbs when I did, had worse luck. His never came up; they rotted in the ground. In certain favored areas, *auratum* is apparently easy to grow. In Oregon, it grows twelve feet tall, with nearly half of that bearing flowers.

Adaptable to a bigger area is *speciosum,* the Japanese lily, either the rubrum-red type or the album white. But more dependable are hybrids between *speciosum* and *auratum,* which grow better than either parent; they come in a wonderful assortment of colors and intensities. I have half a dozen kinds. A few of them, though, are beginning to drop their lower leaves before blooming, and the flowers are twisted. This probably means mosaic, an incurable disease, so that if my early diagnosis is accurate, I must dig them up and discard them.

Somewhat less glamorous but far more disease-resistant are some old favorites. Maxwill is a stiff-stemmed vigorous orange-red plant that forms a big clump of flowers. *Amabile* is a short, deep-red variety that blooms in June without fail. The brilliant little coral lily is an easy one to grow, and it returns year after year if you keep it from setting seed. The Hanson lily sends up its shoots so early that frost sometimes kills them, but otherwise it is an easy plant to grow. Its decorative whorls of leaves are reason enough to grow it. The wild American lilies—*superbum and michiganense*—are beautiful and easily grown. *Formosanum* is an easy plant to grow from seed, and its six-foot stem with white trumpets is beautiful, but its flowers bloom too late for Minnesota. Its candelabrum of pods is an artistic triumph. (How's that for a seed catalog phrase!)

To me, the most satisfactory of all lilies is the *Lilium regale* and its many hybrids. These plants grow tall and healthy, their trumpets are commanding, their heavy fragrance makes the evening garden seem like something out of the Arabian nights.

When regals start growth too early and their tops freeze, I find that the main bulb dies and only little bulblets regrow. In our area, snow generally prevents that early growth, but as insurance, I blanket at least part of them with slabs of foam insulation. An especially vigorous lily resembling the regal but somewhat more dependable is one that de Graaff calls Black Dragon. Of all lilies I think it is my favorite.

Where they prosper, madonna lilies are a great addition. Mine, planted in accordance with the best advice—in full sun, with perfect drainage, and only two inches deep—sometimes manage a single flower stalk, but more often succumb to disease before that time.

There is much more to say about lilies. I hope I have encouraged you to try growing them. They're one of the finest garden adventures.

Lilies from seed. Here is something for the expert—or, at least, the patient— gardener. With luck, growing lilies from seed to bloom takes two years for the fast-germinating kinds, three years for the slower kinds. My friend Minerva Christofferson does it routinely.

There are several advantages to seed-grown lilies. First and most important —you can brag about it. Second, if you figure your time at roughly five cents an hour, the cost is somewhat less than that of buying bulbs. Finally, you get disease-free plants, without the scourges that sometimes wipe out an entire bed of lilies.

I get my seeds from Park's or from Rex Bulb Farm of Newberg, Oregon, and I immediately put them in the crisper of the refrigerator for a month or two. It seems that a cold snap like that shocks more of them into germinating, One lily hybridizer says that soaking the seed for a day in a .5 percent water solution of thiourea—a chemical used to speed up germination of lettuce—boosts germination from half to nearly 100 percent as well as speeding up the time. This is something I haven't tried.

Some people start lilies in peat moss, others in various blends of vermiculite, sand, and peat moss. I much prefer the decomposed heart of a hardwood stump, when I can find it, using that soft, absorbent fiber without adding anything to it. If I can't get that material, I buy a bag of African violet soil, potting soil, or, better yet, Jiffy Mix. It's important that soil be sterile. Damping-off is the worst problem of lily seedlings, and a sterile soil prevents that condition. I plant in shallow trays, barely covering the seed (which I have coated with a disinfectant like Arasan. Then I put the whole tray in a plastic bag and stow it in a warm place out of sight (like under a bed). As soon as sprouts appear, I remove the plastic cover and put the tray under fluorescent lights, an inch or so below the bulbs. Sometimes the seeds sprout more quickly than I expect. Generally, though, they straggle along a month or so after planting, and sometimes two.

Besides keeping the plants close to the fluorescent bulbs (or in a bright window), it is important that you not disturb the young plants by trying to transplant them into better quarters. No matter how careful I am, they generally die off. Obviously, it's important not to overwater so that the tray gets soggy, but with fluffy leaf mold or decayed wood, drainage is simple. When spring comes, I plant the lilies in the shade of an apple tree, without separating them or disturbing the roots. In the fall I move them to permanent quarters where they bloom the following year.

If all that sounds simple, let me say it's not. Cutworms and slugs are fond of young lilies, and so are heavy-footed human visitors, who insist they aren't standing on anything but grass. A dog or even a cat can scratch out a year's work. But the rewards are worth it.

Seedling lilies vary in color and form, some resembling one parent and some the other. Last fall two seedling lilies bloomed that looked blue to my color-blind eyes, but friends said they were deep orchid.

For those who want to try growing the Mount Everest of lilies from seed, order *auratum* and its hybrids, which take two years to put up a leaf. You might be able to trick them into believing they are spending the winter outdoors by chilling them in the refrigerator for a couple of months—something I haven't succeeded with. In any case, after planting and chilling either indoors or out, plant them in small trays that you can stack away in the basement, checking only to see that they don't dry out. It's amazing that a seed can germinate and begin forming a small bulb before a single leaf emerges, but that is what happens. With considerable luck, you ought to have a few leaves emerging the second spring.

If you can grow lilies from seed, you're no longer an amateur gardener. And if you can grow the slow germinators without much trouble, you're out of my class.

Lily of the Valley

In a shady spot under a tree, you might put in a clump of lily of the valley. There are many reasons why you shouldn't. It spreads and crowds out anything in its way, its season of bloom is short, it's generally stingy with its bloom, and, at best, not at all spectacular. But if you're sentimental about it, then get a friendly grower to spade up a small piece of it for you. Plant it in good rich soil. Certainly it makes a more interesting ground cover than that presently fashionable pachysandra.

Lysimachia, or Golden Loosestrife

Here is an unsung beauty of the border. From the time it pushes up its fascinating, pagodalike stems in spring until it flowers, it is handsome, clean, and orderly. Its yellow blossoms never fail; it never needs staking or any attention. Although easy to grow, it can easily be kept within bounds. Plant it anywhere, even in boggy soil. In spring, spade off the edges to keep it to whatever space you have.

If golden loosestrife had a better name, were harder to grow, and came in pink instead of yellow, I believe it would be one of America's favorite perennials. Without those changes, it is already one of mine.

Lupines

This sumptuous flower should have sued the Romans for libel. They named it after *lupus*, "the wolf," believing that the plant wolfed down soil nutrients, thereby causing other plants to starve. Actually, the lupine grew in soil too poor for almost anything else, fixing its own nitrogen from the air and forever looking well fed and well groomed.

Lupines are unpredictable about germinating. Nicking through the hard coat of the seed with a file helps; so, probably, does freezing the seeds in a cube of ice for a few weeks. Mixing them in a package of inoculating bacteria often helps them get started, too. The most important requirement to keep lupines thriving is a well-drained soil. Without it, they disappear fast. In my sandy garden they seed themselves and grow without any encouragement.

Flower arrangers like the stiff, showy stalks. With the usual care—cutting off old stems—lupines keep blooming all summer. One of my friends has lupines growing in her lawn, like shrubs that she carefully mows around until they begin looking weedy, then mows them off. Undaunted, they flower again the following year.

Along the Alaska Highway, wild lupines bloom all summer, like the finest specimens in English parks, their green dressing gowns circling the clean white gravel at their feet.

Lychnis

The trouble with scarlet lychnis is that it's too easy to grow. For most gardeners, there is no distinction in having a clump of it in the perennial border. But, believe me, it's one of the first plants you ought to put there. Get a start from your neighbor—who probably calls it Jerusalem cross—and by summer you'll have a clump of flowers nearly waist-high, so vivid that even I can see why the Greeks long ago gave it the name *lychnis,* which means "lamp." An older name given by pioneers is scarlet lightning. Both Washington and Jefferson wrote of it.

Lychnis has no faults. It seeds itself but isn't weedy; it never gets ragged-looking and never needs staking. It never fails to perform. You can use it as a stand-in where temperamental perennials failed you.

Lychnis Viscaria

I can't understand why nearly everyone walks past the vivid scarlet lychnis to exclaim over its weak-kneed cousin, *Viscaria.* Is it, once again, that Americans are hung up on anything pink? The plants I have are double, rose-red, and bloom in July for only a couple of weeks. The flower heads are so dense that the first rain or watering flattens them, and even though they're little more than a foot high, the stalks don't spring up again. This flower is frankly a mess, but if you're determined to have rose-red blooms, go ahead and plant it.

Lycoris, or Surprise Lily

When you find bulbs of this hardy kind of amaryllis for sale, pick them up by all means. Plant them in a slightly shaded spot. Unless you are the kind who carefully marks each plant with a permanent stake (and I hope you do this), you will forget all about the bulb. In the spring you'll wonder what exciting flower is pushing up its big straplike leaves. You wait in vain for a blossom stalk. By midsummer, the leaves are brown and dried off.

Then, on a day in August, watch out. Suddenly, you'll have a waist-high lily in full bloom that wasn't there two or three days before. You'll swear someone moved it in as a gag. That's about the way it looks, poked into the ground like a bare stalk of flowers at a cemetery lot. Someday I want to time a Surprise lily from emergence to bloom. I suspect it all may take place in three days, certainly in less than a week.

The flowers are a delicate lilac-pink, but on the stiff bare stalk they aren't exactly beautiful. In the right location, though, they're something else. At the Aullwood Nature Center, Marie Aull has naturalized them among low ferns that cover up the leaves as they brown in summer, and hide the long bare blossom stems. Under small trees behind a brook, the Surprise lilies appear to arise from the ferns, and are a striking sight.

The only trouble that hits Surprise lilies are people like me who forget where the bulbs are planted, and hoe them out during their resting stage in summer.

Lythrum

Nongardeners are taking to lythrum like prospectors to Sutter's Mill, and I can't see why. To me, lythrum, though big and dependable, is strictly Plain Jane. At a distance, its five-foot wands are pleasant enough, but close up, they look weedy. My un-enthusiasm grows, I suppose, from my inability to see the beauty of pink, and yet the purple varieties aren't any better.

Lythrum grows without any care. In fact, it thrives in the marshes of much of the East. Capitalizing on this ease of propagation, a New York merchant is promoting it in full-page ads as a "steeplechase lily of the Orient, suitable to the penthouse gardens of Manhattan."

Few gardeners would give it that acclaim, but most would say that it is one of the best perennials for a mass of color, and it blooms from midsummer to fall. It never needs staking, doesn't need lifting or thinning, has no disease or insect problems, enjoys soggy soil but survives drought. Wht more could you ask? If only I could see pink!

Mertensia, or Virginia Bluebells

"Apr. 16, 1766 a bluish colored, funnel-formed flower in low grounds in bloom." So wrote Thomas Jefferson of Virginia bluebells the year he began the garden diary he was to keep for the next fifty years. "May 7. blue flower in low grounds vanished."

You can tell that Jefferson was fond of mertensia, and rightly so. Early in spring its pale green foliage pops up almost overnight and grows to a foot or two, bearing chains of pink buds that open into fine blue flowers. Around clumps of tulips or daffodils, it is beautiful, and it rapidly seeds itself and spreads over whatever area you permit it.

It has one fault that may or may not be serious to you. After it blooms, the leaves turn brown and eventually die, and during this period you have a raunchy-looking area—unless you buy flats of annuals and interplant them.

Mertensia grows best in moist rich soil in shade or semishade. If you have a marshy area or a lightly wooded area, try starting it there. In wild-flower gardens in Pennsylvania I have seen whole bogs of blue mertensia—a magnificent sight. My own plants are beginning to take hold along a path to the lake. If they can compete with quack grass, they will be a fine addition.

Monarda

If you've never been able to attract hummingbirds, by all means plant a few monarda, and the birds will come like drunks to free booze, and stay to sample your delphiniums, larkspurs, and other flowers.

Besides the bright red monarda, I have three others that I have found wild along prairie roadsides. One is purple (I am told), another is lavender, and the other pink. All are equally pretty to me. Monarda are members of the mint family—you can tell by the square stems, as well as by the scent of the leaves and stems. They grow about three feet tall and flower much of the summer.

The only trouble I think you'll have with monarda is that you need to dig it up each spring—early—and discard the matted old center, and replant only the outside, active roots. If you don't, you may find that, husky as your plant was, it will die out. That little work is small effort for a plant so eager to grow, flower, and play host to hummingbirds.

Monkshood

This is a big, showy flower a little more dependable than delphinium, but with somewhat the same habits. I like plants like monkshood, which grow vigorously, come up every year without fail, and give height to a perennial border.

In rich, deep peaty soil. monkshood will tower above your head, especially if it is partly shaded and has good moisture. Often the tall wiry stems stand without staking. More often they need a little help.

Not much troubles monkshood, except that occasionally the stems die off (from verticillium wilt and from crown-rot fungus, in case you want to be clinical). When this happens, dig up and destroy the plants and try fresh ones in a new location.

Monkshood belongs in every perennial border, as a friend that will greet you every year, growing a little broader and more stately with every season. Just one caution: it's dangerously poisonous (not to the touch), so better hold off planting it until the kids are past the nibbling stage.

Paradisea

For no more than two weeks or so in June, this foot-high member of the lily family—also called St. Bruno's lily—has white, funnel-shaped blossoms, each about two inches long, that make the plant sparkle.

St. Bruno's is easy to grow, doesn't die even in the roughest winters, and, to my knowledge, hasn't a single enemy. It is reasonably tidy, doesn't spread or sprawl, but keeps to its allotted square foot of garden space. What's more, you can give seeds to your friends, pieces of the root to your close friends, and all will have St. Bruno's lilies as a constant reminder of your generosity and garden virtuosity.

Why then have you never before heard of it? Because you can't get hold of it. I ordered mine from a Canadian firm; shipments require a permit from the United States Department of Agriculture, and such permits take as long as a month to receive.

Peonies

Now there are hybrid peonies. I couldn't believe that our fine old varieties could be improved upon until I saw Red Charm, which my fellow garden club member, Beatrice Welte, brought to our flower show. It's a rich red double with such a velvet gloss to the petals that it stood out among all others at a recent flower show. There are hybrids that are pink, salmon, cherry, scarlet, and orange-red—a color new to peonies. They bloom ten days or so ahead of nonhybrids, and so extend the wonderful peony season. Don't expect your neighbors to give you a start of hybrid peonies, though, because they won't have them yet. And be prepared for a shock at their price: they range from five dollars up.

If you don't already have peonies, plant some this fall, in full or nearly full sun. As a friendly border between city lots, you can't beat them. They're handsome from early spring when their red stalks spring to life until fall when their foliage once again turns red. And for a couple of weeks in spring, they put on a razzle-dazzle show, a more exciting display than that of almost any other flower you can plant. You'll need to wait a couple of years before the peonies come into their own, but even during the first year, you'll have flowers. Add to all this fragrance—in many varieties—that is fresh and fruity.

I'm sentimental about peonies for another reason. They care for themselves. You'll find them in abandoned gardens and old farmsteads where everything else has died out except lilacs. And they continue to mark the graves of people long forgotten. They do best, though, when weeded, fertilized with bone meal, and watered during dry spring weather. In general, peonies are plants for northern gardens, since cold is necessary to let them go dormant.

Now then, for some adventuring. Get hold of the true fern-leaf peony that blooms before most others. Its bright red double or single blooms against the delicate foliage are handsome. Try Japanese-type peonies with sparkling stamens, or anemone-flowered ones with a mount of petallike stamens, or plain singles, some of which are giant-sized and open out flat into blazing platters of bloom like tree peonies. These big singles don't need staking, and that's a real plus. Prairie Afire is a splendid anemone-flowered kind. Krinkled White is one of my favorites of all singles. There are many others, all worth growing.

The biggest blooms of all come on so-called tree peonies. If you haven't seen them, to go your nearby arboretum during flowering time in June, and prepare to be surprised. At Swarthmore College outside of Philadelphia there are tree peonies five feet tall, with fifty giant flowers to a bush. Each blossom with its intricate form and penciling is a minor work of art.

Tree peonies have survived several winters for me in weather forty degrees below zero, and my Scottish gardening friend, Margaret Sletten, induced her peonies to bloom, but they are somewhat out of bounds this far north. The first year after planting, give peonies a little mulch of leaves or hay or evergreen boughs. This is especially necessary, I am told, for the new hybrids.

Phlox

In rich soil and full sun, with plenty of moisture in the ground and not on the leaves, and with air circulating around the lower leaves, perennial phlox may well be the "queen of the border." If you keep picking off flower heads before they go to seed, phlox often bloom from summer till fall. if you lift and divide them with your friends every couple of years, they'll prosper year after year.

Phlox take work to keep them coming, more than many people want to volunteer for—witness the beds of magenta phlox in many gardens. The plants you buy don't change color—only an act of God or atomic radiation will do that—but if you allow flowers to set seeds, those seeds produce plants that revert to a more primitive color, usually magenta. The primitive types are more vigorous, too, and without your knowing it, they crowd out their parents. So watch out for seedlings.

Like most vigorous perennials, phlox tend to choke themselves out in a couple of years, and when you lift them, you'll find a mass of old and dead roots. In early spring, pull the clumps apart and discard the old roots. Replant only the vigorous young shoots, preferably in a new location, and water them well. In any case, keep down the number of stems in an old clump to eight or ten.

In some climates, phlox have no troubles other than degenerate offspring and overcrowded roots. But for most of the country, they get mildew and leaf spot, especially in hot, humid weather. For this reason, when you give them their weekly soaking, let the water run on the ground and see that air can flow around the bottoms of the stalks. It's a good idea to carry along your all-purpose fungicide and give the leaves a light dusting now and then, even before mildew appears.

Don't give up on phlox before you try them. Maybe you have just the climate, location—and temperament—for them. In that case, you'll have color in your border from June almost till freeze-up.

Phlox Subulata, or Moss Phlox

Those startling carpets of pink or blue or white at tulip time are *Phlox subulata,* or moss phlox, and one of the first plants that the amateur rushes to buy.

They are rewarding. The following spring they are loaded with bloom, and a joy to the homeowner. However, they are soon loaded with something else—a crop of weeds, mostly grassy weeds that defy my most determined efforts at eradication. The cool, moist ground beneath a mat of moss phlox is the perfect seedbed for every noxious weed I know. You can lift up the carpet and massacre the weeds that way, or you can cover the ground below the mat with black plastic. I have tried both.

My best suggestion for handling moss phlox is to be a generous neighbor, dig it up for the man who has so long admired it, and let him figure out ways of weeding it.

Physostegia

Stay away from this one—regardless of what the catalogs tell you about it. The flower stalks aren't worth the gamble you take by introducing this garden thug onto your place. The roots spread and smother anything in their path. Plant it in the weeds, if you must. Some flower arrangers like it for the way they can bend each flower on the stalk and have it stay bent—hence the common name: obedient plant. For fear you might grow interested in anything more about it, let me conclude by saying that nothing else about it is obedient.

Platycodon, or Balloon Flower

One of the pleasantest blue flowers for the border is platycodon, or balloon flower. Plant it from seed. It's easy to start either outside or inside under lights. Or pick up a root at the nursery. Just make sure you know where you want to plant it because once it starts growing, it's not easy to move.

Platycodon is Greek for "broad bell"—a good description of the upward-facing blossoms that come for much of the summer, especially if you keep the pods picked off. It will grow fairly well in semishade, but in such a spot it will probably need staking.

Only one caution about platycodon. It starts growth so late in spring that you're likely to hoe it out, concluding that it's dead. A good idea is to leave the stalk or else mark the place where it will be appearing.

I have the low-growing and the double-flowering varieties, but I find them not nearly as good as the traditional kind, which runs about twenty inches tall. I consider platycodon one of the finest perennials in the border. It doesn't get weedy, always looks neat and trim, and is one of the few perennials that doesn't need dividing or lifting. To me, a border isn't complete without platycodon.

Poppy, Iceland

In my garden I have only to leave an open space uncultivated, and before I know it, Iceland poppies are growing there. In this climate, they seem to grow spontaneously. Beginning with the earliest tulips, these flowers bloom from spring and continue all summer until frost. So many flowers are supposed to do that, but how few there are that really do! In warmer areas, Iceland poppies don't perform so tirelessly, but in the northern United States they are stars in a border. Mine generally die off after the second year, but it requires no effort to keep a constant supply of them.

The most dramatic Iceland poppies are at Lake Louise, where they are almost as much a part of the landscape as the mountains and the reflecting lake. They'll probably never bloom as luxuriantly in your garden, but they're worth a trial.

Someday if you should find yourself in tundra-land, look for the miniature Iceland poppies springing out of the barely thawed earth. I shall never forget the tiny tufts of green—scarcely bigger than a boutonniere—crowded with thirty to forty blooms.

The best way to get a start of Iceland poppies is from seed. That way you get the new varied colors, which range from white to scarlet. Or you can get plants from a neighbor. In either case, plant them in full sun. Snip off the seedpods when you get around to it and they'll flower better. A flower that thrusts up a bud just after the snow disappears and is still blooming at freeze-up is quite a flower!

Poppy, Oriental

If Oriental poppies bloomed for something more than ten days, I'd be more enthusiastic about them. Certainly their giant blossoms are handsome and arresting, and in good well-drained soil, there is no trouble growing them. But in short order, they're over and done with, and you must police up after them since the foliage and stems brown and die. In fall they thrust out basal foliage that crowds out everything around it and becomes a favorite hangout for slugs. I just don't like Oriental poppies, and I have grubbed out all but one plant in my garden. If you must plant them, see that each plant has plenty of room around it. Try some of the new, less violent colors.

Primroses

Perhaps you can't grow primroses in your climate. I was sure I couldn't, and for years I didn't even try, even though I knew that most of them come from cool, alpine climates. One year I took a plant from Philadelphia and divided it into fifteen or twenty plants and put them down in the cool, moist soil north of my house. Every one of them lived through the winter under the blanket of snow and bloomed. Now, years later, they are fine clumps of yellow that bloom soon after the snow disappears, and though not as spectacular and smothered in bloom as those in my Philadelphia garden, they are still one of my favorite small perennials.

If there is a secret to growing primroses, it is simply that they can't tolerate full sun, and plants that barely survive in sun will thrive when moved into partial shade. They do like rich soil and lots of moisture. Their wilted leaves are quick to tell you when they need a fresh soaking.

A few years back I decided I wanted every kind of primrose that grew, and I ordered seed of everything available. A few plants came up, varying in germinating time from one to three months, and all were temperamental. From these plants I got a range of colors from red, white, and blue to pink and rose. They were somehow a little disappointing. None came up to the old original *Primula veris*, or cowslip, for putting on a show.

In milder parts of the continent, there's a fine bog garden primrose—japonica—that stands three feet tall and has whorls of blossoms around the tall stalk. Might it not grow in the far North, too? It is magnificent in the right marshes of the Philadelphia area.

One of the fascinating things about primroses is the way a clump will divide. Like the fish that fed the multitudes, a primrose can be pulled apart into as many plants as you have need for.

Pyrethrums, Painted Daisies

Painted daisies are some of the most pleasant flowers in the early summer border. They're easy to grow, they bloom for a long while, and they don't crowd their neighbors. The tall stems sometimes fall over but generally keep upright.

New varieties come in good reds, deep pinks, and white. The new crested and doubles are especially fine. All of them start easily from seed. You might do better to buy the particular color and type you want from the nursery. A plant or two is all you will want, since each one quickly forms a big clump. As you do with most fast-growing perennials, lift and divide this one every couple of years.

Ranunculus

Be warned. See Anemone, Tuberous-Rooted.

Rudbeckias

You would hardly guess that purple coneflower, Golden Glow, Gloriosa daisy, and the golden daisies of the hardy border are all cousins. All are obviously daisies, all are hardy and easily grown, but there the similarity ends. All are worthy of planting, though, unless your yard is very small.

The old-fashioned Golden Glow towers six and eight feet high, nearly always needs to be staked, and needs lower plants to hide the dead leaves at the bottom of its stalks. The flowers are double, golden, and pleasant. I like it for old time's sake.

Shorter rudbeckias are better in that they bloom all summer and don't get ratty. One, called Goldsturm, has the charm of the wild black-eyed Susan and seems just as hardy.

My favorite rudbeckia is the purple coneflower. The big pincushion center is maroon red, petals are rose-red, and flowers sit on three-foot stalks as stiff and erect as palace guards. Nothing fazes them: heat, drought, sun, or insects. They'll care for themselves and always look neat, even after the flowers have faded.

Gloriosa daisies are so temporary that I have included them under annuals.

Salvias

For a short time in summer, the perennial salvia is a dense clump of bright violet-blue. That's about all I can say in its behalf. Shortly, the long blue wands droop with seed, which scatters and starts up everywhere. I'm sure that salvia has its adherents somewhere, but not at this spot, although I must admit that I keep a plant of it in an isolated part of my garden.

Scabiosas

This perennial version of the more common annual scabiosa is a good one in that it blooms a little all summer. Stalks are two feet or so tall, and flowers are a soft lavender color. In light, well-drained soil the plant persists for a few years. See if you can get this one free from a neighbor. That's about what it's worth.

Sedums

Old gardeners: before you sneer at lowly sedums, look back. Didn't you go through a phase when you collected every new kind you saw? And may not that compulsion for sedums have been what catapulted you into your current infatuation with growing things?

Children and nongardeners alike often get caught up with plants when they see the almost infinite variety in the little prostrate sedums. Some are gray carpets, some pale green; some are little pine forests, some seem pure moss. Because they can perch on rocks and survive, they get the name of sedum, from the Latin word for "sit," from which our word *sedentary* also derives.

That cousin of the sedums, the sempervivum called hen-and-chickens, is a charming novelty. Keep one in a teaspoonful of soil on top of a rock for the sake of visiting children.

Except for rock gardens and rock walls, the low-growing sedums have little garden use. But the tall "live-forever" types are fine, shrublike plants that are handsome at the edge of the lawn, the end of the border, in a pot on the patio, or wherever you need their crisp, tailored look. Newer kinds have fine red or pink flower heads in fall. I like the little fountainlike rosettes that the six-inch sieboldi makes.

Shasta Daisies

Most gardeners don't realize that the Shasta daisy is more biennial than perennial. Unless divided every year, it tends to die out after its big second year of bloom. Like other members of the chrysanthemum family, it tends to choke itself out, so that every spring you ought to dig it up, toss the center section away, and replant the outside sprouts. Only in this way can you hope to keep it alive and healthy. This is small labor for such superb plants. Some new singles have giant-sized blooms that completely cover a mound of green two feet high. Others are quilled, some shaggy, and all of them make ideal cut flowers, lasting for a week or even two.

Spirea

At the rear of my garden zoo, this spirea stands six feet high, trussed up with stakes, its frothy pink flower heads—ugly to my eyes—causing most people to gasp with pleasure. A careless kind of plant, it rises tall and lanky, and bedecks itself with feathery bloom like that of the astilbes. It blooms in July and August; it likes plenty of moisture, full sun, and considerable room to sprawl. Perhaps in some climates it needs no staking, but for me it always needs a little help.

Stokesia, or Stokes Aster

This one grows wild across the Deep South, and that's a fine place for it, growing wild. At its best, the big blue blooms look as if grasshoppers have been chewing on them.

Thalictrum, Meadow Rue

The meadow rues are good additions to the perennial border, since they stay in place, always look well groomed, and bedeck themselves with pleasing feathery blossom heads, which may be white, cream, yellow, or lilac, depending on the variety and species. There is nothing spectacular about them. But it is pleasant to have plants that always put in an appearance—like those good friends who show up at a club meeting when the speaker (maybe it's you) doesn't have much razzle-dazzle to offer.

Meadow rue sprang suddenly into the news in 1973 when researchers disclosed that the seeds contained materials that showed promise in work with cancer. In our area, combines harvested wild plants growing along the roadsides in marshy ground.

Thermopsis

Maybe with a better name, this one might have gone further in the world, but I doubt it. Thermopsis, a native of the Carolinas, looks for all the world like a giant yellow lupine. In a sunny, dry border, it grows up to five feet tall, and late in June or early July it is studded with blooms. Unfortunately for such a pleasant, willing plant, its flowering season is over before you know it.

Don't refuse a free sample. Your garden and you are richer for every different species, and thermopsis will be a well-behaved member of any border.

Tradescantias

How I wish I didn't feel compelled to testify against this beautiful wild flower, otherwise known as spiderwort. Its vivid purple blossoms surmount a fine, upstanding stalk two feet tall. Plant breeders have added white and orchid kinds that also are handsome. Tradescantia grows and blooms everywhere, but it does best in a little shade and with plenty of moisture.

It has no enemies—except me. In my light, loamy soil it comes up everywhere, crowding out everything nearby. Digging it out doesn't help. I suspect that the smallest fraction of its spidery roots will generate new plants. Most weeds you can outwit, eventually, but tradescantia masquerades as a seedling lily or an early spring bulb. Worse yet, it seeks out the heart of a clump of phlox or other perennial where it is impossible to extract it without digging up the whole clump and shaking off all the soil. After fifteen years of battling it, I finally know the snakelike stems and respond to them as a fireman does to a siren. Sadly, some are still with me.

If you have an Ellis Island in your yard where you can keep it strictly confined, you might try tradescantia. But don't say you weren't warned.

Tritomas

Just because I have never been able to grow tritomas like those in pictures, doesn't mean *you* shouldn't try. I have once seen them flowering in the far north, and only a few times in the East. More often I have seen scruffy, pallid flowers surrounded by dying, grassy foliage.

If tritomas thrive in your climate, you'll certainly know it by their flaming red-hot pokers of bloom. Go ahead and try them. But if they are as scarce and inferior as those I have seen, better experiment with another flower.

Trollius Ledebouri

The trollius known as Golden Nugget is one of my favorite perennials. Its blossoms are golden explosions, and though the blooming season isn't long, it's spectacular. Petals are split into shreds that look like yellow stamens.

A Siberian import, Golden Nugget survives, regardless of cold. For best performance, it prefers plenty of moisture. Trim it back after flowering; it's inclined to look somewhat scraggly. With a little encouragement, it will provide seedlings for your favorite gardening neighbors.

Tuberose

One of the first words I learned to read was tuberose—and then, no one could tell me for sure how to pronounce it. Only lately have I learned that either *tube-rose* or *tuber-ose* is acceptable. By neither name, though, will it grow in any of the gardens I have tried it.

As a six-year-old, I was intrigued with the photograph of tuberoses and resolved to grow them. The dried-up root that arrived by mail never came to life. And neither did others I have tried in the years since. I began to think that the whole plant was a myth until the evening I saw one growing in a North Carolina garden, a sadly bedraggled plant. It did have the fragrance that I had read about, though, so it was no disappointment. If you are lucky enough to live where the tuberose blooms, be glad. And if a big man stops by your yard for a smell, it might be me.

Veronicas

Admirers of veronica call it the backbone of the perennial border; they might rather have called it the neckbone. Tall and scraggly, every veronica I own (except for the variety called Icicle) is weedy and scraggly. Veronica belongs to the Scrophula family, which seems appropriate. They're scrofulous. Their skinny necks fall to the ground. They reproduce like Kallikaks, and unfortunately they never die in winter.

Why then do I keep them—every last one of them, from light blue to purple, green foliaged ones to gray? Because I feel the way Noah did when he must have considered tossing pocket gophers out of the ark: certainly, even they must have some purpose on earth. I keep hoping that some visitor to my garden will express a deep affection for them, and I can pawn them off. But so far I have found no one who wants them.

Perhaps in some more favored climate, they come to look like pictures in the nursery catalogs.

The variety Icicle grows to the respectable height of a foot and a half, and its blooms are dense enough to suggest its name. It sprawls, but not as much as the rest of the clan.

Vinca, or Creeping Myrtle

The vinca vine or creeping myrtle, is a pleasant evergreen ground cover, easy to start, quick to cover a shady or semishady spot beneath trees, yet easy to control. In spring, light blue flowers appear everywhere, and they look especially good with daffodils emerging through the cover. Vinca will cling to almost any shady slope, and it eliminates erosion.

Violets

To most of us, violets are the wild flower, and viola the larger-flowered, cultivated one. Violas are good but temporary plants that spring up from seed without encouragement. They are listed under annuals in this book.

If you are thinking of introducing the wild blue violet into your perennial border, don't. Beautiful as it is in the wild, in cultivation it runs to leaves with few flowers. But more important, it will take over your garden. You will never be rid of it. I wouldn't even grow it in a wild flower garden because there, too, it tends to smother out everything in its path. There is nothing shrinking about a violet. Certain wild kinds—the yellow, white, bird's-foot and tiny Johnny-jump-ups—are safe enough for the wild flower garden.

12
annuals— for quick color

There is a special excitement about annual flowers, which germinate, grow, blossom, and die all in a single season. For the most part, they are more generous with bloom than perennials. With no need to return food to an overwintering root, they can throw their all into blossoming, and they do.

A garden of annuals lets you start fresh every year, with new kinds and new combinations of colors. Plow or hoe under the old rows, and the slate is clean. Hybridizers are creating new varieties fast, nearly all of which are worth trying. After all, the big seed houses stake their reputations on their introductions.

In this list of annuals I have omitted a few that I have tried and found wanting, I have passed over most annual vines like canarybird, *Cobaea scandens*, momordica, and cypress, to name a few. They simply haven't been worth the space or effort. I have passed over most of the everlastings, too, like globe amaranth, statice, and strawflower, largely because they take too long a growing season for me. (I wish it were otherwise, after seeing the spectacular dried arrangements that Bert Schmidt of Vermont makes, using her husband Art's everlastings.)

I omit nemesia, nemophila, and nierembergia, any of which might please you. Nor have I mentioned layia, or tidytips, a nondescript plant that keeps seeding itself among my perennials where it is a charming little waif. You might try venidium, a daisy from the African veldt; for me, it died when it had barely started to bloom. Lavatera, an annual mallow, is one my friend Elmer Walde swears by, since it never fails, with its rose-pink hollyhocklike blooms from midsummer on.

Biennials are in this list, largely to underline their impermanence. So too are summer-flowering bulbs and corms that you can pick up at the nursery or dime store for blooming this year.

Achimenes

Don't let seed catalogs fool you into planting this perky little houseplant outdoors. It can't stand the vagaries of the outdoors. Even inside, it's temperamental. The original blue-flowered plant generally prospers, but I have never known a gardener who has been able to get one of the newer hybrids to grow, let alone flower.

Ageratum

Take home a flat or two of ageratums next time you see them. It doesn't matter if you haven't prepared a bed or a border for them. They'll look good anywhere, and they even thrive in part shade. Few plants go all out in flower production the way the ageratum does. Its leaves barely show when the blue haze of flowers envelops the plant. New hybrids have enormous flower heads and come in white and pink, besides the usual powder blue. Seeds are quick and easy to grow indoors. Start them six weeks or so before the time you would normally plant corn in your area.

Alyssum

This is the edging that catches the eyes of visitors to formal gardens. Alyssum is a neat little plant, wherever you put it. With room to stretch out over the ground, it forms a perfect circle of lace, in white, purple, or pink. Its fragrance is pure honey, and strong enough to perfume the whole yard. That's what I like best about it.

Alyssum comes up fast, then rests for a spell before it decides to strike out and bloom. You'll get quickest results if you start a flat indoors and move the seedlings out after the ground has warmed a bit. In most areas, alyssum slows up its blooming during late summer, but then it revives and is again a sheet of white during the fall.

Amaranthus

I have tried this so-called "summer poinsettia" for several years without success. In the North, the season seems too short. Generally these flowers are just coming into color when frost strikes them down. In Virginia they are superb.

Arctotis

This is an annual to try when you've experimented with most others. Be sure it gets a sunny spot; otherwise it will look pretty scraggly. I have found arctotis to be erratic. Sometimes it covers itself with pleasant flowers; other years it just sits, at least in the North. Occasionally, self-seeded plants make the finest show; this suggests that fall seeding is a good idea.

Asters

Every package of aster seed ought to bear this label: GROW AT YOUR OWN RISK. They're beautiful, extravagantly so. There's probably no finer cut flower in existence. But they're disease-prone. In fact, they seem in love with tragedy. There they are, popping out of the ground and growing fast, and you think this year they'll make it. Then cutworms start beheading them. The survivors grow fast, then one after another starts turning yellow, and though they try to put forth flowers, the blooms are misshapen and yellow. Their martyrdom is even immortalized in the name of the disease: aster yellows. Rust hits them, too, and so does wilt, but wilt-resistant varieties take care of that. For me, it is aster yellows that makes me reluctant to try them again.

Still I plant them, hoping I can keep off the leafhoppers that spread the infection from one plant to the next. But I can't, and the disease (or something akin to it) seems to spread to calendulas, which keep trying to bloom, too, but can't, and to cosmos and marigolds and occasionally to petunias, even though I pull and burn each plant as it gets infected. Leon Snyder, director of the Minnesota Arboretum and perhaps the best-informed horticulturist I know, says that the virus lives in the soil and awaits only the right conditions to spread via leafhoppers to asters and other plants.

I tell myself that next year I won't try asters again, but when the new catalogs arrive and I remember how beautiful asters can be, I order another package or two. At a distance from weeds—where leafhoppers flourish—and surrounded by a clean-shaven lawn, perhaps asters will flourish for you. If so, be glad.

Bachelor's Button

This old-timer has been glamorized by hybridizers into a delightful flower, with deep purples, deep blues, pinks, and whites, and with double the petals of the old one.

This is a flower for amateurs and children. Nothing much goes wrong with it, and it's quick to grow and bloom. When it passes its peak, yank it out. It gets to look pretty weedy. But, for a month or more, you'll have some of the cleanest blue and pink and white blooms in existence, fine for cutting. It germinates best in the cool of the spring, so plant it as soon as you can get a rake into the ground.

Balsam

Balsam—or the touch-me-not of Grandma's garden—is something different today. Grandma used to pick off the crisp stalks, then pull off the leaves so the flowers would show. Today's blossoms aren't hidden like the old ones, but protrude beyond the leaves. They come in a splendid assortment of colors, including glamorous doubles. Do I begin to sound like a seed catalog? Perhaps because this year balsams did particularly well and, as frost approaches, are still in full bloom.

Try balsams, at least once. They're easy to grow and they don't need full sun; such virtues will recommend them to some. In fact, they do best in a little shade. Don't bother to start them indoors. They get lanky and will topple over with the first stiff breeze when placed outside.

Begonias

Small-flowered begonias are those you buy in flats for bedding and are commonly known as fibrous-rooted begonias. Many kinds do well in full sun, if the sun isn't boiling. Generally they do better in light shade. Once they start blooming, they never stop. Hybridizing has produced some absolutely fantastic new kinds, with far more blossoms, which rise well above the foliage; some are two-toned, others marbled, and there are elegant little doubles. There's only one trouble with them. You'll want to take them all inside to escape frost. So why not build yourself a greenhouse and do it?

A remarkable new type of fibrous-rooted begonia has been developed in Germany and is known as Rieger's; it is probably best suited to indoor culture.

Begonias, Tuberous

Giant-flowered begonias have tuberous roots, and are called, logically enough, tuberous begonias. You can buy tubers mail-order or locally from a nursery house or even the dime store. The biggest tubers aren't necessarily the best. Choose those that are 2 1/2 inches or more across, and thick. Pick those with some of last year's roots still adhering. They start faster. Or pick those that show short sprouts. Put them in a warm dark place to encourage those that haven't sprouted. Ron Hanson of the men's garden club of Minneapolis says it's important that tubers develop a sprout before you put them in their starting medium. Dormant ones are apt to rot. As they are starting to grow, put them in a porous substance (without fertilizer or manure) like well-decayed leaf mold mixed with ten to twenty percent coarse sand. Peat moss is all right, but mix it half and half with coarse sand. Pure peat is inclined to keep the tubers too wet, according to Lottie Walde, who seldom fails to have magnificent begonias. Your aim is to promote lots of roots with the least amount of top growth. Another reason for leaving tubers out of the ground until they start is that you won't plant them upside down—as many people do. The saucer side is the top.

Cover the tuber with half an inch or so of soil, and when the sprouts surface, move your tray of tubers into a bright spot but not in sunlight. Fluorescent lights are ideal.

Ron Hanson says that tuberous begonias can't stand direct sunlight during the heat of the day. Ideally, they want early morning sun, early evening sun, and either filtered sun or open shade during the day. The more sunshine you can give them without burning the leaves or blossoms, the more abundantly they bloom.

A few tips about growing them: some experts break off all but one sprout and plant the extra sprouts in moist earth where they quickly take root. When you put out your plants, position them so that the leaf tips point in the direction you want the flowers to face. More often than not, it works.

The only hard part about begonias is keeping the tubers alive and healthy through winter. I follow these rules: take the plants indoors before frost and let them ripen; this means watching them grow increasingly scraggly. Hold back on water until the stems die down and the foliage drops off; then wash off the dirt and any remaining stems. Dry the plants in the sun for a few days and store them in a cool, dry place until spring when the buds start coming again.

Begonias have only three pests, really, and these are dogs, small children, and winds. If you have no more than a single prize begonia, any or all three of these pests will be sure to find it and break off parts of it. Believe me, begonias are brittle at their point of attachment to the tuber. If a stalk does break off, don't toss it away. Sink it into the earth a little; it will keep on growing, forming new roots and a tuber, and perhaps continue to bloom.

The most important part of growing begonias is to lash each stalk to a bamboo stake imbedded deeply in the soil alongside it, and to keep lashing the stalk as it grows taller.

The right spot for your begonias is any shady spot protected from wind and kids and dogs. Begonias are beautiful on the patio, on the porch, or out under trees. A favorite spot seems to be a window box on a shady wall, safe from small feet and wagging tails.

Louise Bush-Brown had the most beautiful setting for begonias I have ever seen. On her place outside Philadelphia are the remains of an old barn's stone foundation, and one whole shaded wall had pots of begonias pegged to it. To water, she sprayed the plants with a hose.

In a climate like England's, tuberous-rooted begonias seem to grow and bloom like weeds. They like cool, humid weather. I haven't seen Copenhagen lately, but the last time I was there, the begonias in Tivoli were hard to believe.

Try some this year. There are few more sumptuous flowers in existence. They're really not hard to grow, and if they succeed at all, your nongardening friends will say you're a genius. Begonias are that spectacular.

Bells of Ireland

Plant this one early, while the ground is cool. It's often slow in germinating, so don't give up on it. Bells of Ireland trade on their excellent name, but they are actually better than novelties. They're pleasant in fresh or dried bouquets. Remember, though, that you need to pull off all the leaves before you get a stalk to look like those on the packet cover.

Brachycome, or Swan River Daisy

Ah, flower of my childhood! As a six-year-old, I thought that Swan River daisy was a work of magic. Minute feathery seedlings grew almost overnight into foot-high mounds of dainty blue daisies the color of the sky. Every plant was a work of art. There are many things wrong with Swan River daisies, but it seems sacrilegious to mention them. Plant a row of these flowers, and share them with a child.

Caladiums

You'll see these big tubers for sale in dime stores as well as nurseries, and if you find good ones—without a trace of rot or softness—pick them up. Choose those that are already starting to sprout, if you can find any; otherwise you may not get action until the summer is half over.

Caladiums are beautiful for shady, cool places. Their leaves are incredibly colored—splotches of red, yellow, crimson, and scarlet, with veins of contrasting colors. One has big white leaves with green veins and a narrow green border.

Start the tubers indoors in peat, and keep them moist and warm (eighty degrees or so). Under the bed beside a hot-air vent is a good spot. Lift them out of the peat occasionally to make sure you haven't planted them upside down. I still do that now and then. When they're ready to set outdoors, choose a shady spot in rich soil that you can keep well watered. Most important, keep out kids and dogs, who break the lush stalks.

A planting box three or four feet long on a shaded part of the patio is a great spot for them. See that the pot has drain holes, though, and use the best earth you can lay hands on.

In the jungles of Ecuador on a visit with Frank and Marie Drown, missionaries to the headhunters, I found caladiums growing wild in the shade along a rushing river. It's always a pleasure to see familiar garden plants in their native homes.

Calendulas

Here is one of the finest flowers in any garden. Be sure to have some this year.

I used to think of the calendula as a beautiful old-timer, friend of my childhood and the standby of old ladies in bonnets, but no longer. I have found this plant in the gardens outside my hotel at Aswân, Egypt, where it reflected back the desert sun, ray for ray. (This was the plant we said did best in cool weather!) I saw it again in formal gardens in Cairo, Beirut, and Bern, where it was the mainstay of almost every planting. And in Katmandu, Nepal, in view of the Himalayas, I found it resplendent on New Year's Day, flowering with the same prim certainty in the Rana family gardens as in my own garden when I was a child. Worldwide, I think no flower is used as universally as calendula.

Part of the reason is that it blooms under any day length. Its name, drawn from the same Latin roots as the word "calendar," suggests its long blooming period. Calendulas never sprawl or grow untidy, and, as cut flowers, they easily last a week.

Let your child plant the nubby little ram's horn seeds. They'll be up in a few days. Before the seedlings begin to elbow one another, thin them out so the survivors can expand into broad bushy forms. What's that fragrance you get when you're pulling them up? It's the smell of rhubarb, a completely different plant.

Even the best flowers have weaknesses, though, and calendulas have two insect pests that plague them: aphids and leafhoppers. Watch closely for both, and at the first sign of either, use nicotine sulphate as a spray or dust. Generally that will stop them easily. Plants heavily infested may be hard to save, particularly since insects spread a mosaic disease from which they can never recover. Pull up the infected plants and see if you can keep the disease from spreading. Don't let me discourage you, though, from growing one of the best half-dozen flowers in any garden.

Calla Lilies

If you insist, try growing the yellow calla lily outside beside the pool, as some books suggest, but remember it wasn't I who told you to. They will bloom, but pretty sparingly, and each flower is short-lived. In California and Florida, however, they might be well worth the effort.

For you readers who live in Quito, Ecuador, by all means grow calla lilies. The big white kinds are magnificent. They go almost wild, on unused lots, at the corners of parking areas. Tiny Quechua Indian women carry armloads of them down the street for sale and for decking church altars.

Calliopsis

This perky little flower of the Coreopsis clan is easy to grow and blooms all summer. Two to three feet tall, its rich mahogany and yellow blossoms come on wiry stems, which make them fine for bouquets. Newer kinds are much less than a foot tall, and are covered with blossoms. I like the tall ones better, though. A row of calliopsis among the vegetables is a mighty pleasant sight.

For those who hate to thin any plants, calliopsis is one that does better when somewhat crowded.

You may not want calliopsis every year, but try it once and see. You'll find it a friend, so dependable it will make you feel like an expert. Calliopsis is a favorite of mine because its colors are those I can see, there's nothing temperamental about it, and it always looks well groomed.

Candytuft

Here's a flower for your child. It really does bloom in six weeks from the time you plant it, and that's something of a record. It comes in pink, red, violet, lilac, and white. Nothing seems to bother it, and though it's seldom spectacular or of much value for arrangements, it's pleasant and reminiscent of old-time gardens.

The new tetraploid kind called Iceberg is something else. Its pure white spikes are double ordinary size, and it does indeed seem like a hyacinth, as the catalogs claim. Most candytuft is through blooming when hot weather comes, but this one is still fresh and pleasant in September, growing taller as the summer lengthens.

Canterbury Bells

From the time they poke through the ground until they bloom, Canterbury bells look as undistinguished as pigweeds, and they often get pulled out as weeds. But rabbits make no such errors, and they need no stakes or markers to designate the row. I have tried chewing the rough, hairy leaves of Canterbury bells to see what taste—sweet or pungent or buttery—is so alluring to the rabbit, but my practiced tongue yields no clue. If you have no more than a single plant living through winter, trust a rabbit to smell it out and eat it to the roots. To a bunny, it is caviar or filet mignon or cherries jubilee. Need I caution you about trying Canterbury bells in rabbit country?

At age six, I planted my first package of Canterbury bells and wondered why they never bloomed. As I say, I had learned to read from poring over seed catalogs, but I didn't yet comprehend the word "biennial." The next spring I was so caught up in the social whirl of second grade that I forgot my garden until late June when my sister called me out to look in my weedy patch.

There was a fairyland of deep blue. Each plant was a little tree hung with bells; some had a saucer behind each bell. Where had they come from? I couldn't have planted them. It was a long time before I realized that my older brothers hadn't moved them in to please me. Several times a day I went to admire them. After a few weeks, when they began to wither and brown, I watered them again and again, grieving because I couldn't keep them alive. I believe it may have been from my Canterbury bells that I first learned about the inevitability of death.

Nearly every year since then I have tried to grow these flowers, but in most winters they freeze out, whether in Minnesota or Pennsylvania. Yet at Kalispell, Montana, they seed themselves and are resplendent.

Besides rabbits and winter, Canterburys have one failing: they get to look raunchy after a few weeks and ought to be pulled out, but they keep on sending out new buds and blooms that argue most effectively for a stay of execution. Plant some Canterbury bells this year. Come on, gamble a little. Even with one to five odds, this flower is worth the effort.

Carnations

Year after year we have tried carnations—the annual and biennial kinds—with little success. The season is too short in the North, and carnations rarely live through the winter. I wish it were otherwise.

Castor Beans

If it weren't that the seeds of castor beans are poisonous, this plant would be a good one for youngsters. It grows fast, and its handsome big leaves make a play jungle out of a corner of the yard. In rich soil, it will grow up to twelve feet high. Older gardeners will remember that it is from this plant's seeds that the infamous castor oil—that vile-tasting purgative of a generation and more ago—was extracted.

Celosia and Cockscomb

Celosia is so bright that even color-blind people like me can see it. My friends say that most celosia reds are tinged with orange, and that what my eyes react to is the yellow. In any case, I like this flower. The trouble is I can't decide whether I prefer the knight's plume type or the cockscomb type, so I generally wind up ordering both. Children like the strangely convoluted cockscomb heads that look so much like the comb of a rooster. The only kinds I don't like are the new improved ones only a few inches high, which look to me like underfed dwarfs.

Celosia is easy to grow, and it takes heat and drought in stride. If you don't mind the trouble, start plants indoors and have them in bloom that much earlier. For winter bouquets, cut flowers at their peak, strip off the leaves, and hang them upside down until they're dry and stiff.

Chrysanthemums

There are annual or summer mums, and one year when I set out started plants they were fine. But something has kept them from prospering when I sowed them in the garden. Perhaps it was aster yellows, or else they were unsuited to this climate. Before condemning these flowers, I must try them several more times.

Clarkias

These pleasant annuals waste no time in coming up and flowering, covering their two-foot plants with double flowers. Clarkias are good flowers for children to plant. They seem to do best in dry soil and are one of the strange annuals that enjoy being crowded. Unfortunately, the plants die fast. One year, ants chose to pasture their aphids on the roots. Another year, hard winds whipped the plants enough to tear loose small feeding roots, and the plants declined fast. Perhaps they are better in more favorable parts of the country.

Cleome

A single plant of this flower is like a shrub that blooms all summer long—and I mean all summer, practically from the time you plant it until freezing. A flat of them will make an airy background for your garden. Cleome—also called spider-flower—is a favorite in city parks because it grows three to four feet tall, is constantly in bloom, and always looks well groomed. Cleome likes light, sandy soil in full sun, but it will thrive almost anywhere. I haven't found that diseases or insects bother it, either. If you're planting from seed, do so while the ground is still cool.

Coleus

The trouble with growing coleus from seed is that all two hundred seeds grow, and that's about one hundred and ninety-five more plants than a person generally needs. I could see my crisis approaching during the spring that I planted the whole packet. While the plants were still pinpoints of green (they don't take on color until they're somewhat larger), I began talking up coleus among my friends at the office. The name coleus didn't mean much to them, but "the plant with the colored leaves" did. They said they'd be glad to take one. Just one is what I distinctly didn't want them to take. I don't have one hundred and ninety-five friends, I'm sure of that. So I laid down the rule of twenty plants or none. I didn't get many takers, even when I brought trays full of perky plants to the office.

Few people realize how coleus plants brighten shady corners around the house, or light up a shady patio, growing luxuriantly in planting boxes that are supplied with holes for drainage. Nothing much bothers them, either. The only maintenance they need is to have the flower heads pinched out as they appear. To increase a favorite plant, all you need to do is to pick off a shoot and keep it in water until the roots form.

Exotic in color and form as coleus already are, they are probably due for even bigger changes. The plant reacts strongly to radioactivity, and at the atomic radiation center outside Knoxville I have seen many new forms. Some plants so treated, however, seem to resort to primitive, less colorful, and weedy ancestral types.

Cosmos

At the back of your garden, where there's plenty of room, plant a few cosmos. Better yet, let your child or grandchild plant them. Within a few weeks you'll have tall, airy, fernlike plants studded with lavender, white, pink, and red flowers. The name cosmos, from the Greek word meaning "order," is an apt one.

Nothing much goes wrong with cosmos, except for occasional infection with aster yellows, in which case you pull up the plant and burn it. (You can tell when cosmos are sick by a yellowing of the new growth at the center of a branch.) Generally cosmos are in bloom when frost strikes down the garden. Enough seed falls to reseed the same area.

The yellow-orange cosmos are also excellent, their bright blooms lighting up their corner of a garden. Many blossoms are smoke-tinged, and seem to belong outside a desert wigwam.

Dahlias, Dwarf, from Seed

Start these early, in the house under lights, to get bloom by midsummer. Or if you're too late this year, get started plants at your nursery. You'll probably need only a flat or two because each plant will quickly fill a square foot or more of space.

Dwarf dahlias make a splash with their clean reds and yellows against shiny foliage. They're short enough so that they don't need staking, and they bloom with abandon all summer and fall.

Unfortunately, slugs like them, too. Some years my dwarf dahlias are superb; other years, for reasons I can't quite discover, they seem to loaf, offering only a few blossoms.

You can lift and store roots (called tubers) of the colors you especially liked. But generally those tubers won't produce bigger—or even earlier—blooming plants than those from seed. Unless you have a cool basement (thirty-five to fifty degrees), you'll probably have trouble keeping the tubers alive.

Dwarf dahlias are for amateurs. The big exhibition-type dahlias are for experts—and those who don't mind midwifing a few plants to amaze friends and neighbors. (My gardening friend Ruth Kragnes disagrees; she insists that exhibition dahlias are simple to grow.)

Dahlias, Exhibition-Type, from Tubers

You now have in your hands a remarkable object: a tuber with an eye in its neck and food in its foot. Potatoes are tubers, too, but their eyes are all over their body, and any eye with a small amount of the starchy body will take off and grow. But a dahlia foot is lost without its neck and at least one eye (or bud). So treat your tuber with care. Plant it horizontally in the best soil you can muster, about six inches deep, and drive down a four-foot stake alongside it. Keep moist but not wet, and when it's growing fast, feed it weekly with a mild solution of plant food. Pinch off all but one or two buds in order to get those mammoth blossoms.

As a dahlia grower, you have only these things to fear: dogs and kids and slugs and that neighbor who is sure to say, "You ought to see the dahlias my cousin in Peoria grows."

Have fun with that dahlia. And if you decide to expand to other varieties, go visit an expert who can fill you in on plant sites, soils, and fertilizers for your area. From there, you might join the American Dahlia Society.

Dahlias, incidentally, are from Mexico, but Linnaeus named them for his Swedish friend, Anders Dahl.

Daisy, English

This prim, orderly little plant is a biennial or short-lived perennial that you occasionally see in well-tended city parks. Only six inches high, its flowers arise out of a tuft of green; this makes it a good edging plant, especially where summers are cool. Daisies are easy to grow from seed, and they winter without care. The trouble with all biennials is that you have to plant and then transplant them every year, so they require some extra care. In the summer heat I find they not only stop blooming, but often die. I suggest you enjoy them in someone else's garden.

Dianthus, Annual

How can I recommend a flower that always eludes my best efforts at growing? Some years it blooms in a sprawling kind of way generally just before frost cuts it down. Some of the newer midget ones do bloom, but they are so short they seem grotesque to me. I'm always conscious of how much better Sweet William would be in the same spot, and of how much finer the perennial kinds are.

Four-o'clocks

Not many flowers are as rewarding for kids as this one. Its seeds are charming little beer barrels, easy to plant and quick to sprout and grow. And though the four-o'clock doesn't get around to blooming until late summer, once it starts it never stops. In hot sunny weather, don't set your watch by its four-o'clock opening. My neighbor says that the first week her plants started blooming, they opened at eleven o'clock, just as she came off her shift at the hospital. As the plants grew older, the blooms opened in late afternoon, as they're supposed to.

Four-o'clocks in the South are perennial. I have tried saving the tuberous roots, thinking they would produce blooms earlier than seed, but the plants lacked the kind of get-up-and-grow vitality that makes the four-o'clock fun to raise.

Foxgloves

This one is a biennial, producing foliage the first year, blooming, and then dying the second year. On Cape Cod I have seen magnificent foxgloves that are forests of bloom, each stalk taller than your head and solid with flowers, seeding themselves so that they bloom year after year. Along the Oregon and Washington roadsides they are superb.

In much of the Midwest and elsewhere, foxgloves die out over the winter, so they are something of a gamble. I have tried various mulches to help them out, including bat-type insulation, but they haven't worked. Perhaps the foam-type might work; I haven't had enough experience to say.

Where foxgloves do persist, they are fine flowers and give vertical accents that do so much to dramatize a garden. Try them, by all means. I have a perennial foxglove that persists, but it doesn't come up to the biennial kind.

Gazanias

Here's a great new flower. Each plant is a fountain of fresh-looking leaves, deep green above and felty-white below, and out of that mound come long-stemmed daisies, a few blossoms all summer long. Most remarkable, each petal has several bands of color, some as many as five distinct bands. The plant always looks clean and well groomed. I was reluctant to let mine freeze last fall, so I potted a few that were in bud, and they bloomed all winter long. This fall, the same plants are still blooming, better than ever, indoors in plastic ice cream buckets.

Gazanias are easy to start from seeds. Sown under lights inside, mine bloomed in summer. In regions where summers are long, I am sure they could be sown outdoors and still bloom the same year.

Geraniums

Take home a dozen geraniums for your planter, for the bed outside your picture window, or for wherever you'd like a guaranteed flood of color all summer. Geraniums are as easy as that, and as sure, too. There's just no other flower you can bank on that way—not even petunias. The only reason you don't see geraniums used as generously as in California is that, to many people, geraniums still belong on Grandma's kitchen window along with the cat, where they grow tall and scraggly.

Geraniums do belong with cats, actually. Both of them seek the sun. And though searching for the sun doesn't bother a cat much, it's hard on a geranium's figure. Outdoors, there's seldom a shortage of light, but indoors, in the short days of winter, geraniums scramble for the light. My nearest neighbors were unwilling to pinch back the lanky growth of the first two geraniums of their married life. The plants, growing in pots on the floor, soon reached the window, where they started to flower, then, lashed to bamboo poles, went on up almost to the ceiling, continuing to flower. They are now sturdy tree geraniums that summer on a patio, flowering all summer, and winter indoors, continuing to flower, though less profusely.

To a businesslike, no-nonsense gardener who doesn't mind seeing a bed of geraniums freeze black after they have been performing all summer, geraniums are the ideal summer flower. But I haven't yet found a gardener like that, thank the Lord. Everyone I know asks, how do you keep geraniums through the winter? There is no good answer. I have tried pulling them up and hanging them from nails in the basement, then rooting the tops in the spring. That wasn't very good. I have tried keeping them in tubs of earth in the basement and the root cellar, but most of them rotted. I am told that next to a cool window in a cool basement they will survive without trouble. Perhaps better is an upstairs window in a cool room where they can keep alive without too much active growing. This is where mine are now, and when one of them sends out buds, I take it down to the living-room picture window, returning it to my upstairs purgatory when it has finished flowering.

How do you start new plants from old? When all goes well, it's absurdly easy. You break off six inches of strong young stem, take off the bottom leaf or two and stick it in water or in moist sand until roots form, then pot it and watch it grow. A young plant like this grows faster and generally blooms better than those with old, hardened stems through which nutrients have a harder time passing.

Sometimes the job isn't that simple. In the fall or early winter, cuttings often rot before they take root. Even after they've developed strong roots and you pot them, a rot begins at the soil line and slowly travels upwards, eventually killing the whole plant. The answer is simple. Throw the whole works out, including the soil. There's no saving plants once the rot begins. Root-inducing hormones don't seem to help, either.

Later, as soon as the sun turns the corner in January and the days start to lengthen, a mysterious force takes over. Snap off a short length of new growth from your mother geranium plant and it will set roots within days. It is awesome how geraniums respond to the first prespring days.

Geraniums indoors are easy to grow if you have plenty of light. All you need worry about is keeping them on the dry side, watering just as they begin to wilt or when the pot feels light. Keep sick leaves and old flower heads picked off. If you notice small white flies around them, then you have a problem. The only way I know of to get rid of these insects is to hang one of the fly-killing insecticide strips in the foliage.

New kinds of geraniums to try? I'd say don't bother with the highly touted Carefree. Every gardener I've talked to has been lukewarm about it. Instead, why not try those with ornamental foliage, like Skies of Italy? There are scores of others, striking and clean, as beautiful indoors as outside in beds. Where you have room, try a few plants with scented leaves. You'll be amazed at how closely one kind resembles lemons, another apples, or nutmeg, or roses. Use leaves as garnish when you have fancy company coming.

Other kinds of geraniums aren't as easy to grow. The Martha Washington types are best left to greenhouse culture. The ivy-leafed kinds, too, are sometimes tricky. My friend, Milton Arndt, developed some dwarf kinds he called "window-ledge," or apartment, geraniums having full-sized blooms, but with small leaves clustered into a tight rosette. They are novel, but they seem harder to keep going than those of normal size.

Geraniums are no longer the exclusive province of Grandma. There are shapes and sizes and colors for everyone. And when the public begins to appreciate their value outdoors, watch out for a geranium bloom boom!

Gladioli

You can call them *glad-ee-o'-lee* or *glad-eye'-olee* or simply *glads* (my preference), but whichever way you ask for them, take home a bag of bulblike corms. Plant them must about anywhere, four or five inches deep, and before you know it, you'll have handsome stalks to cut. Glads are easy to grow, but they do best in moderately rich, well-drained soil.

They don't look like much in the border: their leaves are pale and cornlike (they were once called corn lilies). But if they're cut just as they begin blooming and brought into the house in an arrangement, few flowers can beat them. They last for a week or more, new flowers opening farther and farther up the stem.

Methodical people plant the corms in successive weeks so that they have a constant supply of bloom stalks, and I'm all for that idea. Not being the methodical kind, I plant all I have at one time among the vegetables, and in midsummer we have bouquets for shut-ins, the hospital, and the nursing home.

There's not much adventure in growing glads. They're too easy and foolproof. The only odds involved are in storing the corms through the winter. If the plants didn't grow well enough to mature or if your basement was too dry, the corms may be shriveled and weak. An airy spot with a temperature from forty to fifty degrees and with slighly humid air is best. Before you plant them, dust them with whatever bulb insecticide your nurseryman is currently recommending. Plant in a new spot. And if your corms don't survive the winter, it hardly matters. You can get fine ones at the dime store for very little cost, including some sensationally ruffled and splotched, vividly colored varieties.

By all means have glads every year. No cut flower makes finer gifts.

Gloriosa Daisy

Here's a great one for casual gardeners, children, and amateurs. It comes up fast, starts flowering the first year, and cares for itself. The flowers are extravagantly big, with petals dripping gold and maroon and mahogany; consequently, they are prized by flower arrangers.

Gloriosas are a chemically induced mutation of one of the prettiest of wild flowers—the brown-eyed Susan, which brightens the roadsides and prairies over most of the eastern United States. Gloriosas are beginning to grow wild on my place; finding them on a walk in the meadow is a pure delight.

Even as tough a roustabout as Gloriosa has its weaknesses, though. It tends to sprawl now and then. In staking, the branches break off easily. Sometimes, too, plants suddenly die at the roots in the midst of flowering. I haven't been able to figure out why. They're short-lived and generally last only a couple of years, but unless you're the nit-picking gardener, you'll have plenty of self-sown seedlings for the next year.

To me, the Gloriosa is one of the finest flowers developed in our lifetime.

Godetia

A flat of godetia from the flower market will keep blooming all summer, with satiny blossoms that earn it the alternate name of satinflower. The stalks tend to sprawl and bloom sparsely during hot weather, but they come on strong again in fall. This is a flower to try when you have tried most others.

Gypsophila, or Baby's Breath

The annual baby's breath is easy to grow, but I can't imagine why anyone would plant it. The cloud of white (rose or red) flowers is fleeting and inconspicuous. If you want to try it anyhow, rather get a package of mixed annuals. You're sure to get a few other plants mixed in.

Hollyhocks

When pioneers in Conestoga wagons jogged across the plains with horses and cows and farm implements, they brought seed for field crops and vegetable gardens, but also a few for flowers to help ward off the loneliness of life in a new land. Chief among them were hollyhocks, which struck down deep roots beside sod houses, and the next year sent up stalks eight, ten, and even twelve feet high, covering themselves with red, white, and sometimes yellow blooms. Chickens, scratching the soil bare beside the house to escape the heat, didn't uproot them. Hollyhocks were like the pioneers themselves, sturdy and independent.

Iowa garden clubs have planted hollyhocks along roadsides—a beautiful sight—and let the plants care for themselves. If you have a stretch of waste ground, you might do the same. Although hollyhocks don't generally last more than a couple of years, they reseed heavily and, with a little help in thinning, should take care of themselves. Hollyhocks are fine as a neighborly fence between lots. I plant mine in a single row across the garden.

They're too big and spread too much for the average flower border. And if you're the fastidious kind of gardener, you'll be forever trimming off seedpods. But nothing much beats them as a splash of vertical color.

I thought I knew hollyhocks well, having grown them from childhood. But Park's new strain called Powderpuff, which bloomed last year in my vegetable garden, was something surpassing by far the older double-flowering types. The plants are bushier and no more than five or six feet tall; they carry such a load of densely ruffled double blooms that you can't see the stems for the foot or two of stalks that bloom at one time. The colors are vivid and fresh. The dozen or so plants were the most striking feature of my last year's garden. None of them lived through the winter, however, though I gave them a collar of loose straw to keep them from starting too early in spring. I planted a fresh row of them, but slugs got all but one or two plants.

It seems a little indecent to mention the faults of a pioneer, but hollyhocks look a little raunchy in late summer. You can cut them off, of course, but while there is still a foot of buds at the top of the stalk, not many people will. The glamorous doubles get so heavy after a rain that they topple over. No bamboo stakes are strong enough to hold them up, either. You need a heavy post driven down deep. Rust often makes the leaves unsightly, and especially susceptible to rust is a new dwarf kind that blooms the first year from seed. In spite of those drawbacks, do plant hollyhocks for a real adventure in gardening and to celebrate the memory of your migrant forefathers.

Impatiens

Here's the ideal annual for the shady side of your house. Hybridizers have done good things with this old-time resident of Grandma's windowsill. Some F_1 hybrids are foot-high mounds covered all summer with sizable blooms that may be anything from red, rose, scarlet, purple to salmon, white, and even orange.

Impatiens are easy to start from seed, but they take time. You really ought to start them about three months before you plan to put them out. Most flower markets sell flats of impatiens. Besides shade, what impatiens must have is plenty of moisture. Without it, plants stand still.

Kale, Flowering

You wouldn't believe how handsome this plant is. The crinkled leaves form rosettes a foot or so across that may be red with green borders or white with green borders. They're easy to grow, but they need to be dusted, as all members of the cabbage family do. I potted some for the patio, where they continued to look good until freeze-up. This is one you ought to try, at least once.

Kochia

Give this one the same attention you would a summer guest on parole from Sing Sing. At its best, a single plant of kochia is a handsome cylinder of green, waist-high and perfectly symmetrical, turning in fall to a vivid red. A row of these plants make a pleasant hedge. But if kochia seeds itself—as it will if you permit it to turn red—it will take over any bare spots in your garden, coating them with mossy green seedlings, which return even after clean cultivation for several years. Experiment with it. You'll enjoy it. But keep it in solitary.

Larkspurs

The best time to plant larkspurs is last fall. That's the surest way to get a good crop of them. If that's impossible, plant them as soon as you can dig them into the frosty soil. If the ground is still frozen solid, chill the seeds in the refrigerator. Larkspurs need to be jarred by cold into germinating. Plant them where you plan to let them bloom. With a taproot that strikes straight down, they're hard to transplant.

Most kinds of seeds will sprout on top of the soil as long as they are moist. But larkspur seeds must be covered before they will grow. I had been wondering why larkspurs in my Pennsylvania garden reseeded and grew only in corners where leaves had blown in. Then, at Beltsville, experimenters with the light requirements of plants showed me a list of flowers that positively won't germinate if any sunlight reaches them. Among them was larkspur.

Whether you'll continue to grow larkspur depends on your climate. It's a cold-weather flower, needing ample moisture. In such places it is beautiful. Elsewhere, it looks weedy.

Lobelias

A window box without lobelia is unthinkable, without the deep blue cascade of blooms hiding the raw wood or metal or plastic of the container, and minimizing the failure of tuberous-rooted begonias above it. Lobelia truly blooms all summer and fall, always looks neat and clean, and is practically faultless.

There are compact lobelias that don't trail, and these are said to be good for edging a bed, a walk, or a border. I am not familiar with them, but if they have the virtues of the trailing type, they must be fine.

No need to buy seed of the window-box type. All you need for each window box is two or three plants, and you can nearly always find them at a plantsman's stall.

Love-in-a-Mist, Nigella

This little flower is insipid. Its fuzzy petals blur before your eyes the way TENSION HEADACHE is made to dance out of focus in an advertisement. It is easy enough to grow, though, and a child might like it. And for dried arrangements, its seedpods are interesting. Perhaps I'd like it better if I had learned to know it by its alternate name: devil-in-the-bush.

Lunaria, or Honesty, Silver Dollar, Money Plant, St. Peter's Penny

Any plant with so many nicknames must be popular, and it is, except that since it is biennial, you need to wait two years for results. Lunaria is wonderfully easy to grow; whether it lives through winter without a snow cover is another matter. If it does, it quickly shoots up a fine flower stalk of purple blooms that is reward enough for planting it. But it is in late summer, after it dies, that the transformation takes place. You pull up the plant and rub the flat seedpod between your fingers, loosening the dull outside plates. The remaining membrane is pure silver, and a tall, well-grown stalk used to bring up to fifteen dollars in Manhattan flower shops. Don't expect that much in Grundy Center, Iowa, however.

I like the ritual of shucking hulls from a silver dollar stalk. It's something akin to magic the way the ugly stems begin to shine. Wherever you do the shucking, you can be sure you'll have honesty plants soon springing up. I am fond of this plant, and though I'm not appreciative of winter bouquets, a single stalk of this plant, to me, is arresting.

Marigolds

No flower—even the petunia—gives the grower the same satisfaction that marigolds give. They make the pure amateur feel like a professional. They germinate quickly, grow fast, and always look as if they were posing for a picture. The short French types make an edging that never stops blooming, never sprawls, and almost never bows before bugs or disease. I can never settle on my favorite variety, so I settle on a packet of mixed dwarfs of all types. I plant them as a border to my perennials, and I plant another row in the vegetable garden to draw attention away from my aging peas or beans. The giant African types are the only flowers I know that outdo the seed catalog photographs. Each flower is a glowing masterpiece of yellow or gold. Some are fringed like carnations, others are like dahlias.

If you are confused about which kind to plant, that's normal. Even those men who divided marigolds into the two major classes were confused. The dwarf French types don't come from France. The tall African kinds don't come from Africa. In the dim past, even before Burpee and Park, marigolds were growing quietly from our own Southwest through Mexico and down to the Argentine. As diverse in their genetics as alley cats, they produced tall plants and short ones, singles and doubles, mahoganies and golds. All that plant breeders needed to do was to segregate the best ones and keep them pure. Later, by crossing and recrossing, hybridizers produced more exotic ones.

But plant breeders were pikers compared with the enthusiasm and imagination of catalog writers. Giant marigolds—and perhaps even supergiants—I can understand. But where do you fit in dwarf giants and giant dwarfs? One kind is the marigold of a lifetime. On a facing page is the finest marigold ever produced. Just where do you go from there?

As of now, there is one strain that beats all others: Jubilee, either golden or orange, and for this reason. Most big marigolds have blossoms too big for their necks, and when they are weighted down by heavy rain or watering, they break. Not so the Jubilees. They come through, heads up. They're listed in catalogs as "hedge-type," and this description is an apt one. Planted in full sun, they quickly form a dense, deep-green hedge, eventually so crowded with blossoms that you can keep cutting bouquets indefinitely without seeming to diminish them. And as long as they bloom, they continue to look fresh and neat and orderly. To my mind, there is no more spectacular annual in existence than the Jubilee marigold.

A note to David Burpee: instead of striving for an odorless marigold to win those aesthetes who say they don't like the clean, fresh aroma of the leaves, why not develop a *parfum de marigold?* Or better still, develop a strain of human beings who appreciate diversity in smells.

Mignonette

Gardeners who long for the past should remember to plant a few seeds of mignonette, a low weedy-looking plant with a heavenly fragrance. It's easy to grow, takes little space, and after its short blooming period, you won't grieve at pulling it out. Children will like growing this one.

Morning Glories

To me, there is no more beautiful flower in existence than a Heavenly Blue morning glory. Perhaps I might tire of it in an area where it has more time to bloom, but in the North, it just won't start blooming until right before frost. I have started plants indoors under lights, but when they are moved outdoors, they stand still until those that were seeded outdoors catch up to them. Perhaps morning glories, like chrysanthemums, bloom only after a long period of shortening days, although I don't believe this is the case. In any event, they grow mightily during summer and deck their vines with clouds of breathtaking blossoms. And then comes frost.

I have tried the bush-type glory, and I find it a poor imitation. The moon-flower is an interesting vine resembling morning glories, with enormous blossoms that open only at night. Try it once, if you like; you'll find the blossoms mighty scarce, and it's frustrating to try to appreciate a flower by flashlight.

Perhaps still other kinds are worth growing. My trials with the red ones didn't satisfy me. Perhaps I only resented the wall space they took away from Heavenly Blue.

Morning glory seeds have a hard coat covered with wax. To speed their germination, soak them in water overnight or else scarify them—that doesn't mean to scare them but to scratch them with a knife or file to permit moisture to penetrate the waxy, hard covering. With either treatment, they sprout within a few days.

Nasturtiums

Let your children plant these along the sidewalk in the sun or half-shade. They come up fast and flower fast, and except for occasional aphids, nothing much goes wrong with them. Old unimproved varieties used to ramble and climb, and their flowers were concealed by leaves. New types stay in place, and their big, lush blooms just about hide the leaves. As a bed or a border, you'll find them spectacular. Just one drawback, though: unless you keep the seeds picked, they'll slow down or even stop growing.

Let me translate that line into the gilded language of the seed catalog. It would then read: be sure to try the seeds as a pungent flavoring in your tossed salad. Your guests will marvel at the spicy watercress flavor. And that is true. A few of the nutlike seeds, either whole or chopped, are a gourmet's trick to pep up pallid salads.

To old-timers, nasturtiums are a whiff of the past, a memory of gentle grandmothers in calico.

Nicotianas

Here is an unsung flower. Perhaps if it were hard to grow, it would be more popular. I like the way it fills in the empty spaces, covering up for my many garden failures. It reseeds liberally, but it is in no sense weedy, and it can easily be pulled or hoed out.

I like the handsome, broad leaves that deck the tall stem before blooming. Nicotiana is a flowering tobacco with the same giant leaf. Slow at germinating, it grows at a furious pace once it begins, and that's something rewarding in any garden. From the time it starts blooming, it is constantly in flower until frost, perfuming the garden with a fresh, almost spicy fragrance. Older strains opened only in late evening and night, but new ones now stay open all day. Last fall, a few stalks picked just before frost kept on blooming in water indoors for nearly two months. Nicotiana is one of my favorite plants.

Pansies

These are the "heartsease" of Shakespeare's day, forever popular for their cheerful faces. How long they continue to bloom depends mostly on climate. Cool and even cold weather is what they like, and when they have it, they'll keep blooming like mad. Hot weather turns them off; they sprawl on the ground, managing a feeble flower now and then.

Take home a flat of pansies from your supermarket or nursery; plant them in semishade where you pass by them going in and out. Give them painstaking care. By that I mean make a little ritual of snipping off old blooms whenever you pass them. You may be amazed at how long flower size and number keep up. Before long, you'll get to know each plant as a friend. Somehow the finest pansies I've seen have been in decorative tubs on the patio. Does this say something about the need for drainage or about the care lavished on them? Probably both.

My father enjoyed his backyard bed of pansies perhaps more than any other flower. When frost came, they were blooming with a frenzy, and he covered them with hay he had cut by scythe in the meadow by the lake. Periodically, he would uncover them and see how they were doing. Even under a coat of snow they were fresh and their flowers crisp and vivid. At Christmas when the snow was a foot or more deep, they still greeted him, and in early spring they were triumphant. By summer, though, they were in a decline, and he grieved, unwilling to pull them out. Sadly, he learned that pansies are at their best in their first year.

Pansies aren't hard to grow from seed sown in August. I don't bother, though. It's too much fun to pick up some from the fairyland of color they make at roadside markets.

Petunias

Petunias—for their vivid colors and the way they bloom all summer—probably prompt more people to garden than any other plant. And so they buy a package of seeds and plant them outside—and fail to give them the careful attention they need in infancy. Or they plant them indoors in an egg carton on the windowsill where they dry out. In either case, they conclude they don't have a green thumb. Regardless of the seed catalog's assurance that petunias are easy to grow from seed, it's not true.

The way to start petunias is to take home a flat from the supermarket. Choose those with short, sturdy stems that may or may not be just starting to bloom. Tip them out of the flat, break the roots apart, plant, and water. Now you're in petunias, and if you keep the soil moist but not wet, you'll quickly become famous for your gardening ability. It's as easy as that.

You'll find reasons other than color for having petunias. Plant them close to your back door—or front door, if that's the one you use mostly—and you'll enjoy them by night as well as day. Their perfume is as remarkable as their blooms—so rich after dark that you can almost taste it and a subtle fragrance by day, but never overpowering. If I could find a shaving lotion with that scent, believe me I'd buy it.

The other reason I like petunias near the back door is for the way they attract hummingbirds. I haven't noticed that Mr. Gallup has polled them recently, but I would guess that hummingbirds would rate petunias at or near the top, and I suspect that there wouldn't be a big undecided vote. The nectar supply in a single blossom must be enormous. The same flower that provides lusty sips for the birds throughout the day gives food at dusk to the big sphinx moths that are surprisingly like hummingbirds in size and behavior. Petunias for me are entertainment as well as nourishment for the eye and nose.

Now then, what kinds do you buy?

Someday I'd like to put seed catalog writers and their supervisors into stocks, head and feet stuck through holes in a board and securely locked, then starve them for a day or two and question them. What is the difference between a grandiflora petunia, a supergrandiflora, a giant of California, and a cascade? Why do some petunias sprawl and die out in the summer heat and others—like those in public parks, for instance—keep flowering profusely until freeze-up? What's *wrong* with each kind? How I'd like to see them squirm. Maybe, just maybe, on the fourth or fifth day I'd get the truth. Until such time as I can try the above, let me venture my own analysis.

The cascades are sprawlers. In a bed, they'll try to crawl out. Try weeding them and you step on them, amputating their long arms. Before the end of the summer, they're likely to be dead. Use them only in window boxes.

Bedding type petunias are the clean, compact little plants that you see in parks. They are called F_1 multiflora. They're excellent. The trouble is that you pass them by at the supermarket in favor of those giant-blossomed kinds. These are the flowers to give a big smash effect. The plant doesn't fall over and break apart, but remains a nice mound all summer. These are the most useful of the petunias for those who want to splash color around the place. The variety Sugar Plum is one I like especially.

Now for those who like the giant-flowered ones, pick the grandifloras. Some of them are ruffled, some fringed, but all have big flowers, and all sprawl and tend to play out rather early in life. Such is the price of glamor, I suppose. They are so beautiful, though, that I suspect I will always keep planting them near the door where I can pause to admire them at their brilliant best. The big doubles and the heavily ruffled ones are akin to the grandifloras in that they don't stay put and they tend to age prematurely, but they too are worth it.

The best spot for petunias is in full sun, but don't let that stop you from trying them in part shade. At my back door I have a patio with a big pine tree in the center, and in the few inches of planting space at its base, I have big white petunias that thrive even though they get only occasional sun. The flowers are bigger, although not as numerous as those in full sun. At night, the big white flowers light up the dark and perfume the whole patio.

An excellent place for the biggest, most glamorous petunias is a window box, both indoors and out, and here the weak trailing habit of the big ones is an asset. If you have a window over the sink that opens easily, try a window box below it and see if your sink chores aren't automatically pleasanter.

Planters, too, were made for petunias, and here too is a spot for the most glamorous ones you can find. Put them in early and see how they cover up the browning leaves of tulips and daffodils.

For you purists who must start your own plants from seed, this year try pelleted seed. You simply press the pellets onto the surface of the soil in your flat. You can space the pellets—something I defy you to do with normal seeds, which are like so much dust. Spaced that way, the plants come up with elbowroom. Ordinarily, petunias come up as thick as fur, and it seems downright inhumane —as well as tiresome and, at a penny a seed or so, a little profligate—to tweezer out nine plants and leave the tenth. Pelleted seed doesn't cost much more, and seedlings aren't as likely to damp off during that critical interval before they grow their first true leaves. A chemical in the coating helps prevent that damping-off, and plant food in the coating probably helps the seedling get off to a fast start.

If you can't get pelleted seed, or if you're stubborn against newfangled aids, then moisten the surface of your sterilized soil, sphagnum, or peat, and sow directly on top. Cover with plastic film until germination begins, then immediately place the tray under a fluorescent light within an inch or two of the tube. Few if any seedlings will damp off, given the strong artificial daylight for ten to twelve hours a day.

For a while, petunia seedlings sit on their haunches like a Buddha, reflecting no doubt on the pains and hardships of germination. But once they start growing, their introversion ends and they are all business. Give them a weekly shot of diluted fertilizer, keep them under the light or in a bright window, see that they're moist but not wet, and you'll have plants like the best in greenhouses. By far the most important part is good strong light. Without enough light, they'll keep reaching until you'll be ashamed to show them to visitors.

What can go wrong with petunias once you've set them out? Very little. In my experience, only one thing hits them, and then only rarely. That is a mosaic disease like that of calendulas. The leaves turn yellow, branch by branch, and the flowers abort. There is no cure. Pull up the entire plant at once and hope that the leafhoppers that spread the virus haven't gotten to the rest of your plants.

Right now, after four successive nights of frost that blackened the tomatoes and cucumbers and marigolds, my petunias are blooming as if they never even felt a chill. What a flower!

Phlox

This is a good one for children because it starts to grow right away, it flowers fast, and it comes in a splashy assortment of colors. Some kinds have starred and fringed flowers. The new, bigger-flowered kinds are good for beds. Unfortunately, for me at least, they don't keep blooming in hot weather, although I notice that seed catalogs indicate that they will if you keep the seedheads picked off. Believe me, that would be some job! Last fall, they bloomed best after several hard frosts.

Poppy, Shirley

Everything the seed catalog says about Shirley poppies is true. They grow fast, bloom beautifully, and nothing—not even aphids, slugs, red spider, or hot, dry weather—bothers them. The better the soil, the finer the blossoms. But more important than using good soil is giving each plant plenty of room—that means a foot or more between plants. This means thinning, and thinning hard, because poppies come up as thick as hair, and a gardener must transform himself into Dracula to get the job done.

Plant poppies in the fall for best results or as early as you can find seeds in spring. To germinate with a bang, poppies need cold weather. You can achieve the same effect by chilling the seed in your refrigerator for a few weeks before planting. Then sprinkle the seeds on top of the ground, THIN, and enjoy.

Generally, poppies will bloom a little all summer and you may be tempted to leave them long after their peak. Don't. Pull them out and put in other plants. Next spring you'll have self-seeded Shirleys. All you need do, once again, is THIN them and enjoy. Could you ask much more of a flower than that?

Portulaca

This is the rose moss or moss rose (the old-fashioned name). The first ones I ever saw were under a pane of glass in a farmyard when I was probably four or five. I must have stood transfixed when the farmer removed the glass. In my whole long life I had seen nothing so breathtaking. The flowers lay on their sparkling green blanket of leaves like jewels. It never occurred to me that the glass was protecting them against dogs or cats or sheep or chickens. To me it was logical that any such treasures should be under glass. Never since then have I seen such moss roses, despite newer, bigger, and double blooms.

Moss roses look best in a mass big enough so they can make a mass of color. Since they're prostrate, a raised bed, a mound, or a planter shows them off best. The right setting is important to them. In full sun, they're easy to grow and take zero maintenance. But since they tend to be slow starters, it's best if you pick up a couple of flats at the supermarket or else start them indoors in March or April. Seeds are like shiny steel filings. Plant them on top of the soil and cover by giving them a fine spray of water.

A first cousin of the moss rose is that villain purslane, or pussley, which keeps on growing and seeding itself even after it's been pulled up and thrown out. Moss rose has none of its relative's bad habits. All that can go wrong with a bed of moss roses beside your walk results from dogs and kids and grown-up clods who never stop to look at what's underfoot.

Salpiglossis

The trouble with this flower is its name. By any other, it would have hit the best-seller list long ago—not because it's easy to grow, but because its flowers have the beauty of Persian tapestry. Its other name is no better: "painted tongue" suggests a hangover. Some enterprising catalog writers have tried to popularize it with the name "velvet flower," which isn't bad, but hasn't taken, either, so don't expect to find it under the V's in a seed rack.

I generally start my salpiglossis indoors under lights because it's important that you have good-sized plants before hot weather hits. If you plant it outdoors early, you can often have good success if the weather stays cool until the flower stalks begin to rise. In upstate New York, salpiglossis reseeds and germinates so early in spring that it's considered among the easy flowers to grow. Salpiglossis, like a few other flowers, seems to like to be crowded, at least enough so it doesn't fall on its side during the first stiff wind.

The new F_1 hybrid is shorter, with double the number of flowers. A single stalk makes a complete bouquet that will keep on blooming for a week or more without becoming messy. For grace in the garden, though, I prefer the original flower growing as it must have in its native Chile, its stems decked all summer long with butterflies of gold and blue, red and maroon, and mixtures of all colors, too complex to describe.

Try salpiglossis your second year of gardening. You may consider it well worth the extra effort it generally takes.

Salvias

You can pick up flats of salvia nearly anywhere. They're easy to grow, they do well in bright sun, and they keep a bright, orderly appearance all summer.

To the color-blind gardener, this one is a bust, like so many paper flowers hitched onto stiff stalks, the color blending with the green of the leaves. To the gardener who likes red and can see red, this one is a must. The purple kind is a little better for me. So, too, are the rose, salmon, and white kinds.

Scabiosas

Annual scabiosa is fun to grow. It comes up fast, fends for itself, and keeps blooming all summer. I like the tall kind, which grows nearly waist-high and has long stems for cutting. There's nothing particularly exciting about scabiosa, or pincushion, but it's well worth a try in your experimental garden.

Schizanthus

If you see schizanthus, or butterfly flower, for sale, pick up a flat for fun, and if the summer is cool, you may be delighted at the cloud of blossoms that surround each delicate stalk. Blooms are somewhat like snapdragons, in red, yellow, crimson, violet, and white. My plants always sprawl, practically disappear in hot weather, but then they revive and put on a modest display. Perhaps in your climate they might do better. Actually, schizanthus is a greenhouse plant.

Snapdragons

In cool climates, snapdragons are a good expenditure of your time and space. But in hot summer areas, better leave them to city parks and greenhouses. Snapdragons just don't do much in the heat.

Start seed early under lights. They're slow to germinate but grow fast once they learn which way is up. Pinch out the center stalk to make the plant bush out. To come into their own, snaps need regular waterings and as much sun as possible.

The big problem with snaps is that they topple over. You can stake them individually, but this is a real chore. An easier way is to cut eighteen-inch lengths of brush armed with stiff twiggy side-shoots and push them into the ground between and among your snaps. For a couple of weeks, until the plants grow up through the brush, your bed will look a trifle raunchy, but your plants won't sprawl the way they generally do. The ideal shoots for this purpose are lilac trimmings, which are stiff and strong and have plenty of twigs. I keep a pile of them on hand.

I like the deep green of snapdragon leaves. The blossoms at their best are wonderfully colored steeples, and if spent stalks are cut off, the plants keep on blooming until late fall, sometimes reaching their peak after the first light frosts. The new snapdragon strains are distinctly better than the old. I can't say which I like best: the rocket, ginger, hyacinth, or butterfly type. The little dwarf kind makes a pleasant ground cover. Now and then snapdragons live through winter but mine lack the vigor and fizz of their first year. I don't bother nursing them along.

Stocks

Somewhere in America there must be a place where stocks will grow and flower, but I haven't seen it. From age six on I've tried them, and though they germinate and start growing, and sometimes look almost healthy, it never occurs to them that their purpose in life is to bloom—not just produce a cluster of gray-green foliage.

Improved varieties are "10-week stocks," although seed catalogs rarely specify ten weeks from what to what. Perhaps if you live where the temperature seldom varies from fifty degrees all season long, you can grow them. I'd say that if you are wild about the color and fragrance of stocks, buy them at your florist's.

Sunflowers

Try a few seeds of ornamental sunflowers this spring. The new double ones are as easy to grow as the old giant ones. When they're blooming on the stalk in the garden, they're pleasant, but obviously only sunflowers, and you might dismiss them as a novelty. But pick half a dozen of the perfectly formed flowers—which run six inches or so across—and put them in a big Van Gogh-style jug and you'll razzle-dazzle your friends. Tell them the flowers are a new type of helianthus, which is true, and they'll continue to believe that you're a gifted gardener, that is, until they see the plant in the garden.

Every child deserves enough space in the garden for a few giant sunflowers. The way the flowers turn their heads to follow the sun across the sky is sure to fascinate children. You can explain to them, if you wish, that the side of the stem away from the sun grows faster, thereby pushing the flower sunward, but the mystery remains. I find myself singing along with Thomas Moore: "As the sunflower turns on her god, when he sets,/The same look which she turn'd when he rose." The day comes when the bulging head gets too heavy with seeds to keep turning, and it hangs motionless.

As children, my brothers and I planted a sunflower house on the new land we had just cleared of brush and trees. With hoes we scratched the outlines of a vast entry hall and two rooms. The house would be our hideaway.

That was the summer we changed from children to men and put play behind us once and for all. There was so much work to do on our new farm that we forgot our sunflower house until suddenly there it was, more beautiful than we had dreamed it could be, the walls dense and towering, surmounted by a circle of gold. Inside, the soil was cool and moist, even on the blazing day we discovered it. I can't recall that I was ever inside it more than once because, every day, work began at 4:30 A.M. and ended well after 10 P.M. Someday I want to plant another sunflower house.

Sweet Peas

Try these if you're willing to risk failure. Except where summers are cool, they're tricky, hard to grow. When the temperature gets above seventy-five degrees and stays there, your sweet peas will likely dry up.

But go ahead and try them, if you must. See that the soil is rich and firm, and get them planted early, preferably in the fall before freeze-up. You can accomplish much the same thing by chilling seeds in the refrigerator for a few weeks. In any case, be sure to soak seeds for a day before planting. Any seeds that haven't swelled after that time should be notched with a file to allow moisture through the hard shell.

Plant in the best soil you have, and if the sweet peas ever come up, see that they have a fence to climb on immediately. Sweet peas, in company with most vines, need encouragement to climb when they are very young, and they go into an early decline without a stake or fence to climb on shortly after they emerge. A good idea is to push twiggy branches into the ground beside the emerging plants.

If you think I seem to be discouraging the beginner from trying sweet peas, you're right. I'd rather that you try other flowers first, where the odds aren't stacked against you. More power to you if you can get sweet peas to prosper. There are few more beautiful flowers. Their fragrance alone is worth the effort.

Sweet Williams

Plant these flowers, but remember that they won't bloom until the following year. They're worth waiting for, though. They come into bloom just as the spring bulbs are finishing and before most perennials and annuals are doing much, and they are asplash with color.

Sweet Williams are as easy to grow as radishes, and they germinate about as fast. They'll grow anywhere, even in weeds. The biggest trouble is that they're too eager to reproduce. Around each plant you'll soon have a mat of young plants too good to discard, too thick to do well. What do you do about it? Get tough and hoe them all out, or else transplant a few to a new location and pull out the old plants.

I don't mean to be lukewarm about Sweet Williams. In mixed arrangements, hardly a flower can top them. They're long-lasting, hold themselves erect, and don't get scraggly. A row of them puts me in mind of a prim old-fashioned calico print. But why, with a name like theirs, aren't they fragrant like their close relatives, carnations and pinks?

Tigridias

Grow this flower as you do glads, say the seed catalogs. But don't expect the same results, I say. For one thing, the glad-like leaves are weak and sickly looking. You don't see a flower stalk. And the flowers—if any—bloom only when you're not there to see them. I think the average blooming time for each one must be about an hour or two in midday and, then, only when the sun is shining. I'll admit that on the few occasions when I crept up on a fully opened flower, it was a beauty —nearly five inches across, with each of its three big petals mottled and tigered at the throat.

Unless you plan to work at home this summer and can take time off during midday just to watch your tigridias in bloom, I suspect you can do better than plant this one.

Tithonias

One of the quickest ways of getting a reputation as a gardener—one who raises striking novelties—is to plant a package of tithonias, otherwise known as Mexican sunflowers. They grow well everywhere I have tried them, from the heat of Philadelphia to the chill of northern Minnesota. The blossoms look like vivid orange-yellow zinnias, growing on what seem to be trees. The common variety grows six feet tall; an improved kind called Torch stays within four feet.

It's great fun to have flowers that grow as fast and luxuriantly as giant ragweed and bloom all summer. Makes you feel you know what you're doing. Artistically speaking, the flowers are too small for the size of the plant, but in bouquets the blossoms light up the whole arrangement.

Toward the end of summer the big plants begin to look a bit ratty, with browning lower leaves, but then you can't ask for everything in a flower.

Verbenas

Never once having grown decent verbenas, how can I say anything in their behalf? In some places, no doubt, they warrant their space, but not for me. I have tried them often enough that I won't succumb to the catalog's blandishment of new All-America winners. At least I don't believe I will. Verbenas fall on their sides, and bloom, lifting themselves up on an elbow sometimes, but more often lying on the ground, where they are spattered with dirt after a rain or after a sprinkling. Try them if you must, but don't blame me.

Violas

On the gentle mountain slopes below the Jungfrau in Switzerland, the soggy earth is covered with wild violas as big as those in carefully tended gardens. They bloom all summer, too, as many alpine flowers do. At the hostel farther down the mountain I bought packages of violas in several colors, hoping to introduce something rare and fine to gardens in northern Minnesota where the weather has much in common with the Alps. They grew but didn't thrive. All that remains of them today is a buttery yellow one that sends out a furtive bloom now and then. Perhaps violas are worth the space and time in your climate. Not here.

But one kind is. It's a tiny version that most people call Johnny jump-up— which it does, wherever you don't disturb the soil. Its perky little blossoms spring up in the lawn and especially in waste places. Flowers are all blue or combinations of yellow, white, and blue. Plant breeders have produced named varieties with bigger blooms, and certainly they are fine plants in some climates. But I prefer the vigor of these little ragamuffins that bloom all summer, anywhere, without tending. If you're the kind of gardener who can't stand to see bare soil around your tulips and daffodils, by all means get a start of Johnny-jump-ups from your neighbor. They'll quickly fill in, and yet they won't become a weed to contend with.

Zephyr Lilies

The trouble with these charming little lilies is that they're lost amid all the lush foliage and flowers of summer. Unless you have the right place to show them off—a planter or raised bed—they go unnoticed. For a window box in the light shade, they are excellent, and they bloom much of the summer. Perhaps in a miniature garden, they would be appealing.

Occasionally they live through winter but should be dug and stored like glads to make sure they survive. Flowers which are rose, bright yellow, or white, look like tiny amaryllis.

Zinnias

The trouble with zinnias is that they're too easy to grow; many gardeners even apologize for a resplendent row of them among the vegetables. Such are the perils of overexposure.

For the beginning gardener there is no better flower. Plant them in full sun almost anywhere and they thrive. Keep them well watered and fed, and they produce giant plants and lots of flowers. Pick off old flowers, and they will be in bloom until frost. The only thing an amateur needs to guard against is letting the plants stand too close together. When they are growing well and are past the danger of cutworms chewing them off, thin the giant kinds so they stand at least a foot apart.

Zinnias are one of the few flowers that grow and bloom the way you see them in the catalogs, and you can count on them when you plan the way you want your yard or your garden to look. Since the germination may be a little uneven occasionally, it's best to sow fairly thick. But nearly always, zinnias won't let you down. And each new kind is a garden adventure. Toward the end of the season, mildew may strike them down. The answer is to pull them out.

Miniature zinnias don't look like much in a row in the garden, but before freeze-up one summer, I cut off a small handful for the house. In a bouquet they looked fine and took on the grace they lacked outside on their oversize stalks. They dried slowly, keeping most of their color; at Christmas they were still a pleasant sight.

Long ago my brother's young bride planted zinnias during her first summer on a farm. They grew without much tending. From that year on, she has planted them in her garden wherever they have lived. Now her children and their children, too, grow zinnias—a kind of trademark of her clan. When I visited her and my brother during their assignment on a Church World Service mission in rural Greece, I saw her at a mountaintop mission overlooking the brilliant blue Aegean Sea—but she had her back to it, admiring a bed of monk-tended zinnias.

13
how to beautify your house and yard

As important as paint to your house are the shrubs and flowers beside it. They do more than beautify. They cheer the passerby. They say hello to the visitor. They testify to the kind of people inside.

Besides that, they change the people inside. Who can start out the morning with a grouch when he opens the door to a world of roses or morning glories or happy-looking lettuce? Arriving home at night, how much easier to throw off the worries of the office when you're greeted by an onslaught of geraniums or petunias. On a mercenary note, a house with well-planted grounds is easier to sell than a bare one, and it commands a better price.

Window Boxes

If you live anywhere near Philadelphia, let me ask that you visit the crowded row-house area just south of the heart of the town. Some streets are pure slums—dirty, littered with beer cans and paper—but just as many in this all-black part of town are avenues of window boxes loaded with geraniums and petunias and pansies, without as much as a gum wrapper of litter. You wonder if you aren't dreaming. The streets seem as prosperous and pleasant as the most genteel areas around Rittenhouse Square, where bankers, attorneys, doctors, and members of the symphony orchestra live. Window boxes make the difference.

A charming little woman, Louise Bush-Brown, started the program, which must rank among the twenty-seven—if not the seven—wonders of American metropolitan life. Mrs. Bush-Brown was coauthor with her husband of *America's Garden Book*, which is a must for every gardener's shelf.

Long after she should have retired, Mrs. Bush-Brown interested her wealthy friends in bringing annual flowers to South Philadelphia streets to plant in window boxes that black residents either built or bought. Many residents of the slums were migrants from farms in the South and were hungry for growing things. Mrs. Bush-Brown's only stipulation before passing out plants was that more than half the residents of each block had to agree to have a window box and to keep the street clean.

Through the years, in block after block, window boxes have appeared, and on planting days, matrons from the Main Line arrive with station wagons full of annuals from their greenhouses, and help older black people plant not only window boxes but also vacant lots with hundreds of flowers. It was Mrs. Bush-Brown who stayed, wielding a spade if no one else was around, until all rubbish was cleared and hauled away and the vacant lot transformed into an oasis of beauty.

Mrs. Bush-Brown preferred wooden planting boxes with drainage, with a mixture of garden soil and peat to hold water. Her favorite plantings: a simple combination of geraniums with blue lobelia trailing down the sides.

Getting plants to thrive in window boxes takes careful attention to watering. In a sunny spot with wind, they may need watering twice daily. For ability to stand up to adversity, nothing much beats geraniums and petunias. Good too, are calendulas, marigolds, and ageratum, as well as trailing nasturtiums and snapdragons. The prize for shady places is tuberous begonias, but these must be protected from the wind. Pansies are easier but don't continue blooming when hot weather strikes.

Put your window box outside your kitchen or dining room window, as my gifted gardening friend Lula Spare does. Watering is simple, and the picture is beautiful from both indoors and out.

Planters

Well-designed planters do wonders for a home, helping to make a too-high house settle onto its site, for instance, or uniting house and garage. But—and isn't it sad that so much in the world is beset with buts?—if you decide to have one, better get an architect or an artist friend to design it. The wrong one could botch up your house.

Planters are ideal for the meticulous. Here you can manicure each plant, massacre each weed. Tiny rockery plants—the kind you'd hardly give a second glance elsewhere—look good here, since they're nearer eye level. Snowdrops, crocuses, and the like will open up the show, and later tulips and daffodils and hyacinths. You can lift those bulbs after the leaves have died down, or else plant right over them with pansies, petunias, dwarf marigolds, or whatever fits your fancy.

Planters on the Patio

Here's an easy way to garden, and it's effective, too. Buy a plastic planting box and put in half a dozen tubers of caladium. You'll find them in dime stores as well as nurseries. Pick those that show evidence of starting to grow, and give them warmth to keep them coming. Coleus make another splash of color in patio planters. Make sure there are holes in the planter, though, or you'll have a watery mess after every rain, and your plants will drown out.

In a sunny location, almost anything thrives in a planter, especially in the big, permanent, tub types, where the soil doesn't dry out fast. Try tulips and daffodils in a big, round planter; then follow them up with geraniums. All summer you'll have a delightful show.

A Cornell horticulturist I know suggests that you make plastic sausages for planters. You fill those long plastic bags with good soil, then insert seedlings. No need to water any more all summer. He has grown flowers and even tomatoes on his patio in the strange snakelike bags. Most people, though, will prefer permanent planters.

Don't Smother the Foundation

Unless your house is an architectural monstrosity, don't let evergreens hide it. If you already have a jungle of evergreens or other overgrown shubbery, chop them out. You'll be pleased at the way you and your house can breathe again. A low juniper here and there is all it takes to tie your house to the grounds. If you insist on having spruces or pine or rhododendron, plant them at the edge of your lot.

Put in a patio with flagstones where you chopped out the oversize evergreens, and border it with yew, if you like, or your favorite flowers, in raised platforms that are both seats and planting receptacles.

Up until 1972, there was no book on landscaping worth the name, but with the *Reader's Digest* book on landscaping, that changed. Buy or borrow it and you will have inspiration for redesigning your place and the information for doing it.

What then do you plant along the foundation? I like a clematis vine, but use whatever ivy succeeds in your climate. Flowering or berried shrubs look good. Most flowers are too small to function as foundation planting, and they look scrawny unless backed up by shrubs.

For the Shady Side of Your House

There aren't many flowers that bloom in the shade. There is one, though, that blooms profusely unless the shade is too dense. That is impatiens, which goes by a lot of other names, like patience plant and blooming fool. With rich soil and an occasional soaking, it will bloom all summer, and its fresh green leaves always look neat. You can get plants at your nursery, or you can start the plants from seed without much trouble except that you must start them indoors pretty early. Hybridizers have brought out new colors and heights. Impatiens is growing in popularity. Its name comes from the way the seedpods wait to explode on being touched. A wild flower of the shaded swamps—the spotted jewelweed or touch-me-not—is a close relative.

For many of the same spots, instead of impatiens, you can use fibrous-rooted begonias. These are the small-flowered begonias that you buy in pots already in bloom. Each plant will soon cover a foot width and will continue to bloom with abandon. If you want to try starting them from seed, go ahead. They're not easy. Begonias are a fine flower in beds or borders almost anywhere except in full, baking sun. A few annuals will bloom in semishade, but pathetically. Why not plant wild flowers there instead, those that do their best in shade?

The Most Exciting Garden of All

Be glad if you have a north side of the house to plant. This is where you plant wild flowers, which for my money are the most interesting flowers of all. Perhaps because I am red-green color-blind, unconsciously I appreciate the form of a plant more than its color. And where can you find a more graceful plant than jack-in-the-pulpit? Jacks are so common in most woods that there should be no harm in your digging up a couple of roots for your wild flower border. The flower, which lasts a long while, is replaced by a cluster of brilliant red fruit.

Another wild flower so common that you can get a start of it from the woods is yellow bellwort, sometimes called wood daffodil. There is a certain grace about the way the pale yellow bells droop from the tops of the plants. By midsummer the whole plant disappears, leaving room for unfolding ferns to expand.

Queen of the wild flower garden is the beautiful white *Trillium grandiflorum*, which pushes out of the ground to unfold its umbrella of leaves and then its waxy white blossom early in June. As it ages, it turns pink. This is one plant you need to search nurseries to find, or you can order it from one of the wild flower specialists.

Once you have started a wild flower garden, you will want to add other plants. Jacob's ladder is an easy one to grow, and in some places, so too is the dogtooth violet. I like the little foamflower, and, of course, hepatica, Virginia bluebells, or mertensia, Dutchman's-breeches, squirrel corn, wild ginger, and mountain phlox. Bloodroot blossoms don't last long, but the handsome leaves persist. Mayapple, too, has handsome leaves, and all season, from the time its beautiful umbrella pushes up until it fruits, it is fun to watch.

If you like your wild garden as much as I think you're going to, then go ahead and invest in lady's slippers. The yellow ones are easy to grow, and if your ground is moist and rich in humus, you'll probably say that the glorious pink ones are easy to grow, too. Lady's slipper is the prize of any wild flower garden.

Be wary of violets. Some of them multiply until you're pulling violets from everywhere in the garden. The big yellow ones are safe, though.

I have left until last a mainstay of the shaded garden—ferns. These you can often get from the wild, where they are plentiful, or buy at a nursery. All they require is shade and cool, moist soil. Among the pleasantest sights in all outdoors are the fiddleheads of young emerging stalks, unrolling to become the glamorous stalks that make the north side of your house a cool jungle of green.

The best time to transplant wild flowers—no listen to this—is when they're in full bloom. Most spring-flowering wild plants start their heaviest root and top growth just after they've flowered. So get out your spade, take plenty of soil with the plants, and move them when they're at their height of bloom. They'll probably wilt considerably, but they're more likely to recover and continue growing than if you took them later. There's another reason for moving them then, too. That's when you can find them. Many die down or disappear in the forest of summer plant growth.

Grass—And the Blessed Absence Thereof

If you want a place like everyone else's in town, with a few prim evergreens in studied places, and everywhere else, a lawn as monochrome and monotonous as the fine print on an insurance policy, better skip this section. It's not for you. But if you flourish on excitement, change, riotous color, and personality, and if you dare to be different, read on.

To me a perfect lawn is what's wrong with America—uniformity, dullness, monotony, and all the other epithets that mean wearisomeness. We are a nation of lawn worshipers, and a few errant dandelions are cause for alarm and the topic of hours of boring noon-hour conversation during summer. There is dignity to a sweep of green meadow that yields its crop of hay, but a patch of lawn chewed over and trimmed and spaded and reseeded and de-dandelioned is ludicrous, especially since it more often means headache than pleasure.

A Yonkers executive, Ben Wiener, is apparently as fed up with grass as I am. "Grass is dumb," he says. "It's a lot of green, nonedible stuff that costs me money." He felt drowned in the stultifying conformity of neighboring lawns kept up by gardeners for fifty-five dollars a month. No one walks on those lawns, or sits on them. "They're totally useless," he says. Three years ago he spaded up a patch ten by fifteen feet—as a symbol of rebellion—and planted a few tomatoes and squash. Today, his garden is twenty-four by ninety feet and houses every new vegetable in the book, from orange beets to purple cauliflower and lemon cucumbers, besides forty staked tomatoes of differing ancestry. He weeds for half an hour—Scotch in hand—upon arrival from work at four (he's president of his own company), then picks and prepares the lettuce that has become his special pride—bibb, Boston, buttercrunch, green heart, ice, oak leaf, and ruby. "Next year," he says, "the whole yard is going to be farm."

Ben, I applaud you!

Why not experiment this year? Spade up a spot the size of an office desk. Plant a package of Shirley poppies and forget about them. When they're in bloom, no passerby will ever notice the bald spots or the dandelions in your lawn. Even you may forget them momentarily. More important, you'll find a reason for getting up every morning a little earlier, to see what exotic new color, shade, or crinkled edge may have opened. I'll admit that the feel of thick, dewy grass underfoot is nice, but without any destination, why walk through it? If lawn watchers enjoyed their lawns, it would be different. But how often have you seen one who wasn't grumbling about it or telling you all he needed to do with it?

With gardens and flowers, it's completely different, and Thomas Jefferson put his finger on it: "Some one [plant is] always coming to perfection . . . . the failure of one thing repaired by the success of another." Then he concludes: "Though an old man, I am but a young gardener." That's what growing things, rather than manicuring them, does for the spirit.

I don't say that you should plant your whole yard with flowers. A patch of lawn gives you breathing space, keeps the house from looking unshaven and long-haired, provides room for the kids to play, and gives you the setting that dramatizes your flowers and vegetables. All I suggest is that you shift your energies to pleasanter tasks, so that all or nearly all of your work outside is pleasant.

For Those Troublesome Corners

For hard-to-mow spots, consider flowers instead of grass. In an area bounded by sidewalk, you can plant nearly anything and it will look good. Portulaca grows fine in the hot sun, and is neat all summer.

For a spot that kids and dogs use as a shortcut, put in short stakes and plant any flower you like among them. A spot too shady for most plants, including grass? That's ideal for some of the ground covers I mention under that heading.

Too steep for easy mowing? You can use a ground cover or else you can terrace it, using railroad ties or flat rocks as edges, if you have a source of them. Terracing a hillside takes some digging—but then you know you really need the exercise. Build your terraces wide enough to accommodate the mower if you want them grassed. You can grow plants if you wish, but remember that if they face the street, they take constant weeding. A friend planted strawberries on his streetside terraces which proved irresistible to small passersby. A rock wall with crevices for plants is a tremendous job, but when well made it is a permanent and beautiful solution.

Sometimes a bothersome piece of lawn is better paved, slated, or covered with pea rock and used as an alternate patio and barbecue spot. In a narrow strip you might still have room for a raised planter for geraniums, petunias, or the like. Such a planter near your driveway is a pleasant greeting, morning and night.

A strip between garage and driveway or between house and sidewalk is just the spot for a clematis vine. And if you want to tackle something exotic, try espaliering a fruit tree, tacking the branches to the siding as they grow. But don't come to me for information on that. I've never done it.

A sunny strip alongside the house or garage may be precisely the place for those flowers that can make you famous: dahlias, for instance, the big exhibition type that need staking and protection from wind.

Planting those hard-to-mow strips probably won't save you time or energy in the long run, but I'll bet that it turns a nagging chore into a pleasant one.

Ground Covers

To lawn worshipers there is only one plant for shady places: pachysandra. Everyone has it, so it must be proper. Perhaps the adventurous may someday come to grow crown vetch instead, but that day seems far off.

Other ground covers—the really beautiful ones that give you a lift—are harder to get hold of, except perhaps for periwinkle or *Vinca minor*, the evergreen vine that thrives in dense shade. In spring it is loaded with blue flowers and even blooms, a little all summer; it looks neat all year and never needs mowing. Nurseries sell it, but you can probably get a start from your friends.

My favorite ground cover is Solomon's seal, a wild flower that you can find in nearly any woodland from Maine to Florida and west; with the landowner's permission, you might transplant it. Its arching stems grow knee-high, and at each leaf are small hanging bells, followed by blue-black berries. I like the soft green of the leaves, the elfin bells, and the casual tilt of its stalk. Best of all, I like the way it changes, pushing out of the earth in spring, growing, bearing fruit, and then dying down. It's a splendid plant. Seed sown in autumn is said to give you a start the next year, but I haven't tried it. I simply gather the roots from the woods.

Perhaps equally handsome as a ground cover is another wild flower: wild ginger. Its big heart-shaped leaves rise directly from a creeping rootstock and completely tent over the ground from spring to frost. At the end of each stem, lying close against the ground, is a curious cup-shaded flower, purple and brown. When you break or crush the creeping rootstock, you get the unmistakable whiff of ginger. The plant is easily started from cuttings of the rootstock and spreads rapidly, although it is in no sense weedy and can easily be kept under control.

For those who like an evergreen ground cover, consider the Canada hemlock, a straggling native hemlock that stays below three feet and thrives in shade and moisture, providing the wind doesn't hit it. Its fruit is a handsome scarlet berry. I got my plants from a nearby swamp that was being cut through by a highway; they would otherwise have been destroyed. In milder climates, dwarf forms of either Japanese or English yews are preferable.

Now for you who want something vastly different, try the beautiful little bearberry, sometimes called by its marvelous Chippewa name of kinnikinick. It grows wild on sunny slopes among pines across most of the north. It's hard to get started, and, more than that, it demands just the right sandy slopes with strongly acid soil. Once started, it can take the worst drought, summer sun, biting cold, and even salt spray. Its glossy, leathery leaves make a dense mat that turns deep and crisp in hot weather, but it is generally covered with red berries all winter. A few nurseries sell the plant. Where they are abundant, you might try cutting out a chunk of them after the ground is frozen and planting them in a site similar to the place where you found them. Bearberries are for dedicated gardeners to try.

In sunny, well-favored places you have a choice of a great many ground covers. The place to see them is at your nearest arboretum, and if you don't know where that is, it's time you found out, as I mention elsewhere. The Arnold Arboretum near Boston has a magnificent collection. You'll see a dozen ground covers you'll like better than pachysandra. Minnesota's arboretum at Chanhassen, outside Minneapolis has the start of a good collection, too.

A Quicker Way to Mow

I cut my mowing time fifteen minutes to half an hour with this idea for edging borders, shrubs, and trees. But in the interest of suspense, let me tell you about some of the things that didn't work. I tried edging with limestone rock, but grass and weeds love rocks, and no matter how careful I am, the rotary blade hits them. I tried a soil sterilizer around my power and telephone poles, and that's all right, but I've never dared use it around the dozens of fruit trees and lilacs that dot the yard, or along the quarter mile (or so it seems) of borders. For a while I laid down tar paper around each tree, with a thin layer of soil to hide the paper. But quack grass pierced it almost as if it weren't there; the mower wheel dropped through and the blade shredded it. I put down hundreds of feet of aluminum edging. It was never at the right height. Too low: the grass rambled across it. Too high: the blade cut it up.

I finally have an answer, I think. Bury heavy plastic (four mil) and cover with pea rock or gravel or with peat moss. The gravel or peat protects the plastic from the blade and, at the same time, conceals it. If you sink the plastic a little below the grass level, the blade won't touch it, and if you slope the plastic down toward the tree or shrub, rain will drain toward it. This is the way I have treated all my borders. Around trees and big shrubs, I bring the plastic all the way in to the stem to keep down weeds. Because quack grass with its long searching underground stems is my major weed, I spade the outside edge of the plastic down six inches or so as a barrier. The result is that I can mow at top speed with very little backing up. My trees and shrubs aren't getting their bark scraped, and there's no more hand-trimming or hard-to-reach spots. Installing the plastic takes time. In fact, I haven't yet finished. I'm buoyed up in my labors by the thought that this is one kind of edging that has an element of permanence about it.

For Cautious Lawn Worshipers, an Idea

No need to go overboard about this one. Just try the experiment. Spade up a little strip of your lawn in some sunny back corner. It needn't be more than a foot wide and three or four feet long. That's room enough for you to try planting vegetables and flowers in your lawn. Try three or four tomato plants. See if they don't give you more fun per square inch than the grass in that area did.

I think you'll want a longer strip next year. In fact, you might want to put in two or three such strips, wide enough apart for you to run a lawn mower between. I've seen some beautiful gardens grow between the rows. The vegetables stay clean and the grass serves as a mulch. You can weed and pick fruit without getting mud on your shoes. Of course, you'll need to run a hoe along the grass edges to keep it from closing in and smothering the plants, but that's not much of a chore. If you should grow tired of vegetables—which I doubt—you can simply let the grass grow back in.

Edging Along Your Walks

Use plants that don't sprawl. The tiny marigolds give a prim, well-ordered look, and they bloom all summer long. Ageratums are pleasant and orderly, too. Nasturtiums are fine but tend to play out unless the seeds are picked off. Pansies are good while they last. A pleasant little flower is Swan River daisy or *brachycome*. Portulaca is fun. All these flowers give you plenty of blossoms to watch during spring and early summer. Cushion mums interspersed during the summer will come into their own in late summer. If you want to expand your edging, you can use hardy perennials, and among them you have a big choice.

Garden Gadgetry

So you like flamingos in your yard, and deer with red noses, and fake ducks marching across the lawn. If you're willing to put up with them, and with mowing around them, and if your neighbors don't sue you for breach of good taste, go ahead and have them. I don't happen to fancy them, but then as I always say, or nearly always, impressively, *De gustibus non est disputandum,* which translated freely from the Latin is "what's one man's meat is another's poison"—so I shut up about it. I've seen works of art scattered throughout the shrubbery around Philadelphia's art museum, and they looked great. Which proves, I guess, that good art looks fine anywhere. But most of us aren't ready to chance any art treasures outdoors without an umbrella and an armed guard.

There is a kind of garden gadgetry that will flatter your scrawniest flowers and glamorize your whole yard. And if you dare to disagree, I'll threaten to quote that Latin phrase again. The gadgetry includes some or any of these: a birdbath with simple lines; a fence of any kind; a seat or bench of any kind; or a large pot. If you don't believe it, go out and buy a birdbath. Anywhere you place it, it will look good. In the center of a flower bed it lends grandeur. Alongside irises, its severe lines accentuate the flowing, random iris leaves. A big earthen pot does much the same.

Fences do something else. They give form to a mass of green leaves. Without a fence or wall to climb on, a rambler rose is a shapeless mass. Clematis vines, too, are a jumble unless they can climb up a wall or, better yet, grow horizontally along a fence top; that's when you see their real beauty. A picket fence gives that same form to what otherwise might be a jungle of flowers. More than that, it dramatizes tall flowers like hollyhocks and foxgloves and delphiniums (besides blocking strong winds that would knock them over). Tall plants look good against a picket fence even before they're in bloom.

A seat or bench gives strong, severe lines that contrast with the formlessness of many plants, but adds something else—a sense of ease and relaxation. When you're hot and sweaty with weeding, or tired out from digging in peat moss, you know that you could—if you had the time—sit down and rest. And just looking at an easygoing bench does you good. Benches and seats invite. I brought home four inexpensive redwood benches that were on sale at the end of summer. The trouble with them is that they look good everywhere, and I've never yet decided where they should stay. They're consequently always on the move. One or two out beside the pool invite you to sit and meditate. They're great at the edge of the garden. They light up any part of the yard, and they seem to say stay awhile to visitors. Most of the time, though, they sit on the patio, because anywhere else involves moving them every time the yard is mowed.

To make your yard or garden look really elegant, install a table and chairs and an umbrella. These accoutrements turn an otherwise dumpy lot into a hangout for celebrities.

Fences

A fence you put up to keep out neighbors will look like that. Fences ought to be objects of beauty rather than guardians of your boundaries. Some of the nicest ones I know are split rail fences. Short pickets are pleasant, too. Whatever kind you put up, make sure you use posts made out of cedar, locust, oak, or any other wood treated to prevent rot.

Painted fences are an awful nuisance to keep up. You'd be amazed at how much paint and labor they take. More than that, they suggest wealth. If you've got it, that's probably all right, but if not, you look presumptuous.

If you feel you must put up a high paling fence for the sake of privacy, first talk to your neighbor about it. Unless you do, you'll no longer be well and favorably known in your community. Point out to him how he can plant shrubs on his side to soften the look of the wall. If you're a good enough salesman, who knows but what you can get him to split the cost!

If you wall off the street with a paling, leave room enough on the streetside for a layer of shrubs. Your place will seem less like East Berlin, for one thing, and more important, shrubbery soaks up street noise almost as effectively as acoustical tile.

The Secret of a Distinctive Garden—a Pool

If you have more money than time, don't read this. You can hire a landscape architect and contract for a pool like those on fancy estates. But if a pool is a luxury, read on.

I predict that no other garden acquisition will give you any more pleasure than a small pool—and for fifty to a hundred dollars you can have a fine one that will last for years.

Concrete pools are fine where you don't have deep, stone-shattering frost. In the northern United States, you'll need to make yearly patches over small cracks. I am told that if pools are reinforced with wire and are thick enough, they won't crack. The two I have lived with weren't designed right, apparently.

The pool I recommend is a metal stock-watering tank available at your lumber dealer or farm supply store in any diameter from three to ten feet across and either one or two feet deep. You can install it fast, and it needs no maintenance. And if you want to rearrange your yard, you have no concrete to rip out. Before freeze-up, all you need do is unscrew the plug and forget the pool till next spring. Where your soil is so heavy it won't drain, you might siphon it dry.

Install a metal tank today anywhere on your place, add half a dozen goldfish from the dime store and a few snails from the store or creekside, and you'll have a spot that's supremely satisfying to the whole family. In a week or so, grass will start obscuring the metal rim. Water bugs will collect from somewhere, striding across the surface, plunging below with a silver bubble of air to keep them from suffocating. Toads will sing and mate and deposit strings of eggs that darken and eventually release tiny tadpoles.

Your pool will be headquarters for your youngsters and their friends, and that poses some problems. I happen to think that anything that lures kids away from the street is a safety feature. Your neighbors might not agree. You'll need to take up the question with them. In any case, don't plant lilies in your lily pool until the kids have had their fill of water beetles and snails and water striders and goldfish. And don't spoil their fun with fancy plantings along the edge. Most kids will lie by the hour on the edge, studying the water life. And nearly all will like to puddle and splash and make passes at fish. If your dog likes water, he too will probably establish his own priority over plants and scenic effects.

When the children are older and less likely to trample, buy a start of water hyacinths from your dime store. They're the plant with a bulblike swelling at the base of each leaf that lets it float on the surface. All summer long it sends up violet-colored flower stalks. It grows and blooms best if the roots can strike into good soil a few inches below the surface. This is the same plant that chokes the waterways of the South, requiring vast expenditures to keep them navigable. However, frost knocks them out completely, so they can be safely introduced into most parts of the United States.

The painstaking gardener will want to try water lilies. The big problem is finding roots. Not many nurseries handle water lily roots. They're difficult to keep from rotting, and the demand isn't big. As a child, I have grown them from mail-order roots, but in my last two tries, the big fleshy rhizomes have been rotten on arrival. If you have a local source, and your pool is three feet deep, try a plant, either the hardy kind that you might—with luck—keep through the winter, or the tropical kind that you treat as an annual.

My lilies grew in apple boxes filled with rotted cow manure, but bigger boxes would have been better. Lilies are heavy feeders and need two or three square feet of soil a foot deep. The problem with planting them is in keeping the rhizomes anchored in the soil so that they don't pop up and float, and in keeping a layer of gravel on top of the soil so that your whole pool doesn't become a black mire.

We never succeeded in wintering over the roots in their boxes in the basement. Toward spring, they smelled. I'm not saying you shouldn't plant water lilies. I'm simply warning you that it's not as easy as you might think. My friends in Dayton, Ohio, have naturalized a deep rose kind in their small lake, and it has spread over much of the edge. And in northern Minnesota, my friends the Roy Pottsmiths of Gilbert have naturalized a pink and red hardy variety in a bay of their lake where the water liles bloom from June to October, a pleasant surprise to passing canoeists. The water is about two and a half feet deep, enough so that the roots never freeze. All that keeps the plants from spreading faster are deer, which like both leaves and buds.

In big ponds and pools, hardy lilies aren't too hard to grow apparently, but again I warn you that in little pools like yours and mine, it's something else. Why then have a pool at all? You have asked exactly the right question, of the right person.

A body of water in your backyard is beauty, entertainment, and tranquilizer, all in one. Install a recirculating pump (about thirty dollars) and you can be Louis XIV, with your own Versailles and splashing fountain and perpetual rainbow. I have rigged up my pump so that it delivers water to the top of a stair-step of flat limestone rocks down which the water gurgles in a miniature cascade that transports me instantly to the Canadian north. To the purist, this might seem a pitiful deception, and I admit that that was my first thought. But within minutes after I snapped on the switch that started my cascade running, the spell of the sight and sound of running water had won me over, as I think it will you.

One of my friends, not content with his fountain in the center of his small pool, has built a cascade behind it. In hot midsummer, birds swarm over the rocks to splash and bathe and drink. One time there might be a flock of grackles, early migrants, dropping in. Another time it might be a family of brown thrashers, catbirds, or robins. He leaves his fountain and cascade running all day. The birds from his part of town must consider it their neighborhood pub to which they sojourn regularly for a short refresher.

My cascade has a leak in it somewhere under one of the rocks, and though I have patched the apertures with concrete, it still leaks . . . so that a few hours of cascade drains my pool a foot. Until I remedy it, I am stingy with the birds.

Not content with one pool and cascade, a friend of mine in Philadelphia has a series of pools in his small backyard, interconnected with streams that run over colorful pebbles and rocks. Outdoor dinner parties beside his pools, with the murmur of water all about, are a memorable experience.

The source of the water ought to be concealed, of course, to preserve the illusion of naturalness. In back of my grandstand of flat rocks, I moved in a few red pine and spruce and cinnamon ferns, and almost at once the waterfall seemed to be coming from some cavern hidden in the dense shrubbery.

If all this sounds complicated, let me say that my brother (from Orion) and I stacked and restacked and again restacked flat rocks into what we considered the most pleasing arrangement, cemented them together on a platform of concrete blocks, moved in shrubbery and trees, all in a day's time.

Most garden adventures take weeding, transplanting, fertilizing, and spraying. But pools, once completed, take no other upkeep than an occasional filling and a draining in fall. Perhaps that's another reason why they are so restful and relaxing.

One summer we had a dipperful of bullheads as residents. They were the delight of children and adults as the tiny fish foraged fin by fin in tight formation around the pool. Another summer we had a black bass that my father brought back from a fishing party. On its second day in the pool, it was coming to the surface to take frogs from our hands. By fall when we returned him to a lake, he was a family celebrity. Our usual occupants are goldfish of all ages, sizes, and colors, which we keep through the winter in a tub in the basement.

I like trying to grow different bog and marsh plants in the pool. One year it might be cattails in a box on the bottom, with watercress in a shallow pan above it. You can simply lay sprigs of cress from the market onto wet soil or place them in the water, and they will promptly take root and grow. In pails sunk along the rim I have planted pieces of the mossy crust from a marsh, from which cranberries grew and flowered, along with dainty bellflowers. In the center of the pool right now I have pitcher plants growing on a peach-crate island supported by two concrete blocks. I pulled a clump of pitcher plants from a floating bog two years ago and they thrived, pushing up half a dozen elegant flower stalks. This year there were a dozen. Wild calla lilies grow on the same small island, but their blossoms have little appeal.

More Glamour and Excitement for Your Place

Lights will do it. A pair of outdoor floodlights, attached high in a tree, give your whole front lawn outside the living-room window a soft glow. One light reaches out into the dark beyond the orchard, picking up the white trunks of birch trees; the other brightens the spruce trees to the west. The twin lights are concealed behind the trunk of the tree. Many visitors mistake the soft illumination for actual moonlight. The yard seems to glow. In winter, too, the effect is almost magic. The snow seems friendly, even on nights when the temperature is far below zero.

We had hoped to hold parties outdoors under the lights, but mosquitoes and moths too often have the same idea, and northern nights even in summer are often chilly. It almost always seems pleasanter to sit inside. Looking out through the big plate-glass window when the lights are on, we seem to be outdoors without the annoyances. A strange thing happens when we switch on the tree lights. Our small living room expands. We no longer feel crowded. It seems as if the whole area under the trees is living room, too. All this—lights, when properly placed, can do.

In the wrong place, lights are devoid of beauty or function. I have one pair, head-high, on a pole at a far corner of the yard out front. This was to be the light for a picnic table, but moths circling it churned up a cyclone that practically blew napkins off the table. I tacked up another pair of floodlights high among the branches of a spruce tree, expecting the shadows of the limbs to make a pattern on the ground. I felt pretty arty about that pair until dark when I snapped on the light. No light on the ground. The branches were too thick. It was simply a light in a tree surrounded by scrawny limbs that looked like hairy arms. Sometime I must reposition that one. For now, the only time that light goes on is when we activate the line for the coffeepot that plugs into a socket at the base of one of the trees.

I have temporary lights, the kind you stake into the ground alongside a clump of plants or beside a path, but they're something of a nuisance. If I ever decide for sure where I want them, I'll put them in permanently. Lights below shrubs or in back of walls or steps can be handsome. On a small city lot or row-house postage-stamp plot of ground, lights are especially important to dramatize every square foot of planting space you have.

Take plenty of time to decide where you want your lights. Obviously I didn't. You need bury the wire only a few inches. Aboveground, be sure the wire is enclosed in a conduit. Have switches indoors, if possible. If you want to fiddle with something unusual, try a submersible light in the lily pool, but watch out for shorts. You might electrocute more than your goldfish. In general, I'd say that the most effective lighting I have seen is high, approximating moonlight, or high under a canopy of leaves so that the effect is like being inside a tent.

Postpone Your Rock Garden

As a fourteen-year-old, I wanted a rock garden. What set me off was having found a couple of flat limestone rocks among the two hundred and twenty-two acres of rocks that my five brothers and I had been digging, lifting, and hauling off the fields to fill up marshes and build dams and roadbeds. Those two flat rocks were treasures among all the rounded granites, basalts, and conglomerates. When I laid them flat on the ground, they didn't show off, so I piled earth under them, and though I placed them ledgewise in the dirt, they were still just two flat rocks and a pile of dirt. Then, using a wheelbarrow, I rolled in a mass of the flattest rocks I could find and positioned them on the mound. But, though I planted the pile with what I thought were rock garden plants, it was forever a rock pile, year after year, until as an adult I wheelbarrowed it off. The only rock gardens I have seen that are worthy of mention are in Seattle, and I suspect that they were arranged by Nature and needed only the addition of a few plants to complete the effect. Most rock gardens are as fetching as mine was.

Rock Walls

Rock walls are something else. I've seen beautiful ones, the work of amateurs. Work, I said. If you want to let yourself in for some hard work, try building one. Keep it low, or you'll wear yourself out. A change in level of even three feet will give you a pleasant rock wall, one you can plant with a variety of rockery plants. Flat rock won't slump forward if you tilt each slab backwards a little, and fix the back end in with soil. Chunks of rock are harder to put up, but these too will stay in place if you slant them back into the hill and leave only the face of the rock showing. Remember that frost tends to punch the rocks outward.

The nearer to natural your rock wall looks, the better. A few people try to introduce rocks of all kinds, gathered on trips around the country, but those belong in a museum, not in a rock wall. Round rocks are almost impossible to work with. Split them with a sledgehammer and you'll improve your chances of getting them to stay in place.

The right flower—a midget bluebell, for instance—clinging to a spot of earth in a rock wall is a thing of beauty. I am moved to recite what I can remember of Alfred Tennyson's poem:

> Flower in the crannied wall,
> I pluck you out of the crannies;
> I hold you here, root and all, in my hand,
> Little flower—but if I could understand
> What you are, root and all, and all in all,
> I should know what God and man is.

Railway Ties—Lay in a Few

The easier way to build a garden wall is with railroad ties. Check with your railway agent to see if he knows of any castoff ties that you might have. Our agent says he isn't permitted to sell them or give them away, but that nobody will complain if we simply pile them onto a truck and haul them off. It saves him from having to get somebody to burn them. All of which seems like a strange way to run a railroad.

Lay a strip of heavy plastic below the bottom row of ties, extending it out a few inches to keep the grass from growing in and smothering the base of the wall. Cover the plastic with pea rock, gravel, or tanbark. On the second row, lay occasional ties at right angles, butting them into the bank with only the end showing, to keep the wall from pushing out. Leave an inch or two between the ends of the ties and pack this with good dirt. This is where your choice little plants will go. Putting up a wall of railway ties is like working with Lincoln logs. You can rearrange your wall until it suits you.

Railway ties make fine steps, too. On a gentle slope, space them three feet apart, at regular intervals, or closer for steeper inclines. Ties also make a good edge for your border. On poorly drained soil, fill in good soil and circle it with a row of ties, either flat to the ground for a low edge or on edge for a higher one. Six inches is generally all the drainage you need to grow good annuals, iris, and many perennials.

At the edge of a border, a row of ties two or three high makes a fine seat. Flowers along the edge raised to that height look great. You can use ties to make a planter. The creosote in freshly treated ties is harmful to vegetation, but ties old enough for discard are safe.

If gardeners in the United States only realized the many wonderful uses for railway ties, there'd be no more burning of them. Who knows but that if enough of us nutty gardeners were out after them, we'd pay enough for them so that we'd keep the railroads humming.

What Kind of Flowering Shrubs Should You Plant?

The best answer is the one you get from a visit to your nearest arboretum. Climate is important in all gardening, but in the case of shrubs and trees that can't cuddle beneath a blanket of snow, it means the difference between death and survival. Azaleas, magnificent throughout much of the United States, just won't survive the coldest winters of the North. Flowering dogwood can't take the frigid northland, either.

Some shrubs may live but won't bloom because the flower buds, which were formed in the fall, won't take temperatures lower than twenty degrees below zero, even though leaf buds are undamaged. Forsythia is one like that. Mine grew luxuriantly for many years, but they only bloomed on small branches that had been covered with snow. At the other extreme, some shrubs, like lilacs, won't bloom without being thoroughly chilled.

There are other reasons you should visit an arboretum before buying: Shrubs are long-lived and expensive. You want to be sure you get what you like. You probably won't have room for everything you see at a nursery.

Every region seems to have a favorite shrub or flowering tree. Nothing much can beat crape myrtle in parts of the South. Azalea and rhododendron and flowering dogwood are magnificent in parts of the East and West. So too are the flowering cherries and peaches. Redbud in Kansas and Texas is unforgettable.

For a Wet, Shady Corner

Don't worry if you have a moist, shady corner on your place. Certain flowers may grow to perfection there. Some of the finest of them have no appeal to their names, and you're likely to overlook them. Try bergenia, astilbe, golden loose-strife, lythrum, and the wild flower *Lobelia Cardinalis*, or cardinal flower. Mertensia, or Virginia bluebell, will transform a marsh in spring. For details, see Chapter 11.

14
the
right
trees

There is such permanence about trees that to tell you which you ought to plant is like telling you whom you ought to marry—even more presumptuous. The climate you live in is a big factor. As I have mentioned elsewhere, before you decide on the trees (and shrubs) you want, visit your nearest arboretum. There you can see what trees look like after they've had a few years to grow. This is far better than picking a tree from a nursery lot. Some trees grow too big and need constant pruning. Some shed twigs and bark and fruit. Others aren't quite hardy. I can think of several small trees that in milder climates are magnificent: golden chain, redbud, dogwood, Franklinia, silver bell, holly, rhododendron, and certain magnolias. All easily fit a fairly small place, but none of them survive really frigid winters.

If you have plenty of room for trees, there are superb big ones you can plant: in the North, the pines and spruces, birch and others; in somewhat warmer areas, the tulip poplar, nut trees, the cork tree, beech, paulownia, sourwood, sycamore, and the oaks. But these demand room, and lots of it.

The First Tree You Ought to Plant

Before you sign the deed, make sure your new place has room for at least one tree—a flowering crabapple. If there isn't room, look for another place. If your present yard doesn't have room for one, saw down a tree or two and make room. Don't argue about it, either.

Some people might say there are more beautiful trees—like flowering cherries, crape myrtle, and so on. But where else do you find a tree that gives a feast to the eyes in spring and again in fall, feeds wildlife, and is so foolproof? The only one that comes close is flowering dogwood, and for much of the country, that one is not quite hardy enough. Crabapples will grow and bloom just about everywhere except in the deepest South, and though they are rapid growers, they can easily be kept within bounds. Add to all this the fragrance of apple blossoms every spring, and you've got something more than a tree: a lifetime investment, a part of the family.

Anyone who hasn't seen a flock of cedar waxwings in an apple tree at blossom time has a treat coming. One bird pulls off a petal and passes it to its neighbor, who either returns it or passes it along to still another bird. The petal may be all but worn out before any bird eats it. In the fall, too, the birds descend on a tree and pass small crabs back and forth in a remarkable display of goodwill and affection.

Robins, too, are fond of the fruit. One spring a couple of years ago, cold and snow shut off the normal food supply of robins, and a single crab tree, which had dropped its fruit in November, fed fifty robins for at least two weeks. I have never before seen a carpet of robins.

Deer feed on the fruit every fall, too, pawing through the snow if necessary to find every apple. We watch them from our living room, window, hardly fifty feet away. Ruffed grouse, too, love the fruit, and sit above my head as I walk to my study. One time six grouse walked along the limbs of my red-flowered crab. Most of the fruit they could get by reaching and fluttering a bit. On the slenderer branches they did a real balancing act. Sometimes they fed from the ground, leaping up to grasp an apple and hanging suspended for a moment before the apple let loose.

There are scores of varieties of crabapples to choose from. Take a trip to a nearby arboretum both in spring and fall and decide which kinds you prefer. Just to be sure the apples cling to the tree during the winter.

A generation ago the favorite flowering crab was Hopa. One I like far better is Red Splendor, so hardy that temperatures of fifty degrees below zero haven't bothered it. It's a dainty tree with leaves that keep their deep-red color all summer. The flowers are red and the fruit small and deep red from the time they form. It is the crab that grouse prefer, too. Several nearby villages have planted their streets with it. Occasionally, grouse invade the city limits and raid the trees. More often, the little apples hang on the tree until spring—a bonus for robins arriving early.

Which of the other trees you plant is a highly personal matter, involving your preferences for evergreen or deciduous, nut trees or fruit trees, dense shade or light, not to mention the requirements of your climate and space. But, for now, do plant a flowering crab.

How to Shut Out Street Noises

I was lost, I knew it. Not a sound from my brothers, who had been walking abreast of me on a deer hunt through a wilderness of hardwoods and occasional black spruce. Had I gone too far—or not far enough? The others had vanished, and there I was without a compass to see me back to camp, which was several miles off. There wasn't a road, a field, or even a trail anywhere. I tried calling again. No answer. I looked up a tall spruce beside me and wondered if I should climb it to look for landmarks. But it was too thickly set with branches. I tried yelling again, as loud as I could. Finally, I shouldered my gun and started walking. And not more than a hundred feet on the other side of the spruce was my brother.

"Why didn't you answer?" I stormed. (You know how fast a man turns from fear to anger.)

"What do you mean you couldn't hear me?" I went on.

So we reenacted the situation, my brother on one side of the spruce and I on the other, and what we discovered amazed us. That tree swallowed our yells, caught and impaled them on its needles, or bounced them off into oblivion—or whatever happens when a substance blots out sound. It was downright mystifying.

Back at my job I prepared an article on trees and how they could muffle street noises, and a year later all the home magazines were discoursing vigorously on the subject. I can't quite believe that I was the first person in the world to discover the idea, but it seemed that way.

The best trees and shrubs for this purpose are dense evergreens that function all year round. Hemlock is good where it will grow, and so is yew, and the arborvitae. You can keep them pruned pretty well. It's important that you keep the lower branches from dying off. Near the ground is where most noises come from.

A Tree to Grow Old With

An Indiana farmer wrote a letter I have never forgotten.

I have just turned 70 today, and I sold a walnut tree for veneer that I planted in a worthless gully when I was 25. It brought me $500. I planted 15 others that I am leaving for my grandchildren. I wish I had planted more. There was room enough. Think if I had planted 100 or 1,000. I could have.

Today walnut logs are selling for up to thirty-five hundred dollars for a single tree, and a whole new sophisticated brand of American thievery has sprung up with chain saws instead of pistols.

Walnut grows best in moist ground, subject to flooding—the kind of land a farmer often can't afford to plant. They'll grow, too, on steep and gullied land. Does this suggest a family project for you? Perhaps you can find a few waste acres that you can plant with black walnuts.

If fifty years seems a trifle long to wait, try short-term investments. Christmas trees are ready in five to eight years. Locusts grow into fence posts in ten. Money in the bank earns interest, but trees appreciate in value, too—and inflation only makes them more valuable. It's hard to go wrong planting trees. More important, there aren't many better things than a patch of trees to walk in, and watch, and pass on to coming generations.

Manhattanites—Grow Trees on Your Own Acre

A growing number of my city friends are buying an acre or more in the country, not as a business investment, but simply for fun, to indulge that urge, so deep in most of us, to grow something lasting, you might say an everlasting good. Some people might cloak that urge in lofty motives, might say that they want to "pass on something to the next generation." But my friends say they simply want to grow trees, and they can't do it on a city or suburban lot. They search rural courthouses for tax-delinquent land, then buy it up or have a friend buy it when it comes up at public auction. The price: from five dollars an acre to twenty dollars. The biggest cost could be for a survey, but that isn't generally necessary.

Then comes the day the whole family goes to investigate the tract, turning in on a side road, scraping paint off the car, later scrambling over rocks with lunch baskets for the first look. The first picnic site, carefully chosen, becomes a hallowed site, and every successive visit deepens the family's love of the place. Are there flying squirrels in the hollow tree? How is the black walnut doing? Just look at the growth those white pines have made!

There is no end to the experiments you can try on a country acre. Some friends have blasted out duck ponds from marshes on their property. Others have damned up trickles into acceptable swimming holes. Most of them are planting small forests of red and white pine with seedlings supplied by state nurseries for about ten dollars a thousand.

The urge to manicure the place comes next, and what started out as a wonderful place to escape for a weekend can—if you don't watch out—become a chore. It's hard not to put up a cabin on the place, but this too can turn pleasure into a constant worry. A cabin in the woods attracts thieves and vandals, even if you don't leave much of anything worth stealing. And, believe me, once your shack becomes headquarters for a bunch of goons, the anticipation of a trip to your property disappears.

Have a shelter in case of rain, a safe place for a fire and a place for your tent or camper, but stop there. Spend your time with your trees and experiments, not in keeping a cabin in shape.

Trees That Attract Birds

"We just don't seem to have birds on our place," some people tell me apologetically. Generally there is little or no reason why they should have birds: there's nothing for the birds to eat. Or else their place is so manicured, so devoid of weedy corners or thickets, that most birds would be terrified to stop there.

The best bird-attracting trees are more shrubs than trees, and they offer, as well as food, a tangle of branches for escape from predators. Here are some of the best:

Flowering crabapples. Some crabapples are eaten as soon as they turn color, others not until after freezing. Often the sour kinds turn sweet after being frozen. Try them yourself. Plant several kinds.

Mountain ash. Waxwings go crazy over these trees and lose all caution. A friend of mine has a twenty-one-year-old cat named Dick, who, even though arthritic, has no trouble catching waxwings because of such a tree and often doesn't bother about concealing himself. Robins and many other birds also love mountain ash, especially the native American type that is seldom sold by nurserymen.

Hawthorns. Like the crabapples, these are favorites of ruffed grouse, and they provide nesting sites for many other birds as well. Cedar-apple rust cripples the hawthorns badly, though.

Honeysuckles. These beautiful shrubs give both flowers and fruits; they care for themselves and are beloved by many birds.

Viburnums. After frost, the fruit of viburnums feeds many tourists en route south.

Euonymus. The fruits of this family of handsome shrubs look like those of the bittersweet vine, a relative.

Maples. A new shrub-size one from Manchuria, called Amur maple, is a fine yard ornament, and it has winged seeds that are attractive to grosbeaks in early winter.

15
strictly for serious gardeners

The humbling part about being considered an expert is that you know in your heart you're not. You're simply posing as one. About the time you think you know the secrets, you find that all these years you've simply been lucky, and when a new kind of blight or insect strikes, you're helpless. Slowly you understand how vital the right soil is, the right texture, the right air drainage, the right temperature—by night as well as by day—and how little you know about all these things.

At the risk of underlining the obvious, may I describe in this chapter what may be the most common error in gardening. After that, I'd like to suggest some of my special gardening pleasures, and introduce you to a few of the people who have enriched my life through their love of growing things. This chapter is for those who garden not for food or flowers or exercise or anything but for the fun and excitement of gardening.

Top-Secret Tip

Water makes a jungle; lack of it, a desert. Plenty of water makes one man a "born gardener" while another who shorts his garden on water wonders why he can't grow cucumbers and tomatoes the way they look in seed catalogs. The real secret of luxuriant gardens is plenty of water.

Heavy soils are an exception. You can drown plants in clay soils—the kind you track in on the carpet after a rain and can barely scrape off your shoes.

You may not realize it, but every particle of soil retains a thin skin of moisture around it. This is what supplies small root hairs with their water between rains or sprinklings. The finer the granules in soils, the more surface there is for holding moisture. Clay particles, infinitesimal in size, can hold so much water that there is little room for the air that plant roots need. The result is that plants yellow and fail to grow.

The ideal soil runs about fifty percent solid particles, twenty-five percent moisture, and twenty-five percent air. You can lighten soils with peat or compost or leaf mold. You can improve the water-holding capacity of sandy soils in the same way, and you can slow down evaporation from the soil surface with a mulch.

Water is important to good gardens because only in solution can the roots take in the dissolved chemicals they need for growth. It is also important in that the evaporation of water through the leaves creates a suction that pulls nutrients up the plant stem.

On most soils, an inch of water a week—whether by rainfall or hose—is enough for most plants. Leave an empty tuna-fish tin or cat-food container as a check to see how much water your garden is getting. When you're shy of an inch, turn on the water.

On my sandy soil, it just isn't possible to overwater. My father used to pump water from our lake for his raspberries and strawberries, and the place looked like the Garden of Eden. Walking through his seven acres of raspberries was like a trip through a rain forest. The canes grew far above your head.

My friend and neighbor Pat Tronerud, who with her husband operates a commercial nursery, says that the biggest mistake home gardeners make in outdoor gardens is to starve their plants of water, and their biggest mistake indoors is to overwater. Outdoors, they're misers; indoors, they are so solicitous, so generous, that they kill their plants with kindness—and water.

Permanent Damage from Too Little Water

What happens when plants go thirsty for extended periods? In an effort to slow down transpiration through the leaves, the guard cells on the underside of the leaf close down the size of the openings that permit evaporation. The leaf wilts, reducing the area exposed to evaporation. Some wilting won't hurt a plant. In fact, a plant often wilts just after a heavy rain if the sun comes out hot.

Prolonged wilting, though, causes the cells in the stem to shrink, and what was once a lush, fast-growing stalk begins to harden and shrink. Growth is permanently retarded. Part of this hardening of the stem is a natural part of aging in plants. You'll notice in a geranium that last year's stem is woody and dense, while current growth is soft and thick. Plant juices move more slowly through dense, gnarled stems.

When cucumber vines wilt for very long, the fruit generally becomes bitter, especially at the stem end.

An Easy Way of Starting New Shrubs

Say you have a snowball bush that you'd like to increase. Did you realize how easy it is to do? You simply bend a new shoot to the ground and bury it, leaving only a bit of the tip showing. Before burying it, cut or break the shoot to expose the inner bark. Roots start from that point of break. Use a flat rock or forked stick or piece of coat hanger to hold the shoot firm. Next spring you'll have a fine new plant to set out. Rhododendrons need two or three years to develop a good enough root system to go on their own, but most things are ready in a few months.

Grafting

Here is one of the most fascinating garden hobbies I know. All you surgeons who never went to medical school, here are patients for you to experiment on. All you with strong, intuitive fingers that can make clean, swift incisions—try grafting.

All my life I had wondered if it wouldn't be fun, but government bulletins on the topic were so stuffy, so passive-voiced, so dusty and old, that not until a few years ago did I give it a try.

I bought grafting wax and set out, following precisely the diagrams in the bulletin. My incisions were as practiced as I knew they would be. But when I tried applying the grafting wax to the union of stock and scion, I grafted my own fingers together instead. Trying to pull myself free was somewhat harder than finger-wrestling with a roll of old-time flypaper. Now and then I would succeed in circling the union with wax. Slowly, cautiously, I would try to sneak my fingers away, but snap—off would come graft and wax. Every new bout with grafting wax would take me fifteen minutes of scrubbing to clean myself of it.

Then, four years ago, I discovered rubber electrician's tape, and suddenly I became an expert. On what slender discoveries does brilliance often depend! Rubber (not plastic) electrician's tape binds together the severed ends positively yet flexibly, and seals out air. Yet by the time the union starts growing and expanding, the sun has begun to rot it away.

My gardening friend, Paul Tangjerd, lent me his rubber tape and showed me how when you stretch it (after removing the cloth backing) it follows the contours of the branches and locks itself into place. Without much hope of success, I grafted some of his best French lilacs onto a hedge of my old-fashioned ones. And right away, they started growing. I couldn't believe it. A purple plum grafted onto a wild stem took right off and began growing.

It was too late for any further grafting that year, but the next spring I was out before the snow was all gone, scrubbed up, with my best surgical steel (a short, stiff butcher knife), grafting the finest scions onto wild shoots at the back of the garden. My technique was perfect, I am sure, even though not a single scion took. I was grafting too early, before the sap had started rising in the wild stock.

Later, with apple scions that I bought from the fruit breeding station of the university, I spliced a hundred scions onto the branch ends of three hardy crabapples and a hardy Canadian summer apple. To my amazement, about half of them took. I could hardly believe it when their buds started swelling and coming into leaf.

The following year, two grafts bore fruit. One had two big brilliant red Beacon apples among marble-sized green ones. They seemed as self-conscious as I felt in tails at a black-tie dinner party. The other graft bore one big blush-red apple. The year before, my friends had professed to being impressed when they saw the strong junctions between scion and stock. Now, when they caught sight of the two red apples, they exploded with curiosity. How do you do it? What do you use? When do you graft?

All this you can find in government bulletins and most good garden books. But not one of them mentions the fun of grafting or the satisfaction you get from successful operations. Or the unorthodox ways you can join scion with stock.

Basically, you splice the two ends together so that sections of the juicy underbark (called cambium) make contact one with another. Since long, slanting cuts give more surface for joining, experts—even more experienced than I—recommend cuts an inch and a half long. It takes a stiff, sharp knife to make straight diagonals so that each cut matches the other. Before taping the sections together, I check to see that substantial parts of the cambium will jibe. When scion and stock (better start using those terms, if you're going to become an expert) are the same size, that's easy. I have tried slicing away enough bark from a bigger limb to fasten a small scion against it, and that works, too. Bulletins will all tell you about how to make cleft grafts by sawing off the stem of the stock, splitting or notching the stem, and inserting wedge-shaped scions at each side so that the outer bark of each will join. This is more difficult, I find.

Say you have a tender rose or other shrub or tree that you'd like to graft onto a hardy rootstock. You plant it in a pot (or in the ground) beside the hardy stem, shave off enough of the bark of scion and stock to get a union, and then tape them together. After the union has actually grown together, you lop off the bottom of the scion. You now have your plant on a hardy root. There is no limit to the ways you can graft. You can slip a small sliver of scion into a slit in the bark of a tree and tape it there.

On rubber plantations, some trees are three-way composites. A tree with an especially strong root system is lopped off and a variety with a vigorous, stiff trunk is grafted onto it, then a third variety with superior leaf and branch system grafted onto that.

In a window of our house I have a single stalk of triangularis cactus about a foot tall. When it gets a little longer I am going to graft a Christmas cactus onto it, and so have a tree-style blooming cactus, a kind I saw priced in a Fifth Avenue shop window at twenty-five dollars some fifteen years ago. I am told that all you need to do to graft certain cacti is to slice off the ends and pin them in place. Not yet having tried it, I can't guarantee results.

Dr. Karl Sax of the Arnold Arboretum near Boston showed me how he converted normal-size trees and shrubs into dwarf ones by cutting off a foot or so of trunk, then tipping the piece upside down and grafting it back together again. That's enough to dwarf the tree for several years. Someday I'd like to try that, but for now I am more interested in converting my crabapples into eating apples.

My most willing stock is a Dolgo crabapple that can stand our fifty-degrees-below winters without a murmur; its framework of trunk and branches is sturdy and rarely splits. Nearly all the apples I have wished onto it are compatible. (Some apples reject the strange tissue of other varieties.) Two other crabapples, sprouts of trees my father planted fifty or more years ago, are also fine beasts of burden, and they are now sporting grafts of perhaps twenty-five different apples. I call them my smorgasbord apples.

The easiest grafts to make, I find, are those in which you lop off the entire top of a seedling apple at the ground level or even below, graft on a scion, and mound a little earth around the union to keep the whole thing moist. I have rarely missed this way. I have also made grafts onto seedling rootstocks and buried them in moist shavings in the basement until it was time to plant. This worked well, too. Others I grafted, then planted in pots in the basement for a few weeks before planting. And this, too, worked. These are all techniques used by big nurseries, and, though effective, they don't equal the excitement of making grafts on the branches of sizable trees and getting fruit the following year.

This so-called topworking of existing trees by grafting onto the branches isn't often practiced commercially, since it involves too much labor and requires that competing branches of the original stock be kept from smothering out the scions.

A man who has grafted for thirty years at the University of Minnesota tells me that he prefers scions with three or four buds, in case some get injured. Longer scions than that tend to dry out, and they may break when a bird perches on the end. He says you can graft almost any time of the year that the sap is flowing readily. The scion, though, must be dormant.

This year I found a few scions in a plastic bag in the refrigerator where I had forgotten them. It was July 13 when I grafted them. As late as that, two out of a dozen started growing. To help ensure that air won't dry out the cambium, I sometimes spray over the rubber tape with a tree-wound dressing (which comes in a dispenser).

Several years ago in August I tried bud grafting. The bark is loose then, and you can cut a T in the bark and insert a single bud with an inch sliver of its bark under the bark of the host tree. Budding is fussy work, something for deft fingers. Even though you leave the leaf stem on the tiny shield of bark around the bud, it's not easy to introduce the sliver under the flaps of bark. You bandage the incision with rubber tape just as you do in splice grafting, leaving only the bud showing. I find that a sizable number of buds stay green and fresh but fail to burst and grow in the spring. Perhaps more of them would be successful if I had covered each one with clear plastic to keep them from drying out.

The Mount Everest of grafting to me is lilacs on black ash trees. When I heard it could be done, I couldn't wait for spring to try it. Imagine my forty-foot ash on the lake bank bursting into lilac blooms! I took enough wood from my glamorous French lilacs to make fifty grafts, and I stored them in the refrigerator in a plastic bag with moistened peat moss. Then I waited.

Spring came to every other tree and bush and flower in woods and field and garden, but the ash stood unmoved by all the excitement. I could wait no longer. Its branches were still dry and cold when I grafted on the lilacs. Not until more than two weeks later did sap start flowing in the ash. Not one of my lilac grafts took. Of course I'll try it again.

Down by the lake on a hawthorn tree (or what we call thorn apple) are two Beacon apple grafts, growing. A wild plum outside my study door sports an entire parasol of healthy, green leaves, and its twigs are loaded with juicy purple plums. For every failure, there are more than enough successes to keep me going.

Glamourize Your Old Lilacs

Just a minute before you bulldoze out your old lilac hedge! Save it. Transform it into a glamourous row of French hybrids. It's not easy. In fact, it's a long, laborious job, but at least it doesn't cost anything, and I'm pretty sure you'll like doing it.

Get scion wood from neighbors who have varieties you like, or buy a lilac from the nursery and use the pruned ends as scions. Then graft them on just as you did your apples. The very next year you'll begin to get a few blossoms.

Just remember, though, that converting the top doesn't convert the bottom. The roots and suckers will always be the old-style lilac, and you can depend on old lilacs to keep on suckering and spreading.

My first year I got four out of five grafts to grow. The next year only one in ten took. I wish I knew why. I suspect that hot, dry weather kills off many budding scions.

There are dozens of other pleasures in gardening. Chief among them, as I have indicated throughout the book, is trying the unknown.

Experiment a Little

A word to conservatives: why not dedicate just a single row in your garden to fun. If you're the rambunctious try-anything type, you probably don't need this exhortation. You're already testing every new flower and vegetable that comes along.

The real excitement of gardening to me is growing something I have never before seen. That's what led me to sow a few feet of roquette, a salad green that George Washington used to mention. It came up like the mustard it is, and when I thinned it, I thought I smelled a skunk. A few weeks later, when I brushed against it, again I thought I smelled a skunk. Only when I gathered some of it to cook did I realize that the smell was the roquette itself. I won't plant it again, but at least I know something more about the tastes of Revolutionary heroes.

The lure of the unknown is to me the greatest appeal. Because I've never grown a plant before is the best reason for growing it. No matter that it fails. Consistent success I find a trifle boring.

Here are some vegetables I recommend that you experiment with:

Jerusalem artichoke. You'll have a six-foot hedge in a hurry, plus crisp tubers you can use like water chestnuts. If you live in the country, you'll have deer eating the dried stalks in winter.

Sweet potato squash. Even if you don't care to eat the hull-less seeds, you'll find the flesh superb.

Burpless cucumbers. Amaze your friends with the foot-long fruit.

New Zealand spinach. It keeps on producing all summer.

Among flowers, try these:

Brachycome. A little gem of a daisy.

Four-o'clock. So old, they'll be new to many.

Martynia. An oddball squashlike plant with pleasant flowers and unearthly seedpods.

Among perennial flowers, there are dozens worth trying. Of those that come to mind there are perennial flax, one of the finest flowers in any garden; giant flowering onion, a real knockout; and any of the new hybrid lilies. Try bocconia, or plumepoppy, *Euphorbia epithymoides,* or cushion spurge, and St. Bruno's lily.

All will please you. I'll practically guarantee it. For fun, try helenium, potentilla, and edelweiss.

As a matter of opinion, I'd say there's not a flower in the catalog that doesn't deserve a try. My hangup is that I feel like Noah; I must preserve a piece of everything that grows.

My place is more like Noah's Ark than a fancy piece of landscape. There's a plant of everything that grows in the North—plus some that don't grow here. I feel a compulsion to keep alive a start of everything I've tried, just in case someone wants a slip. I don't recommend the plan for others. I'll admit I'm hooked on plants, especially exotic ones.

Seeds of unusual plants aren't expensive. You can get them from Henry Field Seed Company (Shenandoah, Iowa), from Park's, and from several other places. You can get shrubs to experiment with from one of the mail-order nurseries in Tennessee, and at surprisingly small cost. Perennials worth experimenting with cost more because they're harder to ship. Some local nurseries specialize in exotic plants, and I have picked up good things from them, but for really fine perennials I strongly recommend Wayside Gardens. I have tried everything in their catalogs that might conceivably prosper here, and though many can't take our winters, all have been rewarding.

Don't shy away from plants with Plain Jane names. A few fine plants have languished for lack of a good name. Who would ever plant a gas plant, butterfly weed, globe thistle, ornithogalum, or potentilla? Such lapses will undoubtedly be corrected by a New York merchant who is transforming staid old stars of the flower border into exotic new ones. He reasons that everything but a rose would sell better by another name.

Old-time plants have a place. It's reassuring to have the old lilacs bud and bloom, the peas pop up and flower, the radishes swell, the peonies flower just as they have year after year. But having something new and unknown coming up adds zest and a new dimension to gardening.

Don't forget a mixture of old-fashioned annuals; a row of them is always fun.

The Joys of Smelling

I am a smeller—or I might say sniffer, whiffer, scenter, or breather-in. (Mr. Roget, you're no help!) What I like to do is smell: flowers, leaves, twigs. Perhaps because I'm color-blind, you might say my nose is overcompensating. At any rate, I like to smell each tree and flower I'm planting.

The smell of pine in hot midsummer transports me to the Rockies, to a mountainside in Glacier National Park. I crush the needles of my spruce and I'm in the Manitoba wilderness. A sprig of oregano calls up the mountains of Greece. I keep a plant of costmary near the back door where visitors can crush a leaf and smell it. In an earlier day, hardly a home was without it—for salads and for keeping the linens in dresser drawers smelling fresh, older folks said, though I never knew anyone who used it that way. Perhaps they too kept it just for old time's sake.

You can have a smorgasbord of smells all summer if you put in just a few plants of clove pink, sweet alyssum, regal lily, sweet peas, and the summer herbs.

Don't blame your nose or the plants if some of them don't live up to your expectations. Some give off their scent at dusk, others in the hottest part of the day, others only after a warm rain.

Some of my favorite fragrances are these: tomato leaf, regal lily, apple mint, petunia, hyacinth leaf, sassafras leaf, calendula leaf, sweet pea, moist leaf mold, artemisia (Old Man), oregano, arborvitae (also good to chew), and primrose root.

How to Fool Kids into Gardening

A few beans in a window pot may do it, or a tree planted for a child on his or her birthday, or a two-by-two-foot patch of earth that a youngster can weed in ten minutes. It's hard to kill a child's interest in growing things, unless you force him into gardening.

The first plants a child should grow are sunflowers. To a five-year-old, sunflowers appear to scrape the sky, and they make him wonder if Jack's beanstalk might not really have happened. Have him watch the way the big golden heads follow the sun across the sky.

Let him plant pole beans, and help him to put up a tripod of sticks for the plants to climb on. For quick results, let him plant radishes. Watermelons are seldom disappointing, even if they don't survive long enough to ripen. There are flowers, too, that are quick and almost foolproof: calendulas, zinnias, bachelor's buttons, cosmos, nasturtiums, poppies, and candytuft.

Whether a child's enthusiasm grows from here on depends on his parents. Alone in a patch of weeds, a child feels lost. But doing a little weeding along with his parents is a companionable, grown-up thing to do. Once a child discovers the thrill of bringing in food from his garden for the family meal, or his own flowers for a bouquet on the table, he is probably hooked on the glorious habit of growing things, an activity that will enrich his whole lifetime.

Spend a Sunday at an Arboretum

If you don't already know where your nearest arboretum is, it's high time you found out. This is where you can find out what the most beautiful tree, shrub, or flower is for your climate. It's a kind of Sears Roebuck of the horticultural world, where you can see and feel and smell the merchandise—and check on faults as well as virtues.

Arnold Arboretum at Jamaica Plain, Massachusetts, is justly famous. Here you can see trees from almost every land, many at their ultimate height and beauty. The collection of flowering crabs is magnificent. The ground covers I remember especially; there were scores of beautiful ones. The Morris Arboretum in Philadelphia with its giant trees and grassy slopes is splendid. Its collection of Asiatic trees and shrubs is especially worth seeing. Morton Arboretum at Lisle, not far from Chicago, is another fine one. As much as the fine trees and shrubs, I remember the wonderful people who lectured there, as friendly as they were well informed and eager for gardening converts.

Outside of Minneapolis at Chanhassen is the Minnesota Arboretum, still new but already a charming place where you may plan to spend an hour or two—and wind up staying all day, walking woodland trails and boardwalks over marshy ground. You wonder what plants will grow in the frozen North? You see them there at the arboretum. Some rhododendrons make it and some azaleas, too, in the right location. You find out which ones and where.

Much farther north is an arboretum at Morden, Manitoba. This is where that gentle man, W. R. Leslie, a plant wizard, spent much of his life, hybridizing lilies and other plants for the Far North. In the vast treeless prairie, the aboretum seems unreal—an Eden of luxuriantly blooming trees and fruits and berries. Of special interest is an acre or more of nothing but hedges and arches trimmed in the conventional English manner. The most unlikely shrubs and trees—including even birches and oaks—have been induced to become hedges. Morden is worthy of a pilgrimage, as are many other arboretums.

Phone your library for the location of your nearest arboretum, and visit it any time of year. Once you go there, I think you'll become a frequent visitor.

Good Garden Books

The most enjoyable garden book I have ever found is one called *How to Have a Green Thumb Without an Aching Back,* in which Ruth Stout relates how she discovered the value of mulching, and that the proper place for compost is right in the garden surrounding her plants. It is a book of sheer pleasure.

My fountainhead of garden wisdom is *Taylor's Encyclopedia of Gardening,* first published by the Riverside Press, Cambridge, Massachusetts, in 1936, but periodically updated. It is both technical and easy to read and amazingly complete. I have thought sometimes that I'd find it had missed an obscure flower that I discovered in some foreign garden, but I have hardly ever found a flower missing. More than that, it directs me to the proper name of every flower.

Let's look up St. Bruno's lily, for instance, that pleasant plant with starry white fragrant blossoms. It's actually *Paradisea Liliastrum*, a hardy perennial "native of the Pyrenees, Apennines, Alps and Juras," says Taylor, "of easy cultivation either from seeds or division." He goes on to tell how and when to plant it, what kind of soil it prefers, its height and flowering time.

The book is so packed with information, in readable, easy-to-use form that I am forever finding out new knowledge in it. In his precise, scientifically honest language, Taylor describes petunias as "weak, straggling, clammy or sticky herbs, nearly all from the Argentine. They have soft, flabby leaves. . . ."

Another book I can hardly get along without is *America's Garden Book* by James and Louise Bush-Brown. This precise, accurate book is easy to use because it's well organized and well edited and thorough. The trouble with it is that friends ask to borrow it and I can't keep it on my shelves. In fact, my copy has been lost somewhere among my friends for the last year.

Perhaps because dainty little Louise Bush-Brown was such an ardent activist, I like the book all the better. She is the one who helped turn dreary blocks of Philadelphia rowhouses into bloom.

Edited by Fred Rockwell, *10,000 Garden Questions Answered by Twenty Experts* is another fine book, loaded with information. Reading it is like listening in on a meeting of amateurs making the most of a session with experts. Some of the questions suggest desperation: "I can never get a stand of carrots. Why?" And the answer: "Probably the ground bakes too hard. Try sprinkling some pulverized magnesium limestone over the seed before you cover it. Don't plant the seed too deep; barely covering from sight is sufficient." The Rockwell book is thorough, easy to follow, and has a friendly, neighborly tone.

Apart from the fact that the George W. Park Seed Company, Greenwood, South Carolina, is a good place to buy seeds, their catalog is a must for every gardener, amateur as well as expert. Its photographs are informative rather than arty or misleading. The text is precise, carefully edited, and sincere, although it doesn't suffer from understatement. At the center of the catalog is an amazingly complete index of plants, their germination time, best use, and how to start them. It's not an easy chart to use, but once you decode the signs, you can order seeds according to the ease of growing them, according to whether the plants do well in semishade or full sun. You learn, for instance, that larkspur needs total darkness to germinate, should be planted in early spring or late fall, takes twenty days to germinate, objects to transplanting, and other than that, is easy to grow if given full sun. Larkspur is principally for cutting and as a background or screen. It blooms in summer and early autumn. Equivalent information is given for nearly five hundred species of flowers—on just two pages!

As a guide to perennials, the Wayside Garden catalog, available for two dollars from Hodges, South Carolina, is a fine one, beautiful enough for your coffee table. Good advice is given for each perennial, and unlike many nurseries that supply only common and easy-to-ship plants, Wayside handles difficult ones that often smother when bundled for shipment. However, I have always found Wayside willing to replace any such difficult ones—for example, the double-flowering form of the rose-colored lychnis. I admire the company for sticking its neck out in promoting a new plant or shrub that they sincerely believe in. Such introductions of perennials and shrubs seldom make money for nurserymen until years have passed.

There are other fine seed and nursery catalogs, and still others that are slipshod and misleading. Some neglect to say, for instance, that certain plants are biennial and die after blooming. Some advertise old-time flowers under fake new names. Burpee's is improving fast. In recommending the Park and Wayside catalogs, I am not suggesting that their products lead the field, but only that their catalogs are particularly informative.

Gardeners Are a Unique Breed

The fact that my little neighbor Hattie Anderson was in her late seventies didn't stop her from gardening, nor did the fact that both her legs had recently been amputated. With a hoe across her lap, she wheeled out to the garden, straddling a row and whistling. Once in her enthusiasm for weeding, she fell out of her wheelchair and had to pull herself by her hands, shoving the chair ahead of her until she came to the edge of the garden where the plow had left a furrow deep enough for her to position one wheel in it and tip herself back in. After that, she tied herself in when she had to hang forward to pick cucumbers or beans.

My brother Robert was stationed for a winter on Barter Island at the edge of the Arctic where winds roared almost constantly for most of the months of darkness and paralyzing cold. Few men could endure the isolation and terrifying monotony; many had to be sent home long before their allotted eighteen months were up. The doctor, appointed to judge the mental health of workmen and send home men approaching breakdown, had himself succumbed to alcohol.

During the few weeks of summer my brother had noticed how the tundra burst into bloom. In a place where the wind had swept the snow clear, he chopped out long pieces of frozen ground and took them inside, fitting them into wooden planting boxes he had made to hold them. For a few days he suffered the gibes of his associates, but, shortly afterward, a profusion of green appeared, followed in a few days by dainty Iceland poppies and other Arctic flowers he couldn't identify. His tundra gardens were the delight of the camp for several weeks.

At about the same time, his son, after serving in the front lines in Korea, was stationed along with the rest of his company on the island of Hokkaido in Japan awaiting rotation back home. To battle-hardened soldiers, idling away a year was devastating to morale. There were fights between whole rifle companies; VD cases averaged three per man.

The army asked, what can we do to make the place more livable? My nephew Charles said he'd like to plant a flower garden—which must have been amusing coming from a man who stands six feet two. His request was granted. With a jeep, a tractor, and a driver to help, Charles searched for soil in the area, most of which was covered with three feet of volcanic ash. He found some soil along a highway where the road cut through the ash, and he brought home two trailer loads, which he spaded into the ash down in front of the orderly room. In town, he bought a couple of flats of pansies and carnations from an incredulous Japanese nurseryman. Not a single combat veteran discouraged him as he weeded his flowers. Many asked for flowers to send in letters to mothers and wives to reassure them that life wasn't all bad. One day a replacement, newly arrived, taunted him as he weeded: "Mistress Mary!" Promptly, the toughest veteran in the company grabbed the recruit by the neck and told him about Charles's combat record under fire. In all the 1st Cavalry Division that General Matt Ridgway reviewed that year, there was only one flower garden, but it was a celebrated one, revered and defended.

Gardeners are a strange, irrational branch of the human race, and I love them.

16
farewell
to
summer

As the summer—and this book—approach their close, I can't say good-bye without a few words of advice, like a parent seeing his children off on a long trip or a teacher admonishing his class on the last day of school.

To You Graduates

A short review before you get your diploma from the Davids School of Practical (and Impractical) Gardening. I trust you will never be guilty of these blatant mistakes.

Planting in the shade. My peonies don't bloom—what's the trouble? Too much shade (although it also could be that they're planted too deep). My lilacs don't bloom? Too much shade. My seedlings grow lank and spindly? Too much shade.

Plants get their power to grow from sunshine, the same way that your beater, refrigerator, and sweeper need electricity. Unless plugged in to plenty of sunshine, plants don't grow. It's as simple as that. There are a few exceptions, which I have noted already. The surest mark of the amateur is that he tries to grow things in the half-dark. And at this point in your education you must certainly never be mistaken for an amateur.

Failing to thin. One summer I walked to work past a window box of marigolds almost as thick as hair. Certainly they'll be thinned, I thought, but when they weren't, I wondered if I shouldn't do the job myself on my way—or else sneak over after dark and do it. I was a coward. I didn't want to get involved, even with a window box. So the plants grew yellower and sicker, struggling bravely to produce a few sick blooms. I told myself it was too late to help, that the plants were already stunted beyond saving. I still feel guilty about that window box. I hope you, as graduates, will have more courage.

Thin marigolds as soon as they get their first true leaves. Then thin them again when they begin to touch one another. Then thin them again until they are as far apart as recommended on the package. If your heart bleeds for the uprooted ones, put them in your compost and let their lives go toward the greater glory of succeeding generations. But THIN!

Too little water. During water shortages, you are excused. Otherwise, see that an inch of rain or spray falls every week on most soils, more on hot, sandy ones. In between times, don't touch the hose. A light sprinkle will revive wilted leaves—and cool you off—but it's of no value to the garden and it can even do harm.

Not pinching off seedpods. When I see tulip and daffodil seedpods growing, I conclude that the gardener either doesn't know better or doesn't care. The little coral lily often dies if its seedpods aren't removed. Many annuals, like snapdragons, shut down blooming when seed stalks are left.

Getting in a rut. The saddest mistake of all is this—that a gardener plants the same things, the same varieties, year after year. You might not believe it, but some people I know are still asking for Rosy Morn petunias, simply and purely because that's the kind they grew twenty years ago. Don't they feel the excitement of the bigger, more floriferous hybrids? Or do they fear failure so much? To me, part of the charm of gardening is its unpredictability. Often seeds don't even sprout. Sometimes they barely live. Sometimes they beat the pictures in seed catalogs.

For the rare gardener caught in a rut: grow tithonia this year, starting it indoors for early bloom. For bloom next year, plant the double hollyhock Powderpuff. And for your vegetable garden, plant Golden Nugget squash.

It's Going to Freeze Tonight

Sometimes, just as your garden is at its height, frost warnings come. There is a way of saving your prize plants, if you don't mind the effort. Cover them with sheets, newspapers, or other light material to keep the heat of the earth from escaping into the air. Often a newspaper sheet on top of a zinnia plant will save it, even though the sides are unprotected.

Cold weather often comes by the week, so you may have to cover every night for a spell, in hopes of a week or more of good weather later. In northern Minnesota, covering the garden is a long shot; still we do it—with cardboard boxes, tea towels, slips, and old shirts.

Certain vegetables give up growing when cool weather sets in—among them cucumbers. You may as well gather up the crop and forget them. Melons give up, too, and so do squash, pumpkins, and beans. If you haven't harvested all your tomatoes and stored them on the basement floor—on papers—to ripen, cover the plants until you can harvest them. Most other vegetables can take a large amount of frost.

Now then, as it's growing dark, what about the flowers? Take inside any tuberous begonias or caladiums and let them start drying off. Cover or take inside the geraniums you want to keep. Cover ageratum, coleus, cosmos, dahlias, four-o'clocks, portulacas, nasturtiums, and zinnias. Most others can take a surprising amount of frost. Petunias sometimes put on their best show in the fall after a light frost or two.

In any case, don't take your annuals into the house and expect them to bloom. Their place is outdoors. The shock of coming inside will throw them out of bloom.

Maybe it won't freeze after all. Go outside and check the night sky. Are there clouds? Then it won't freeze. Clouds are a warm blanket. Any breeze stirring? Again, it probably won't freeze.

Farewell to Summer

There comes a day in fall when a gardener knows in his bones, even as he awakens, that the first killing frost has come. As he looks out the window at daybreak, things seem untouched, but the moment the sun comes out, the dahlias droop, the marigolds wilt, and the whole garden looks limp and liquid. This is the dreariest hour in a gardener's year.

But something happens in the garden, and just as E. B. White's old dog gained strength as the family pig grew steadily weaker, so certain juices flow stronger in the flowers remaining. The calendulas are never so fine as now. The alyssum is whiter than ever. The roses are as big as in early summer. Shastas and gloriosas are radiant. Delphiniums bloom on short but sturdy stalks, and petunias make a fresh start. Phlox keep on flowering even after nights of twenty degrees, and gazanias keep sending up fresh glowing stars of bloom. After two weeks of almost constant freezing with intermittent snow, the lupines stand erect in full flower. "You never can tell," I say to myself as I cover the begonias in a window box. "There's always the chance of an Indian summer."

I sense that same optimism in the snapdragons, which send out buds as they never did in summer. The Iceland poppies keep opening new blooms, too. They were blooming just after the snow left this spring, and still are at it. That doesn't surprise me much, though, because I have seen the tiny wild ones in full bloom at Point Barrow, Alaska, only inches above the frozen tundra.

The asters, too, come into their own now that summer is done. But it is a fragile-looking annual outside the window that surprises me most—godetia, also called farewell-to-spring, a flower I have never before grown. During summer I barely noticed it, but now its satiny blooms are pink mounds. There are flowers that really do bloom—to use the language of the seed catalogs—until frost.

With most greenery turned black, there are unexpected spots of color. The day lily foliage is yellow, and so too are the tall blades of Siberian iris. And my friends who see colors a trifle differently from the way I do, say that the euonymus is a splash of fire.

The Eternal Promise

Finally, the snow falls. The garden is dead and buried. I am never quite ready for winter, much as I try to be. I yearn to prolong the grandeur of life and its beauty.

Death is there beneath the snow, but so too is life and another spring, not far off. Seeds are waiting to be born. Dormant roots are waiting only for the warming soil to rouse them. As sure as winter is spring, too. This is the eternal promise of gardening.

To a gardener, life after death is a bottomless mystery, but one he accepts pretty much as a certainty . . . so that snow comes as a promise of new life ahead. Snow covers the failures of the past, too. The weedy corners are obliterated, the rough brown lawn is smooth and clean. Last year is forgotten. We look ahead. Next year is going to be better. We start planning for a year like nothing we ever knew before.

Flowers and Plants for Every Purpose

(Courtesy of the Burpee Seed Company)

PLANTS FOR PARTIAL SHADE

Ageratum	Lily-of-the-
Anchusa	Valley
Astilbe	Lobelia
Azalea	Mock Orange
Begonia	Nemophila
Bleeding Heart	Nicotiana
Boston Ivy	Pachysandra
Caladium	Pansy
Coleus	Periwinkle
Columbine	Plumbago
Coral Bell	Polyanthus
Ferns	Sweet Violet
Forget-Me-Not	Torenia
Foxglove	Vinca
Impatiens	Viola

PERENNIALS FROM SEED

Achillea	Geum
Alyssum	Gloriosa Daisy
Anchusa	Gypsophila
Anemone	Helianthemum
Anthemis	Hemerocallis
Arabis	Hibiscus
Aster (Hardy)	Hollyhock
Aubrieta	Iberis
Campanula	Lathyrus
Candytuft	latifolius
Carnation	Lavender
Centaurea	Lilies
Cerastium.	Linum
Cheiranthus	Lupine
Chinese	Lychnis
Lantern	Nepeta
Chrysanthe-	Penstemon
mum	Polyanthus
Columbine	Poppy
Coral Bell	Pyrethrum
Coreopsis	Rudbeckia
Daisy,	Scabiosa
Shasta	Statice
Daylily	Tritoma
Delphinium	Trumpet Vine
Dianthus	Verbena
Forget-Me-Not	Venosa
Gaillardia	Viola

TALL FLOWERS FOR BACKGROUNDS

Celosia—Tall	Marigold
Cleome	(Tall)
Cosmos	Nicotiana
Dahlia—Tall	Snapdragon
Delphinium	(Tall)
Foxglove	Sunflower
Gladiolus	Sweet Sultan
Gloriosa Daisy	Tithonia
Hibiscus	Zinnia (Tall)
Hollyhock	

HANGING BASKETS

Asparagus Fern	Nasturtium
Begonia	Petunia
House Plants	Thunbergia
Lobelia	

LOOKING FOR FRAGRANCE?

Alyssum	Peony
Carnation	Persian Lilac
Clematis	Petunia
paniculata	Phlox
Heliotrope	Rose
Lavender	Stock
Lilies	Sweet Pea
Lily-of-the-	Sweet Shrub
Valley	Sweet Sultan
Mignonette	Tuberose
Mock Orange	Wallflower
Nicotiana	Wisteria

DWARF PLANTS FOR EDGING

Ageratum	Marigold
Alyssum	Dwarf
Begonia	Pansy
Daisy—	Portulaca
English	Viola
Lobelia	Zinnia—Dwarf

WINDOW BOX

Alyssum	Ivy
Asparagus	Lantana
sprengeri	Lobelia
Begonia	Marigold
Celosia	Petunia
Coleus	Verbena
Geranium	Vinca

DRY OR POOR SOILS

Achillea	Godetia
Alyssum	Gypsophila
Brachycome	Helianthemum
Bridal	Honeysuckle
Wreath	Iris
Cactus	Lathyrus
California	latifolius
Poppy	Linum
Calliopsis	Lupine
Candytuft	Lychnis
Celosia	Marigold
Centaurea	Mugho Pine
Montana	Nasturtium
Cleome	Petunia
Coreopsis	Phlox
Cosmos	Poppy
Dianthus	Portulaca
Euphorbia	Potentilla
Four O'Clock	(Gold Drop)
Gaillardia	Verbena
Gloriosa Daisy	Vinca

PLANTS FOR BEDS

Aster	Pansy
Balsam	Petunia
Begonia	Portulaca
Dahlia	Salvia
Geranium	Snapdragon
Impatiens	Verbena
Iris	Vinca Rosea
Marigold	Viola
Nicotiana	Zinnia

BEST FLOWERS FOR CUTTING

Achillea	Gypsophila
Anchusa	Heuchera
Anthemis	Iris
Arctotis	Larkspur
Aster	Lathyrus
Bells of Ireland	Marigold
Calendula	Nigella
Carnation	Pansy
Celosia	Peony
Chrysanthe-	Poppy
mum	Pyrethrum
Columbine	Rose
Coreopsis	Salvia-blue
Cornflower	Scabiosa
Cosmos	Shasta Daisy
Cynoglossum	Snapdragon
Dahlia	Stock
Delphinium	Sweet Pea
Dianthus	Sweet Sultan
Forget-Me-Not	Sweet William
Foxglove	Verbena
Gaillardia	Viola
Gerbera	Wallflower
Geum	Zinnia
Gladiolus	"Everlasting"
Gloriosa Daisy	Flowers

EASIEST TO GROW ANNUALS

Alyssum	Marigold
Anchusa	Mignonette
Aster	Nasturtium
Balsam	Nigella
Calendula	Night-scented
California Poppy	Stock
Candytuft	Phlox
Celosia	Poppy
Cornflower	Portulaca
Gaillardia	Scabiosa
Godetia	Sunflower
Larkspur	Sweet Pea
Linaria	Zinnia

ROCK GARDENS

Ageratum	Gazania
Alyssum	Helianthemum
Arabis	Heuchera
Aubrieta	Juniper, Andorra
Brachycome	Linaria
California	Lobelia
Poppy	Nemophila
Candytuft	Nierembergia
Cerastium	Phlox
Dianthus	Portulaca
Dimorphotheca	Verbena
Forget-Me-Not	Zinnia—Dwarf

PLANTS FOR MOIST PLACES

Astilbe	Lily-of-the-Valley
Caladium	Nicotiana
Ferns	Polyanthus
Forget-Me-Not	Sweet Violet
Foxglove	Vinca
Impatiens	Viola

Germination and Cultivation Guide

(Courtesy of the George W. Park Seed Company)

When sowing seeds it is always best to divide the packets and sow at different times. Note the time and give good care until the plants have had time to appear. The following tables give the time normally required for germination of each variety of seeds. This time may vary as much as 25% either way. Do not discard seeds until you have given them at least two or three trials. Those marked (c) or having the dagger (†) beside them may lie dormant for a year or more. The other tables are self- explanatory, and while they are somewhat complicated, do give a great deal of information about each of the hundreds of species listed.

SYMBOLS USED IN TABLE

Classification
ha, hardy annual
hha, half-hardy annual
hb, hardy biennial
hhb, half-hardy biennial
hp, hardy perennial
hhp, half hardy perennial

Germination Time
a—5 days
b—8 days
c—10 days
d—15 days
e—20 days
f—25 days
g—30 days

z—50 days or may lie dormant a year or more.
†—dagger added means seed may take much longer than time indicated.

For Fluorescent Light Gardeners
L—Needs light for germination
D—Needs total darkness for germination

Best Use
Hb—Hardy border
B—Summer bedding
C—Cut flower
E—Low edging or border
D—Drying, for use as everlasting
F—Foliage or Seed pod
G—Ground Cover
S—Background or Screen
Sp—Specimen
W—Window Garden or Porch Box
R—Rock Garden
V—Vine

Time to Bloom
a—Early spring
b—Late spring or early summer
c—Summer
d—Late summer early autumn
e—All autumn
f—Late autumn
g—Tends to be everblooming
h—Winter blooming indoors, or can be forced into bloom
i —Perennials, blooming first season if started early

Culture
1—Of easy culture for beginners.
2—Soak seeds before sowing.
3—Sow in early spring while soil is cool.
4—Sow in early spring or latest fall.
5—Sow in heat in sunny window, frame or greenhouse. Sowing may be done at almost any season.
6—Sow in spring or summer, up to September. Be sure seedbed is shaded if sown in heat of summer.
7—Sow in late autumn or early winter in open beds. Germination will take place in spring. Cold is needed to start them. May also be sown in early spring if given refrigerator treatment.

8—Resents transplanting, sow in permanent location.
9—Sow where plants are to bloom after soil has warmed up in spring.

a—Very fine seed. Carefully sow on top of soil and water with misty spray to cover.
b—Sow indoors 6-8 weeks before planting out time for earliest bloom.

⊙—Sun S⊙—Sun or partial shade.

S—Semishade.
M—Requires extra moisture.
D—Will grow in rather dry soil.

Name	Germination	Best Use	Bloom Time	Culture Symbol
A				
Abu'til on, hhp . . . . e		W	gh	51
A ca'cia, hhp. . . . . d		W	ac	⊙52
Ac anth'us, hhp . . . . e		FWB	d	⊙31
A chille'a Milfoil, hp Lc		CHb	bd	⊙4a61D
A chim'en es, hhp. . . . . d		CBW	de	S⊙5a
A co ni'tum, hp . . . . . . e		CHb	d	S⊙7
A cro clin'i um, ha . . . . . b		CD	c	⊙31
Ad o'nis, hp c		CHb	b	S⊙4b
African Violet, hhp . . . . . Le		W	g	S5a
Aga pan'thus, hhp. . . . . . e		W	c	⊙M5
Ag ath ae'a, hhp. . . . . . . e		B	b	⊙3
Agera'tum, hha . . . . La		CRE	gc	⊙19ab
Agros'tis, ha . . . . Le		F		⊙3
Al li'um, hp . . . . d		CHbR	c	⊙4
A'loe, Tiger Aloe, hhp . . . . . g		W	c	D5
Al stroe mer'i a, hhp . . . . . d		CSp	cd	⊙3
Al the'a, hha, hb c		SHb	bd	⊙61
Alys'sum, ha, hp . . . . a		EB	bd	⊙31a
Amaran'thus, hha. c		B	c	⊙9b1
Am ar yl'lis, hhp . . . . g		CW	h	S⊙5
Am'a zon Lily, hhp, bulb		W	ch	S⊙5
Am mo'bium, hb . . . . a		CD	c	⊙61
Am so'nia, hp . . . . e		Hb	bc	S⊙4M
A'na phalis, hp c		D	c	⊙4
An chu'sa, ha, hp c		CHb	bd	S61
Andros'ace, hp . . . . d		ER	a	S4
An em'on e, hp . . . . d		CHb	b	S⊙4
An'themis, hp . . . . b		CHb	b	⊙61
An thu'ri um, hhp. . . . . . †g		CWSp	h	S5M
An tig'o non, hhp. . . . . . . e		WS	bdi	⊙5
An tir rhi'num, ha. Lc		CWB	bd	⊙9b1
Aphan'o ste phus, ha . . . . . b		BC	c	⊙9b1
Aph e'lan dra, hhp		W	g	S
Aq uil e'gi a, hp . . . . Lg		CHb	bc	SM631
Ar'abis, Rock Cress, hp. . . . Ld		BHb	a	S61
A ra'li a, hhp. . . . . La		WF		5
Arc to'tis, ha. c		CB	ce	⊙31
Ar e na'ri a, hp . . . . b		R	c	31
Ar me'ri a, Thrift, hp c		EHb	bc	⊙D612
Ar'nic a, hp . . . . f		CRHb	bc	⊙41
As cle'pi as, hp, hhp . . . . Lg		CHbW	ib	⊙61D
As par'a gus Fern, hp . . . . . g		FWHb		M56S
As pho'del us, hp . . . . g		E	b	⊙61
As'ter, annual, ha. . . . . . . b		CB	de	⊙9b
As'ter, perennial, hp . . . . . d		CHb	ei	⊙3
As til'be, Spirea, hp. . . . . . f		CHb	ch	S3M
Au bri e'ta, hp. . . . . e		E	a	S⊙6
Av'ena, ha . . . . a		DC		⊙91
A'zalea, hp. . . . . †z		HbS	abh	7SM
B				
Baby's Breath, ha, hp c		CB	c	⊙61
Baby Blue Eyes, ha c		E	ab	⊙41
Bachelor's Button, ha. c		CB	bc	⊙31D
Bal'sam, hha. . . . . b		BW	g	⊙9b1
Bap tis'i a, hp . . . . e		CHb	b	⊙41
Bar to'ni a, ha c		B	bd	⊙a3D1
Bas'il, hha c		FB	c	91
Be go'ni a, hhp . . . . Ld		WB	gh	S5a
Bel am can'da, hp . . . . d		CHb	d	S⊙691
Bells of Ireland, ha . . . . L†f		CBD	cd	S⊙31
Bellflower, hb, hp, ha. . . .		CHb	bc	S⊙61
Bel'lis, hp . . . . Lb		BWE	abi	S⊙41
Ber ge'ni a, hp . . . . d		Hb	b	S4M
Beverly Bells, hhp. . . . . . . d		BCS	bci	⊙9ab
Big no'nia, hp . . . . d		VS	c	S35
Bird of Paradise, hhp . . . . . z		CSpW	h	⊙25
Blackberry Lily, hp . . . . . . d		CHb	d	S⊙691
Bleeding Heart, hp . . . . . . †z		Hb	ab	S7
Ble'til la, hp		SpC	c	S⊙
Bou gain vill' ea, hhp . . . . . g		VW	b	⊙51
Bou var'dia, hhp. . . . . e		CW	h	S⊙5
Brachy co'me, hha . . . . d		E	b	⊙9b1
Bri'za, ha. c		CD		⊙31
Bro wal'lia, hha . . . . Ld		WB	g	S⊙5b1
Budd'le ia, hp . . . . e		CHb	c	⊙51
Buph thal'mum, hp . . . . . . e		Hb	d	⊙41
Butter Daisy, ha . . . . b		CHb	cd	⊙91
Butterfly Lily, hhp . . . . . . f		SpW	c	S⊙5
C				
Cabbage, Flowering, ha. . . . Lc		FB	df	31
Cac'tus, hhp . . . . †d		W		S⊙5
Ca la'di um, hhp.		BW		S⊙
Cal an dri'ni a, ha c		E	c	⊙D9
Cal ce o la'ria, hhp . . . . . Ld		W	h	S⊙5a
Ca len'du la, ha . . . . Dc		CBW	gh	⊙4b1
Cal'la "Lily," hhp. . . . . g		CWSp	h	⊙51
Cal li op'sis, ha . . . . b		CB	cde	⊙9b1
Cam el'li a, hhp . . . . †g		CW	h	S25
Cam pan'u la, ha, hp . . . . . e		CHb	bc	S⊙61
Candy tuft, ha, hp		See Iberis		
Can'na, hhp . . . . †z		B	cd	⊙259
Can'ter bury Bells, hb c		CHb	c	⊙61
Cap si'cum, hhp. . . . . . . †e		WF	c	S⊙5
Car na'tion, hp . . . . e		CHbW	gi	⊙561
Cas'sia, hhp		Sp	c	⊙
Cast' or Bean, hha. . . . . . . d		SF		⊙91
Cat a nan'che, hp . . . . e		CHbD	bc	⊙31
Ce lo'sia, hha c		CBD	cd	⊙951b
Cel si a, hhp . . . . a		W	c	⊙5
Centau'rea, ha c		CB	bc	⊙91
Cen tra'therum, hhp c		BW	g	S⊙5
Ce ras'tium, hp . . . . d		HbRg	b	⊙31
Cheiran'thus, hhp, hb. . . . . a		HbR	ah	⊙631
Che lo'ne, hp . . . . e		HbC	c	⊙6
Chry san'the mum, ha, hp . . . b		CHbB	defi	⊙561

Name	Germination	Best Use	Bloom Time	Culture Symbol
Ciner a'ria, hhp Lc		W	h	S561
Cla dan'thus, ha . . . . g		BE	bd	⊙9b1
Clark'ia, ha . . . . a		CB	cd	⊙91
Cla'ry, hha . . . . L†d		See Salvia		
Clem'at is, hp . . . . †z		VS	cg	⊙7
Cle o'me, Spider Flr., ha . . . Lc		CB	cd	⊙31
Cli an'thus, hhp . . . . e		VW	a	S⊙5
Cli tor' ia Butterfly, hhp . . . . d		VW	hg	S⊙52
Cli'via, hhp . . . . g		SpW	h	S5
Cob ae'a, hha . . . . d		VW	c	⊙9b1
Cobra Orchid, hhp . . . . . . †g		SpW	a	M5
Cockscomb, hha		See Celosia		
Coff'ea, hhp . . . . Lz		FW		S52
Co'le us, hhp Lc		FWB		S⊙51
Col'um bine, hp . . . . Lg		CHb	bc	S⊙61
Con valla'ria, hp		b		S
Coral Bells, hp		See Heuchera		
Cor dy li'ne, hhp . . . . . Lg		WF		S⊙5
Cor e op'sis, hp . . . . La		CHb	cdi	⊙461
Cornflower, ha, hp . . . . . D†c		CB	bc	⊙91
Corn, Ornamental, hha . . . . . a		FS	c	⊙91
Cor o nil'la, hp c		EG	c	⊙D3
Cor yd'al is, hp . . . . g		HbR	a	S⊙4
Coryno car'pus, hhp . . . . . . d		WF		S51
Cos'mos, hha . . . . a		CSB	bd	⊙91
Cotton, Ornamental hha . . . . h		SpF	b	⊙9b1
Cot y le'don, hp . . . . g		R	b	⊙4
Crape Myrtle, hhp . . . . d		SpW	cd	⊙5b
Cre'pis, ha . . . . a		E	e	⊙91
Crossan'dra, hhp . . . . . L†f		W	g	⊙5
Crot al a'ria, hha c		CB	cd	⊙231
Cro'ton, hhp . . . . g		FW		S⊙5
Crown Vetch, hp c		EG	c	D3
Cu no' nia, hhp . . . . f		FW		SM5
Cu phe'a, hha . . . . L†b		B	g	S⊙9b1
Cyc'lam en, hhp . . . . Dz		WR	ah	S⊙5
Cyn o glos'sum, ha, hhp . . . Da		CB	gi	⊙31
Cy pe'rus, hhp. . . . . f		SpWF		S⊙5M
Cy'press Vine, hha . . . . a		VS	cd	⊙981
Cypho man'dra, hhp . . . . . . e		WSp	bf	S⊙5
Cy'tis us Broom, hp . . . . . . g		CHb	a	⊙42

D

Name	Germination	Best Use	Bloom Time	Culture Symbol
Dahlborg Daisy, ha . . . . . . d		EW	g	⊙3
Dah'lia, hhp . . . . a		CESp	de	⊙951
Daph'ne, hp . . . . †z		RHb	a	S⊙7
Dar ling ton'ia, hhp . . . . . †g		SpW	a	M5
Datu'ra, hhp . . . . d		WSp	ci	⊙9b1
Daylily, hp . . . . d		CHb	bc	S⊙41
Del phin'i um, ha, hp . . . . . e		CHb	bdi	⊙6
Di an'thus, ha, hp . . . . a		CEHb	gi	⊙69b1
Di cen'tra, hp . . . . z		Hb	ab	S⊙7
Di chon'dra, hp . . . . d		G		91
Dic tam'nus, hp . . . . †z		Hb	bc	⊙7

Name	Germination	Best Use	Bloom Time	Culture Symbol
Di dis'cus, hha . . . . Dd		BC	de	⊙9b1
Dig it a'lis, hp, hb . . . . . . Le		CHb	b	S61
Dim orph oth e'ca, ha c		Hb	c	⊙9b
Do'de cath eon, hp . . . . . . †g		RGC	a	S⊙7
Dom'b eya, hhp . . . . †g		WF	h	S3
Do ro'ni cum, hp . . . . d		CR	a	⊙6
Dry'as, hp . . . . z		ER	b	S⊙7
Dusty Miller, hhp Lc		See Cineraria		

E

Name	Germination	Best Use	Bloom Time	Culture Symbol
Ech ev e'ri a, hhp . . . . d		WF	c	DS⊙5a
Echin'ops, hp . . . . d		CHb	c	⊙61
Ech'ium, hha . . . . b		R	g	⊙D31
Eggplant, Ornamental, ha . . .		Sp	c	⊙1b
E mil'ia, ha . . . . b		SD	bcd	9b1D
English Daisy, hp . . . . a		BWE	abi	S⊙41
Ep i' sci a, hhp . . . . g		W	g	S5a
Er'anth is, hp . . . . †g		GR	z	S⊙4
Ere mu'rus, hp . . . . g		CHb	b	⊙7
E rig'er on, hp . . . . d		CHb	c	⊙41
Er i'nus, hp . . . . f		R	bc	S⊙61
Eryn'gi um, ha, hp . . . . z		CHbD	c	⊙37
Eryth ri'na, hhp c		W	cd	S25
Er y thro'ni um, hp . . . . . . z		R	a	⊙S7
Esch scholtz'ia, ha c		B	g	⊙481
Eu ca lyp'tus, hhp . . . . e		WF		5
Eu'cha ris, hhp, bulb		W	ch	S⊙5
Eu'co mis, hhp . . . . e		HbW	c	⊙51
Eu pa to'ri um, hp c		HbC	a	S⊙4
Eu phor'bi a, ha, hp. . . . . . d		B	d	S39b
Eu toc'a, ha . . . . e		B	c	9D
Exa'cum, hhp . . . . Ld		WB	g	S5a

F

Name	Germination	Best Use	Bloom Time	Culture Symbol
Fat'sia, Aralia, hhp . . . . . . d		WSp		S⊙5
Fe lic'ia, ha . . . . d		E	c	⊙51
Ferns, hp, hhp . . . . e		WHb		S5a
Fi'cus, hhp . . . . Ld		WSpF	b	⊙5
Flag of Spain, hhp . . . . e		VS	d	⊙9
Flax, Linum, ha, hp . . . . . . d		RHb	bcd	⊙61
Forget-me-not, hb . . . . . . Db		CR	ai	⊙S61
Four O'clock, hhp . . . . a		B	de	⊙9b1
Foxglove, hp, hb . . . . Le		CHb	b	S61
Frank'lin i a, hp . . . . †g		CSp	d	S⊙7
Frees'i a, hhp . . . . f		CW	h	⊙51
Fuchs'i a, hhp . . . . L†f		W	gh	S⊙5
Funk'i a, Hosta, hp . . . . . . †d		E	c	S⊙7

G

Name	Germination	Best Use	Bloom Time	Culture Symbol
Gail lar'di a, ha, hp . . . . . . e		CHb	cdi	⊙69b1
Gal to'ni a, hp . . . . d		Hb	cd	⊙6
GARDEN MIXTURES				
Ga za'ni a, hhp . . . . Db		BW	ghi	⊙9bD
Gen'tian, hp . . . . g		RHb	cd	S⊙7
Gera'nium, hp . . . . †e		RHb	bc	S⊙41

Name	Germination	Best Use	Bloom Time	Culture Symbol	Name	Germination	Best Use	Bloom Time	Culture Symbol
Ger'be ra, hhp. . . . . Lg		CWB	chi	⊙5	Jacob'inia, hhp . . . . Lg		WF		S⊙5
Ges ne'ri a, hhp. c		W	h	S⊙5a	Jas i one, hp. . . . . f		RHb	bd	6⊙
Ge'um, Avens, hp. . . . . . . f		CHbR	bc	⊙61	Jas mine', yellow, hhp . . . . . g		SW	d	S⊙5
Gil'i a, hb, ha c		Hb	cd	⊙31	Jewels of Opar, ha . . . . d		CHb	c	9b1D
Gladi' olus, hhp . . . . e		C	c	⊙3	Job's Tears, Coix, hha . . . . . e		SpF	c	⊙9
Glob u la' ria, hp c		R	a	S4					
Glo ri o'sa Daisy, ha, hp . . . e		CHbB	bci	⊙61	**K**				
Gloriosa Lily, hhp. . . . . . . g		BW	ch	S⊙5	Kal an cho'e, hhp Lc		WF	h	S⊙5a
Glory Flower, hhp . . . . . . f		VSpS	ci	S⊙5	Kale, flowering, ha c		FB	df	⊙31
Glox in'i a, hhp . . . . Ld		W	gh	S5a	Koch'i a, Cypress, ha . . . . Ld		S		⊙9b1
Gode'tia, Satinflower, ha. . . d		CB	cd	⊙31	Kud'zu Vine, hp. . . . . d		VS	c	⊙5
Gom phre'na, ha . . . . . . Dd		CBD	cd	⊙9b1					
Gom pho'car pus, ha . . . . . d		FS	cd	⊙9b1	**L**				
Gourds, hha . . . . b		SFD		⊙9b1	La bur'num, hp . . . . †g		SpC	a	S⊙9
Gre vil'le a, hhp . . . . . . L†e		FW		D5	Lan ta'na, hhp. . . . . †z		CWB	gi	⊙51
Grass, Lawn & Ornamental . .					Lark'spur, ha . . . . De		CS	cd	⊙481
Gyp soph'il a, ha, hp c		CHbD	bd	⊙661	La ta'ni a, ha. . . . . z		WSp		S5
					Lath'yr us, hp . . . . De		CSV	bci	⊙312
H					Lava'tera, hhp. . . . . e		Hb	bc	⊙b1
Har pe phy'llum, hhp. . . . . d		WF		S⊙5	Lavender, hp. . . . . d		FR	bci	⊙61
Heather, hp . . . . g		ER	b	⊙3	Lay'ia, ha . . . . Lb		BC	b	591
He dych'ium, hhp. . . . . . . f		SpW	c	S⊙5	Lazy Daisy, ha. c		BC		⊙9b1
Hele'ni um, hp. . . . . a		Hb	d	⊙61	Le'on to po'dium, hp Lc		RF	c	⊙D4
Helian'the mum, hhp . . . . . d		HbE	bc	⊙D6	Leucan'the mum, hp c		CHb	bc	61
Heli an'thus, Sunflr., hha. . . a		CS	d	⊙D91	Lew is'i a, hp . . . . g		R	b	⊙S7
He li chry'sum, ha. . . . . . La		CDB	c	⊙9b1	Li'a tris, Gayfeather, hp . . . . e		CHb	cd	⊙41
He li op'sis, hp. c		CHb	cdi	⊙61	Lil'i um, Lily, hp . . . . †g		CHb	bc	⊙77
He'li o trope, hha . . . . f		BW	gh	S⊙51	Lily-of- the-Valley			b	S
He'lip ter um, hha. . . . . . . d		CD	c	⊙9b1	Lin a'ri a, Toadflax, ha. c		RE	bc	⊙31
Hel leb'o rus, hp. . . . . . . †g		SPHb	a	S7	Lin'um, Flax, ha, hp . . . . . . f		BR	bc	⊙69b1
He mer o cal'lis, hp . . . . . d		CHb	bc	S⊙41	Lir i'o pe', hp . . . . g		E	d	S⊙234
Her ni a'ria, hp c		E	c	⊙3	Living Stones, hhp . . . . . . d		W	d	S⊙5
Hes'pe ris, hp . . . . Lf		CHb	ci	⊙61	Lo be'lia, ha, hp . . . . Le		WEHb	gci	S⊙7a
Heu'che ra, hp. Lc		CRHb	bc	S⊙4	Lotus, hp. . . . . f		Sp	c	⊙5M
Hibis'cus, hp. . . . . †d		Sp	ci	⊙61	Lu na'ri a, hb c		CDB	c	⊙361
Holly'hock, Althea, hp. c		SHb	bd	⊙61	Lu'pine, ha, hp . . . . e		CHb	c	⊙8321
Hop, hha c		VS	c	9	Lych'his, Campion, hp . . . . Lf		CHbR	cd	⊙D61
Ho'sta, hp . . . . †d		E	c	⊙S69	Ly co'ris, hp, hhp, bulb		WSp	d	S⊙
Hoy'a, hhp.		W		S5	Ly'thrum, hp . . . . d		CHb	d	S⊙M41
Hun nem an'nia, hhp . . . . . Ld		CB	ci	⊙61					
Hya cinth', hp. . . . . d		Hb	cd	⊙4	**M**				
Hyp er'icum, hp. . . . . e		ER	a	S6	Mach'oeranthera, ha . . . . . g		CB	bcd	⊙31
Hy po estes, hha. c		WE	f	S⊙51	Mad ei'ra Vine, hhp.		V	d	⊙59
					Maltese Cross, hp . . . . . . Lf		CHbR	cd	⊙D61
I					Mal'va, Mallow, hp . . . . . . a		Hb	bc	⊙61
Ib e'ris, Candytuft, hb, hp . . . e		ER	b	⊙59b1	Ma na' os Beauty, hhp c		BW	g	S⊙5
Ice Plant, ha . . . . D†d		BWF	g	⊙5a1	Man de vil'lea, hhp c		VW	h	⊙5
Im pa'tiens, hhp. . . . . . . Ld		WB	gh	S⊙51a	Marble Vine, hha . . . . b		SV	c	⊙9
In car vil'le a, ha, hp . . . . . †f		Hb	bc	⊙46	Mar gue rite', hp. . . . . a		CHb	b	⊙61
I pom oe'a, hha . . . . a		VS	cd	⊙9812	Mar i gold, Tagetes, ha . . . . a		CBW	g	⊙9b
I'ris, Flag, hp . . . . †e		CHb	ab	S⊙M7	Mar tyn'i a, hha . . . . e		RF	c	⊙9b
Is me'ne, hhp, bulb		W	c	⊙	Ma tri ca'ri a, ha, hp Lc		CBE	g	9ha⊙31
					Mathi'o la, ha . . . . La		B	bc	⊙51
J					Mau ran'di a, hhp . . . . d		VW	h	⊙5a
Jac a ran'da, hhp . . . . e		W	h	S⊙5	Me con op'sis, hp . . . . e		Hb	d	S4M

Name	Germination	Best Use	Bloom Time	Culture Symbol
Mer i on Blue Grass, hp. . . . . f				
Meryta Sinclair, hhp . . . . . . f	Sp	c		S
Mes em bry an'the mum . . D†d	BWF	g		⊙51
Mich'ael mas Daisy, hp. . . . . d	CHB	ei		⊙3
Mi cro sperm a, hha. . . . . . d	W	h		S⊙5a
Mig non ette', ha . . . . a	BW	gh		S⊙318
Mi mo'sa, hha . . . . Db	FW	d		⊙95b1
Mim'u lus, ha, hhp c	WBR	gh		S⊙5Ma
Mi rab'il is, hhp . . . . a	B	dei		⊙9b1
Mom or'di ca, hha. . . . . . d	VSF	c		⊙9
Mo nar'da, hp . . . . d	CHb	c		S⊙61
Mont bre'tia, hhp	CB	c		⊙5
Morning Glory, hha. . . . . . a	VS	cd		⊙9812
Mu'sa, Banana, hhp . . . . . z	FSp			S⊙5
Myoso'tis, hb . . . . Db	CRHb	ai		S61
N				
Nae'gel i'a, hhp . . . . . . Ld	W	h		S5a
Nas tur'ti um, hha. . . . . Dc	BE	be		⊙91
Nem es'i a, hha . . . . . . Da	EBR	bc		⊙9b5
Nem oph'i la, ha. c	E	a		⊙41
Nep'eta, Catmint, hp c	ER	bd		S⊙61
Ner te'ra, hhp . . . . e	W			5
Ni can'dra, ha . . . . d	WSP	c		5⊙
Ni co'tia na, hha. . . . . . Le	B	cd		⊙9b1
Nier em berg'i a, hhp . . . . d	EB	c		S⊙61
Ni gel'la, ha . . . . b	DB	c		⊙318
O				
Oen oth e'ra, hb. . . . . . . a	RB	c		⊙D61
O pun'ti a, hp . . . . d	W			S5D
Or'chis, Orchid, hp . . . . . z	CW			S5
Or ni thog'al um, hhp. . . . †g	CW	b		⊙5
Ox'alis, hhp c	WE	gh		⊙5
Oxypet'alum, ha c	WB	cd		⊙9b1
P				
Pae o'ny, hp . . . . z	CHb	b		⊙7
Painted Daisy, hp . . . . . . e	CHb	b		⊙61
Palms, hhp. . . . . z	WSp			S5
Pam'pas Grass, hhp . . . . . e	CB	d		⊙59b
Pansy, Heartease, ha . . . . Dc	CEB	agh		S⊙6b1
Pas si flo'ra, hha. . . . . . . g	WSp	hd		S⊙59
Pel ar go'ni um, hhp . . . . †d	WB	gh		S⊙51
Pent'a petes, ha . . . . a	S	c		⊙25
Pen'tas, hhp . . . . Le	W	g		5
Pent'ste mon, ha, hp . . . . LDc	CHb	bi		DS⊙49
Pep er o'mi a, hhp. . . . . . e	FW			D5
Pepper' Ornam., hhp . . . . L†e	WF			⊙5
Per il'la, hha . . . . Ld	FB			⊙9b1
Peri'winkle, Vinca, ha . . . . Dd	WB	g		⊙9b15
Petu'ni a, ha, hhp Lc	BW	g		⊙1ab
Phil o den'dron, hhp . . . . †g	WF			S5M
Phlox, ha. c	B	bc		⊙31
Phlox, hp. . . . . D†f	CHb	a		⊙7
Phy ge'lius, hhp c	Hb	b		S6
Phy'sa lis, hp. . . . . Ld	F	d		⊙5
Phy sos te'gia, hp . . . . . . d	CHb	c		S6
Pi'lea, hp. . . . . d	FW			5S
Pineapple Lily, hhp . . . . . e	HbW	c		⊙51
Pinks, hb, hp. . . . . b	CEHb	bci		⊙6b1
Pitcher Plant, hhp. . . . . †g	See Cobra Orchid			
Pla ty co'don, hp Lc	CHb	bci		⊙61
Plum ba'go, hhp. . . . . . f	VW	h		⊙5
Poin ci an'a, hhp . . . . . . d	W	c		⊙25
Poin set'ti a, hhp . . . . . e	SpW	h		S⊙5
Pol em o'ni um, hp . . . . . e	Hb	bc		S⊙41
Polka Dot Plant, hha c	WE	f		S⊙51
Po lyg'o num, ha . . . . . . e	E	d		9b
Pop'py, ha, hp. . . . . . Dc	CHb	c		⊙3618
Por tu la'ca, ha . . . . . LDc	RBE	cde		⊙D91a
Po ten til'la, hp . . . . . . d	Hb	g		4
Primrose, hhp . . . . Le	W	h		S⊙5a
Prim'u la, hp. . . . . . . L†f	HbE	ab		S⊙4
Pseudopanax, hhp. . . . . d	WSp			S⊙5
Pu'ni ca, hhp. . . . . . . Le	WSpE			⊙5
Pyre'thrum, hp . . . . e	CHb	b		⊙61
Q				
Queen Anne's Lace, ha Lc	CD	c		⊙9b1
R				
Ra mon'da, hhp. . . . . . . f	R	b		S3
Ra nun'cu lus, hhp . . . . . d	HbR	bbi		⊙9
Re chsteiner'ia, hhp. . . . . e	SpW	h		S⊙5a
Rhod an'the, hha . . . . . . d	CD	c		⊙5b1
Rho'do den dron, hhp . . . †z	S	ab		7SM
Rho i cis'sus, hhp . . . . . g	SPWi	h		S5
Ri'ci nus, hha . . . . d	SF			⊙91
Rom'ne ya, hhp . . . . . . g	CSp	d		⊙9
Rose, Rosa, hp . . . . z	CSpW	gi		⊙7
Royal Red Bugler, hhp. c	W	g		S5a
Rud beck'i a, hp. . . . . . . e	CHbB	bci		⊙61
S				
Sa gi'na, hp . . . . f	RE	d		⊙3
Saint paul'i a, hhp. . . . . . Lf	See African Violet			
Sal pig los'sis, hha. . . . . Dd	CB	cd		⊙9b1
Sal'vi a, hha, hp . . . . . L†d	CBHb	g		⊙961
San gui na'ria, hp . . . . . . d	R	e		S4
San to li'na, hp . . . . d	HbEF	c		⊙6D
San vi ta'li a, ha Lc	RE	cd		⊙91
Sap on na'ri a, hp . . . . . Dc	R	b		⊙61
Saxi f'ra ga, hp. . . . . . . d	RE	b		S9
Scab i o'sa, ha, hp. c	CHb	cde		⊙96b1
Scarlet Sage, hha . . . . . Ld	CBHb	g		⊙961
Scheff le'ra, hhp. . . . . . . e	FW			DS5
Schizan'thus, hha . . . . . De	CWB	hc		S⊙5
Sed'um, hp. . . . . a	FHbR	g		⊙5
Sem per vi'vum, hp . . . . . d	ER	g		⊙5

Name	Germination	Best Use	Bloom Time	Culture Symbol	Name	Germination	Best Use	Bloom Time	Culture Symbol
Sen'sit ive Plant, hha . . . . . Db		See Mimosa			Thymus, Thyme, hp . . . . . . e		ER	a	S⊙41
Sham'rock, hp. . . . . Dc		WB	b	⊙5	Ti grid'i a, hhp. . . . . g		B	c	⊙9
Shas'ta Daisy, hp c		CHb	bc	⊙361	To bac'co, Flowering, hha . . .D		See Nicotiana		
SHRUBS.					Tor e'ni a, hha. . . . . d		WB	bg	S59b1
Si dal'ce a, hp . . . . d		Hb	c	⊙6	Touch-me-not, hha		See Balsam		
Si le'ne, hp. . . . . a		F	de	⊙61	Trad es can'ti a, hp c		HbW	d	S⊙4M
Si nnin'gi a, hhp. Lc		W	h	S5a	Trans va'al Daisy, hhp		See Gerbera		
Smi'lax, hhp. . . . . Dg		CWF		S⊙5	Trill'i um, hp . . . . z		E	a	S7
Snap'dragon, hhp L		See Antirrhinum			Tri to'ma, hhp. . . . . e		CHb	cd	⊙61
So la'num, hhp . . . . . . L†e		WF		S⊙5	Trol'li us, hp. . . . . z		HbC	bc	S⊙M4
Spider Flower, ha.		Cleome and Lycoris			Trumpet Flower, hhp.		See Datura		
Spre ke'lia, hhp . . . . g		CW	h	S⊙5	Tuberose, hhp, bulb		C	b	⊙
Stachys Lanata, hp . . . . . . d		HbF	b	⊙6	**V**				
Star of Texas, ha . . . . f		CB	g	⊙9b	Val er i a'na, hp c		Hb	ci	⊙61
Stat'ice, hha, hp. . . . . d		CDB	bc	⊙9b	Ve nid'i um, ha . . . . Lb		C	g	⊙9b
Steph a no'tis, hhp . . . . . . g		CWV	g	SM5	Venus Fly Trap, hhp				1S
Stocks, Gilliflower, ha Lc		WCB	ch	⊙9b1	Ver bas'cum, hb. . . . . e		SF	c	⊙61
Sto ke'sia, hp . . . . e		CHb	ci	⊙61	Ver be'na, hhp. . . . . De		CB	cde	⊙9b
Straw'ber ry, hp. . . . . g		BF	gi	⊙4	Ver be si'na, ha . . . . b		CHb	cd	⊙91
Strawflower, ha. . . . . . . La		CBD	c	9b1	Ver on'i ca, hp. . . . . d		CHbR	cd	⊙61
Strel itz'i a, hhp. . . . . . . †f		CW	h	⊙52	Vin'ca, Periwinkle, hhp. . . . Dd		BW	g	⊙59b1
Strep to car'pus, hhp . . . . Ld		W	h	S5a	VINES				
Succulents, hhp . . . . f		W		S⊙5	Vi o'la, ha, hp . . . . Dc		BEW	gi	S⊙61
Sultana, hhp. . . . . Ld		See Impatiens			**W**				
Sun'flower, hha		See Helianthus			Wahl en berg'i a, hp. c		CHb	bci	⊙61
Sweet Pea, ha, hp . . . . . . Dd		CV	ab	⊙412	Wall flower, hb, hp . . . . . . a		CW	gc	⊙31
Sweet William, ha, hp. . . . . a		CHb	bi	⊙96b1	Water Lily, hhp . . . . e		i		5
					Wild Flowers.				
T					Wis te'ria, hp. . . . . †g		SpV	b	S⊙7
Ta ho'ka Daisy, ha . . . . . . g		CB	bcd	⊙31	Wood Rose, ha . . . . b		WD		25
Ta li'num, ha . . . . d		See Jewels of Opar			**X, Y**				
Tet ra nema, hhp . . . . d		W	h	S5a	Xer anth'em um, ha. c		CD	c	⊙91
Teu'cri um, hp. . . . . g		ER	b	⊙6	Yuc'ca, hp . . . . z		Sp	d	⊙7
Thal ic'trum, hp. . . . . d		CHb	c	S⊙4	**Z**				
The'a, tea, hhp . . . . z		WSpF	h	S72	Zeph yran'thes, hhp . . . . . f		WBR	g	⊙5
Ther mop'sis, hp . . . . d		CHb	bc	⊙61	Zoy'sia Lawn Grass. . . . . . . g				⊙6
Thistle, hp . . . . d		CSp	d	9b1	Zin'ni a, hha. . . . . a		CB	g	⊙91b
Thrift, hp		See Armerea							
Thun berg'i a, hp, hha c		VS	c	⊙9b1					

SELECTING AND SOWING

If you wish seeds to sow in a garden bed or to present to children, or if you have had but little experience in raising flowers from seed, select such flowers as Alyssum, Aster, Balsam, Cosmos, Calendula, Candytuft, Oriental Pinks, Gaillardia, Helianthus, Marigold, Mignonette, Bedding Petunia, Pansy, Phlox, Scabiosa, Nasturtium, Valeriana, Verbena and Zinnia; for vines get Cobaca, Cypress, Jasmine, Gourds, Morning Glory, Thunbergia. Even in sowing these, it is well to prepare the bed carefully in a sunny exposure. Keep constantly moist until plants appear.

TO CONTROL "DAMPING OFF"

"Damping Off" is a microscopic fungus growth which attacks the baby plants just as they emerge from the ground or while they are still small and is the reason for many failures which are blamed on the seed, especially where very small seeds are concerned.

Sphagnum Moss is an excellent, natural growing medium for sowing any kind of seed. It promotes germination and inhibits the growth of "Damping Off" fungi.

To prevent damping off of seedlings, drench seed flats after sowing with Benomyl. Oz. makes 12 gallons.

HARDY FLOWERS, with symbol h, may be sown in early spring as soon as the ground may be worked, or in fall to come up with the first breath of spring for earlier blooms. Hardy perennials and biennials may be planted in July or August and transplanted to permanent location about 1 month before frost where they live over with the protection of a mulch to give bloom in spring. We think it best to sow perennials and biennials in the spring so that they can become better established before winter.

HALF-HARDY FLOWERS listed with the symbol hh may be started early indoors for early bloom, or may be planted outside when danger of frost is over. Half-hardy perennials need winter protection in the Northern states.

TO INSURE SUCCESS. Many failures with seeds are due to lack of knowledge of the time required by the seeds to germinate. Study the table on these pages to avoid failures from this cause.